UK TAXATION
FOR
STUDENTS

A SIMPLIFIED APPROACH

MALCOLM FINNEY

FINANCE ACT 2005 EDITION

Third edition

First published 2004 by Management Dynamics

This (third) edition published October 2005 by
Spiramus Press Ltd
The Boathouse Office
57a Gainsford Street
London SE1 2NB
Telephone +44 20 7357 0861
www.spiramus.com

Visit web site www.mgtdynamics.co.uk

ISBN 1 904905 23 4

Printed and bound in Great Britain by Cromwell Press, Trowbridge, Wiltshire
Cover design: David Shaw and associates

Dedication

I dedicate this book to my two sons Matthew and Nicholas.

Dad

ABOUT THE AUTHOR

MALCOLM FINNEY

B.Sc M.Sc (Bus Admin) M.Sc (Org Psy) MCMI C Maths MIMA

Malcolm Finney is an international tax consultant and founder of Management Dynamics which specialises in both tax and management training and consultancy. Malcolm has also lectured on taxation at many of the London-based accountancy colleges.

Formerly, Malcolm was Head of Domestic and International Tax at the London based law firm Nabarro Nathanson; Head of International tax at international accountancy firm Grant Thornton; and prior to Grant Thornton worked for J F Chown & Co Ltd, J Henry Schroder Wagg & Co Ltd and Duncan C Fraser & Co.

Malcolm is joint editor of the leading text *International Corporate and Personal Taxation* published by Tolley/Butterworth and has recently published *Inheritance Tax for Students: A Simplified Approach* a book also intended for accountancy students (Spiramus Press, 2005). Malcolm has written extensively for numerous tax journals both domestic and international and has also spoken at both domestic and overseas conferences on a variety of taxation topics.

PREFACE TO THIRD EDITION

Another twelve months have passed and a new update of my book is needed.

The amendments required have been significant due not only to changes in the rates and allowances between tax years 2004/05 and 2005/07, but to the new Income Taxes (Trading and Other Income) Act 2005 referred to as ITTOIA 2005.

The first and second editions of the book have been very well received according to the feedback I have received from students and others who have purchased the book.

The book now also appears on reading lists at a number of universities where taxation is taught.

I am of course delighted.

Many commented on the easy to read style and the large number of helpful examples used throughout the text. This approach continues in this edition.

A completely new adition are the 100 exercises produced in Appendix 2 for students to test whether they have undertood the text.

The book's sole purpose is to try to help students sitting the taxation papers of the various professional examinations (e.g. ACCA, CIMA, CAT and AAT).

This edition includes the provisions of the Finance Act 2005 and is thus suitable for students sitting their tax examinations at any time during the calendar 2006. In addition, as mentioned above, full account has been taken of the new Income Tax (Trading and Other Income) Act 2005.

Writing any book takes time and effort and not normally just that of the author. Updating this edition has proved no exception. As before I would like again to thank Karen Donnelly, my still long suffering partner, without whose constant encouragement and hard work this edition would have failed to materialise.

Malcolm Finney

September 2005

PREFACE TO FIRST EDITION

I hope that this is the first edition of many. Only time will tell.

Its sole purpose is to try and help students sitting the taxation papers of the various professional examinations (e.g. ACCA, CIMA, CAT and AAT). I have attempted as best I can to write an easy to understand and read text.

It is not a book for the tax expert.

I have included numerous worked examples as an aid to understanding the text.

I have avoided both specific references to the UK's tax legislation and to reported tax cases. I have done this as to include such matters not only complicates the text but, more importantly, it is not a requirement of any of the examination papers at which this book is aimed.

This edition includes provisions of the Finance Act 2003 and is thus suitable for students sitting their tax examinations at any time during 2004 (normally, in June and December).

Writing any book takes time and effort and not normally just that of the author. This book is no exception. I would like to thank Karen Donnelly, my long suffering partner, without whose constant encouragement and hard work this book would never have seen the light of day.

Malcolm Finney
January 2004

IMPORTANT NOTICE TO STUDENTS: MUST BE READ

For a number of years the tax authority (now known as Her Majesty's Revenue & Customs; formerly the Inland Revenue) has been undertaking a Tax Law Rewrite project.

This project involves the re-writing of all the UK tax law in plain English rather than, as historically, in legalese. It is not the intention that any of the law will be changed just rewritten in plainer and easier to understand English. This is a mammoth task but progress has already been made.

To date, three new acts have been produced. The first was the Capital Allowances Act 2001; the second, the Income Tax (Earnings and Pensions)Act 2003 and most recently the Income Tax (Trading and Other Income) Act 2005.

The latter two acts are commonly referred to as ITEPA 2003 and ITTOIA 2005 respectively.

One of the major effects of the rewrite project has been the abolition of the "Schedules" which were at the core of the law on income tax (paid by individuals) and corporation tax (paid by companies).

Although a number of these Schedules had in fact already been abolished some years ago the following remained in force until recently, namely, Schedule A, Schedule D Cases I, II, III, IV, V and VI and Schedule F (Schedule E was abolished in 2003 by ITEPA 2003).

The Rewrite project has not, as indicated above, changed the law despite these Schedules now having disappeared.

The impact of the Rewrite project will be felt for the first time by ACCA students sitting Papers 2.3 and 3.2 examinations in June and December 2006.

No longer will any references be made to any of the "Schedules" either in the text books or the examination (other than perhaps in text books where the author wants to mention them in passing). Students therefore no longer need to know anything about the "Schedules".

As these changes only apply from 2006 any review of past examination questions will, of course, contain references to the various "Schedules".

This text book in line with the changes no longer makes reference to the Schedules but adopts the new replacement descriptions. Set out below are the old Schedules and how they are now to be described:

OLD TERMS	NEW TERMS
Schedule A	**Property business income**
Schedule D Case I/II	**Trading profit**
Schedule D Case III	**Interest income**
Schedule D Case IV/V	**Relevant foreign income**

Schedule D Case VI	**Other income**
Schedule E	**Employment income**
Schedule F	**Dividend income**

At this stage in your studies all this may seem a little mind-boggling!

You needn't worry as all will become clear as you read the text book.

We are only really talking about labels used to describe things changing; nothing else. A normal person would talk about his/her "employment income" not "Schedule E income"; now, because of the Rewrite project tax advisors/examiners will also no longer talk about "Schedule E income" but "employment income".

CONTENTS

CONTENTS

CORPORATION TAX

GENERAL TAX ADMINISTRATION, NATIONAL INSURANCE CONTRIBUTIONS AND PENSIONS

RATES AND ALLOWANCES

INCOME TAX

Rates

		2005/06				2004/05	
		£	%			£	%
		taxable income:				taxable income:	
Lower rate	first	2,090	10		first	2,020	10
Basic rate	next	30,310	22		next	29,380	22
Higher rate	above	32,400	40		above	31,400	40

Personal allowances

	2005/06	2004/05
	£	£
Personal allowance	4,895	4,745
Age allowance (65 – 74)	7,090	6,830
Age allowance (75 and over)	7,220	6,950
Married couples allowance (65 -74)	5,905	5,725
Married couples allowance (75 and over)	5,975	5,795

Note: Age allowance is reduced by £1 for every £2 by which STI exceeds £19,500 (2005/06) or £18,900 (2004/05).

Married couples allowance may also be reduced but cannot be reduced below £2,280 for 2005/06 and £2,210 for 2004/05.

Car benefit
Petrol
The taxable percentage of list price is 15% for petrol engine cars with a carbon dioxide (CO_2) emissions base level of 140 grams per kilometre for 2005/06 (for 2004/05 the comparable figures were 15% for 145 grams per kilometre).

Diesel
For diesel powered cars the respective figures for 2005/06 are 18% and 140 grams per kilometre (for 2004/05 the comparable figures were 18% and 145 grams per kilometre).

Car fuel benefit scale charges 2005/06
The percentage arrived at in ascertaining the amount of car benefit (see above) is also used to arrive at the measure of the car fuel benefit by applying the relevant percentage to the figure of £14,400 for 2005/06.

Authorised mileage rates: cars and vans where employees use their own cars for business purposes 2005/06 (and 2004/05)

	Rate per mile
	£
Annual business mileage up to 10,000 miles	40p
Each additional mile over 10,000 miles	25p

Loan benefits and the official rate of interest

The official rate of interest applicable to favourable loans to directors and/or employees is 5% effective from 6th January 2002 (prior to this date the rate was 6.25% effective 6th March 1999).

Payments on account: income tax

Payments on account are payable on the 31st January within the tax year and on 31st July following the end of the tax year.

No payments on account need be made where the aggregate of the relevant amount (i.e. income tax liability for previous tax year plus Class 4 NIC less tax deducted at source) for the immediately preceding tax year is less than £500 *or* where more than 80% of the taxpayer's income tax liability plus Class 4 NIC for the immediately preceding tax year was satisfied by tax deducted at source.

Any balancing payment is payable on the 31st January following the end of the tax year.

Personal pension schemes

Maximum contributions into a personal pension scheme are determined by the age of the contributor at the start of the relevant tax year and net relevant earnings as follows:

Age at start of tax year	% of net relevant earnings
35 & below	17.5%
36 to 45	20%
46 to 50	25%
51to 55	30%
56 to 60	35%
61 or more	40%

Earnings cap for 2005/06 £105,600 (£102,000 for 2004/05).

National insurance contributions

Class 1	Per week	Per year
Earnings threshold both employees and employers	£94	£4,895
Upper earnings limit	£630	£32,760

Employee contributions:

11% on weekly earnings between £94 and £630 per week

1% on weekly earnings over £630 per week

Employer contributions:

12.8% on weekly earnings over £94 per week

Class 1A

12.8% on benefits payable by employer only (no minimum or maximum)

Class 2

Flat rate of £2.10 per week payable by the self employed only

Class 3

Voluntary contributions of £7.35 per week

Class 4

Payable by the self employed only:

8% on profits between £4,895 and £32,760 per annum

1% on profits over £32,760 per annum

CAPITAL GAINS TAX

Annual exemption 2005/06

Individuals are entitled to an annual exemption of net gains of £8,500 for 2005/06 (£8,200 for 2004/05).

Rates of capital gains tax 2005/06

Capital gains are taxed as the top slice of an individual's income at rates of 10% (up to £2,090), 20% (above £2,090 up to £32,400) and 40% above £32,400.

The corresponding figures for 2004/05 were 10% (up to £2,020), 20% (above £2,020 up to £31,400) and 40% above £31,400.

Indexation allowances

Individuals are entitled to an indexation allowance on the sale of an asset when calculating any resulting capital gain. The indexation allowance is calculated by multiplying each item of allowable expenditure by an indexation factor. The indexation factor is computed as follows:

$$\frac{\text{RPI (date of disposal)* – RPI (date on which expenditure incurred)}}{\text{RPI (date on which expenditure incurred)}}$$

*or April 1998 if earlier.

Indexation allowances are only available up to 5th April 1998 for disposals by individuals. Thereafter taper relief applies.

Retail Price Indices (RPI)

	JAN	FEB	MAR	APR	MAY	JUN	JUL	AUG	SEP	OCT	NOV	DEC
1982	78.73	78.76	79.44	81.04	81.62	81.85	81.88	81.90	81.85	82.26	82.66	82.51
1983	82.61	82.97	83.12	84.28	84.64	84.84	85.30	85.68	86.06	86.36	86.67	86.89
1984	86.84	87.20	87.48	88.64	88.97	89.20	89.10	89.94	90.11	90.67	90.95	90.87
1985	91.20	91.94	92.80	94.78	95.21	95.41	95.23	95.49	95.44	95.59	95.92	96.05
1986	96.25	96.60	96.73	97.67	97.85	97.79	97.52	97.82	98.30	98.45	99.29	99.62
1987	100.0	100.4	100.6	101.8	101.9	101.9	101.8	102.1	102.4	102.9	103.4	103.3
1988	103.3	103.7	104.1	105.8	106.2	106.6	106.7	107.9	108.4	109.5	110.0	110.3
1989	111.0	111.8	112.3	114.3	115.0	115.4	115.5	115.8	116.6	117.5	118.5	118.8
1990	119.5	120.2	121.4	125.1	126.2	126.7	126.8	128.1	129.3	130.3	130.0	129.9
1991	130.2	130.9	131.4	133.1	133.5	134.1	133.8	134.1	134.6	135.1	135.6	135.7
1992	135.6	136.3	136.7	138.8	139.3	139.3	138.8	138.9	139.4	139.9	139.7	139.2
1993	137.9	138.8	139.3	140.6	141.1	141.0	140.7	141.3	141.9	141.8	141.6	141.9
1994	141.3	142.1	142.5	144.2	144.7	144.7	144.0	144.7	145.0	145.2	145.3	146.0
1995	146.0	146.9	147.5	149.0	149.6	149.8	149.1	149.9	150.6	149.8	149.8	150.7
1996	150.2	150.9	151.5	152.6	152.9	153.0	152.4	153.1	153.8	153.8	153.9	154.4
1997	154.4	155.0	155.4	156.3	156.9	157.5	157.5	158.5	159.3	159.5	159.6	160.0
1998	159.5	160.3	160.8	162.6	163.5	163.4	163.0	163.7	164.4	164.5	164.4	164.4
1999	163.4	163.7	164.1	165.2	165.6	165.6	165.1	165.5	166.2	166.5	166.7	167.3
2000	166.6	167.5	168.4	170.1	170.7	171.1	170.5	170.5	171.7	171.6	172.1	172.2
2001	171.1	172.0	172.2	173.1	174.2	174.4	173.3	174.0	174.6	174.3	173.6	173.4
2002	173.3	173.8	174.5	175.7	176.2	176.2	175.9	176.4	177.6	177.9	178.2	178.5
2003	178.4	179.3	179.9	181.2	181.5	181.3	181.3	181.6	182.5	182.6	182.7	183.5
2004	183.1	183.8	184.6	185.7	186.5	186.8	186.8	187.4	188.1	188.6	189.0	189.9
2005	188.9	189.6	190.5	191.6	192.0	192.2						

Taper Relief

Taper relief applies to disposals by individuals after 5th April 1998. Taper relief reduces any capital gains after indexation allowances and after offset of any capital losses. The percentage of taper relief depends upon the length of asset ownership in complete years and whether the asset is a business or non-business asset. Non-business assets owned prior to 17th March 1998 are entitled to a bonus year.

Number of complete years after 5th April 1998 for which asset held	Business assets % gain relieved %
0	0
1	50
2 or more	75

Number of complete years after 5th April 1998 for which asset held	Non-business assets % gain relieved %
0	0
1	0
2	0
3	5
4	10
5	15
6	20
7	25
8	30
9	35
10 or more	40

Payments on account: capital gains tax

No payments on account are required with respect to capital gains tax liabilities. Capital gains tax liabilities are payable on the 31st January following the tax year in which the gains arise.

CORPORATION TAX

Rates of corporation tax

Corporation tax rates are fixed for financial years:

Financial year 2005	30%
Financial year 2004	30%
Financial year 2003	30%

Starting and small companies rates:

Financial years	2005	2004	2003
Starting rate	0%	0%	0%
First relevant amount	£10,000	£10,000	£10,000
Second relevant amount	£50,000	£50,000	£50,000
Small companies rate	19%	19%	20%
Lower relevant amount	£300,000	£300,000	£300,000
Upper relevant amount	£1,500,000	£1,500,000	£1,500,000
Marginal relief fraction	19/400	19/400	19/400
Marginal relief fraction	11/400	11/400	11/400

Where PROFIT exceeds the First or Lower relevant amounts but not the Second or Upper relevant amounts corporation tax on PCTCT is reduced by:

[Second or Upper relevant amount − PROFIT] x PCTCT/PROFIT x MRF

PROFIT = PCTCT + FII

PCTCT refers to the profits chargeable to corporation tax

FII refers to franked investment income

MRF refers to the Marginal Relief Fraction.

Payment: corporation tax

The corporation tax liability for an accounting period is generally payable by a single payment nine months plus one day after the end of the accounting period.

For large companies (i.e. a company paying corporation tax liability at the full 30% rate) four equal instalments for the accounting period are payable on the 14th of the 7th month of the accounting period and at subsequent quarterly intervals (i.e. the 14th of months 10, 13 and 16).

Capital allowances
Industrial buildings

(all size businesses)

First year allowances	Nil
Writing down allowance	4% per annum

Plant and machinery
First year allowances

Small & medium sized businesses	40%

(increased to 50% for expenditure incurred
between 1st April 2004 and 31st March 2005
for companies or
6th April 2004 and 5th April 2005 for
sole traders who qualify as small businesses)

Small businesses only	100%

(information & communications technology
expenditure incurred between 1st April 2000
and 31st March 2004)

New low emission motor cars (all businesses)	100%

	Writing down allowances
Generally	25% per annum
Motor cars (not low emission)	25%* per annum

* restricted to maximum of £3,000 per annum

Long life assets

	First year allowances
Generally	0%
	Writing down allowances
Generally	6% per annum

VALUE ADDED TAX

Registration limits

From 1st April 2005 where turnover (i.e. taxable turnover at zero and/or standard rates) of past 12 months exceeds £60,000 compulsory registration required unless turnover for next 12 months not expected to exceed £58,000.

Where turnover in the next 30 days likley to exceed £60,000 compulsory registration required.

Deregistration

From 1st April 2005 where future turnover (i.e. taxable turnover at zero and/or standard rates) of next 12 months likely to fall below £58,000 voluntary deregistration may be effected.

Rates of VAT

Standard rate of VAT is 17.5%.

VAT fraction is 7/47ths.

Car fuel

A VAT inclusive car fuel scale charge applies to assess VAT where petrol is provided at below cost for private journeys of registered traders or their employees as follows:

From 1st May 2005	12 months	VAT due per car
Engine size:		
1,400cc or less	£985	£146.70
>1,400cc ≤ 2,000cc	£1,245	£185.43
Over 2,000cc	£1,830	£272.55
Diesel engines:		
≤ 2,000cc	£945	£140.74
Over 2,000cc	£1,200	£178.72

CHAPTER 1

Student Reader

Free standing text book

This text book can be used either on its own or in conjunction with other texts.

It is, however, completely self contained (including at the front of the book all the various allowances, reliefs etc that a student may need).

What is unique about this book?

This book is written in a user-friendly manner. It intersperses numerous examples throughout the text designed to illustrate particular points.

Complex jargon is avoided. Simple English is used.

This book also assumes absolutely no knowledge about UK taxation whatsoever.

How to use this book and how to study tax

This book covers the four main UK taxes, namely, income tax (paid by individuals), capital gains tax (paid by individuals), corporation tax (paid by companies) and value added tax (levied on consumers by businesses).

These are the taxes which typically form the core of the syllabuses for most of the UK's professional examinations in taxation such as those of the ACCA, CIMA, AAT and CAT. The book is also likely to be of help to any student studying tax in whatever form for the first time.

Preferably, the student coming to tax for the first time should read each of the chapters in the order in which they have been written.

This is because to a certain extent each chapter presupposes knowledge of earlier chapters. Having said this, value added tax, as it is a tax so different from the other taxes, could be studied at any point.

(see also Appendix 1).

Tax is not difficult

Many students believe that tax is difficult. This is not so.

The problem, however, is that many tax text books tend to be written in complex language. They tend to introduce the student to too many new facts at the same time leaving the student confused and bewildered.

This book avoids these mistakes. The language is simple and each new issue is followed by an illustrative example.

Many lecturers believe that learning tax is simply about doing lots and lots of examples. This is not true.

INCOME TAX

To pass any tax examination the student needs to understand the basics. Understanding the basics means that the student can cut down the need to simply memorise lots and lots of rules. This book concentrates on the basics.

Tax can be enjoyable

Tax can be fascinating, enjoyable and can offer the student a rewarding career.

Many other countries own tax systems are based upon the UK's tax system. By studying UK taxation the student will also be studying many parts of other countries' tax systems.

In studying this text I would suggest that, first, read the brief "Summary" at the end of each chapter; then read the whole of the chapter relatively quickly; then re-read the chapter slowly pausing to try and understand as much as possible before moving on to the next part of the chapter.

If understanding any particular part of a chapter proves a little too difficult move on and come back to it later in your studies. You will be surprised at how often something that you found difficult at one stage of your studies becomes straight forward when you return a bit later.

So, enjoy the read. Pick up the book when you are in the mood and good luck!

CHAPTER 2

Income Tax: General Principles

INTRODUCTION

This chapter will introduce various concepts including:

- how income is taxed
- the rates of tax which apply
- the categories of income

Who Pays Income Tax?

Any *individual* who is resident (basically someone who lives in the UK) in the UK will pay income tax on their worldwide income. As we shall see later in the book (Chapter 16) a company does not pay income tax but corporation tax on its worldwide income.

What Is Income?

Income includes for example:

- a person's salary/wages;
- a person's trading profits from conducting a business;
- bank interest;
- dividends from companies; and
- rents.

What Is An Income Tax Liability?

An individual's *income tax liability* is the tax liability on his *taxable income*.

Tax on this taxable income is referred to as *income tax*.

In order to work out an individual's income tax liability it becomes necessary to aggregate all his income to which he is entitled in a year (see below) and to then make certain deductions from it. Two types of deduction are made:

- a deduction for charges on income
- a deduction for a personal allowance

The effect of these calculations is to produce the following definitions:

Statutory Total Income (STI) = Total Income – Charges on Income

Taxable Income = STI – Personal Allowance

More will be said about these terms in Chapter 3.

Tax Year

An individual's total income for a year is in fact the income which arises in the *income tax year*. This is the period 6th April in any year to the following 5th April.

For example, the tax year 2002/2003 refers to the period 6th April 2002 to 5th April 2003.

The tax year 2005/2006 refers to the period 6th April 2005 to 5th April 2006.

A tax year is also referred to as a *year of assessment* or *a fiscal year*.

Working Out an Income Tax Liability

Although an individual's income to which he is entitled is aggregated it also needs at the same time to be categorised into one of three categories, namely:

- Non-savings income
- Savings income
- Dividend income

This categorisation is needed as these different categories are taxed at different rates of income tax and in a different order.

Categories of income

Non-Savings income comprises:

- rent from letting out a property
- business profits from the carrying on of a trade
- salary from an employment

Savings income comprises:

- interest income (e.g. from a bank or building society deposit)

Dividend income comprises:

- dividends from shares in UK companies

Order of taxing

- Non-savings income is taxed first
- then Savings income is taxed
- then Dividend income is taxed

Rates of income tax

- for *Non-savings income* the first £2,090 of Taxable Income is taxed at 10%; the next £30,310 is taxed at 22% and everything above £32,400 is taxed at 40%
- for *Savings income* which is taxed after Non-savings income (i.e. on top of it) any amount falling in the first £2,090 of Taxable Income is taxed at 10%; any Savings income which falls in the next £30,310 is taxed at 20% and any such income in excess of £32,400 is taxed at 40%
- for *Dividend income* which is taxed after both Non-savings and Savings income (i.e. on top of both) any dividend income falling in the amount up to £32,400 is taxed at 10% and above £32,400 it is taxed at 32.5%

The 22% rate is referred to as the *basic rate* of income tax.

An individual who is liable to pay income tax at the 40% rate is referred to as a higher rate taxpayer.

Let us look at how all this works in practice. At this stage charges on income and the personal allowance deductions will be ignored (these items will be looked at in more detail in Chapter 3).

First assume that all John Smith's income is Non-savings income.

Example 2.1

John Smith has taxable Non-Savings income of £1,500.

Income tax due = 10% x £1,500 = £150

As John's taxable income is below the £2,090 limit the rate applicable is 10% and this applies to all of John's taxable income.

Example 2.2

John Smith has taxable Non-Savings income of £25,000.

Income tax due:

First £2,090 of the £25,000 taxed at 10%	=	£209
Next (£25,000 - £2,090) = £22,910 x 22%	=	£5,040
Therefore total income tax liability	=	£5,249

Example 2.3

John Smith has Non-Savings taxable income of £35,000

Income tax due

First £2,090 at 10%	=	£209
Next (£32,400 - £2,090) = £30,310 x 22%	=	£6,668
Next (£35,000 - £32,400) = £2,600 x 40%	=	£1,040
Therefore total income tax liability	=	£7,917

John in this Example 2.3 is taxed on a part of his income at 10% (i.e. up to £2,090); the next £30,310 (i.e. the next £32,400 minus £2,090 = £30,310) is taxed at 22%; with only the excess over £32,400 then being taxed at 40%.

Let us now look at the position if John's income is all Savings income.

Example 2.4

John Smith has taxable Savings income of £1,500

Income tax due =10% x £1,500	=	£150

As John's taxable income is below the £2,090 limit the rate applicable is 10% and this applies to all of John's taxable income.

Note this gives the same answer as in Example 2.1 above.

Example 2.5

John Smith has taxable Savings income of £25,000.

Income tax due:

First £2,090 at 10%	=	£209
Next £22,910 at 20%	=	£4,582
Total income tax liability		£4,791

Note

Compared to Example 2.2 above John's tax liability is £458 lower (i.e. £5,249 minus £4,791) This is because some £22,910 of his taxable income has been taxed in this example at 20% rather than 22% as in Example 2.2; thus saving 2% of £22,910 i.e. £458.

Example 2.6

John Smith has taxable Savings income of £35,000

Income tax due:

First £2,090 at 10%	=	£209
Next £32,400 - £2,090 = £30,310 x 20% =		£6,062
Next £35,000 - £32,400 = £2,600 x 40% =		£1,040
Therefore total income tax liability	=	£7,311

Compared to Example 2.3 above John's tax liability is some £606 lower (i.e. £7,917 - £7,311). This is again explained by the fact that £30,310 of taxable income has been taxed at 20% rather than 22% saving 2% of £30,310 i.e. £606.

Let us now assume all of John's income is dividend income.

Example 2.7

John Smith has taxable Dividend income of £1,500.

Income tax due = 10% x £1,500   =   £150

As John's taxable income is below the £32,400 limit the rate applicable is 10% and this applies to all of John's taxable income.

Note in this case up to £32,400 not just £2,090 is taxed at 10%. This is different to the position re Non-savings and Savings income.

Example 2.8

John Smith has taxable Dividend income of £25,000.

Income tax due:

First £25,000 taxed at 10%   =   £2,500

Example 2.9

John Smith has taxable Dividend income of £35,000

Income tax due:

First £32,400 taxed at 10%	=	£3,240
Next £35,000 - £32,400 = £2,600 x 32.5%	=	£845
Therefore total income tax liability	=	£4,085

In this case John is taxed on a part of his income at 10% (i.e. up to £32,400); the balance (i.e. the next £35,000 minus £32,400= £2,600) is taxed at 32.5%.

Now assume that John Smith's income is a mixture of Non-savings, Savings and Dividend income.

Example 2.10

John Smith has the following taxable income:
Non-savings income of £25,000
Savings income of £7,500
Dividend income of £3,000

Income tax due:

Non-savings income		
First £2,090 taxed at 10%	=	£209
Next (£25,000 - £2,090) = £22,910 x 22%	=	£5,040
Savings income		
Next (£32,400 - £25,000) = £7,400 x 20%	=	£1,480
Next (£7,500 - £7,400) = £100 x 40%	=	£40
Dividend income		
Next £3,000 x 32.5%	=	£975
Therefore total income tax liability	=	£7,744

This example illustrates that although each category of income is taxed at different rates of income tax and in a specific order, in working out the total income tax liability each category is stacked on top of the other to ascertain what rate of income tax should apply to how much of that category of income.

Thus, the Non-savings income of £25,000 is taxed at the 10% and 22% rates. This is so because the amount of Non-savings income is not more than £32,400 and thus the 40% rate cannot apply.

However, when the Savings income of £7,500 is added to the £25,000 this gives a total of £32,500. Thus, some part of the Savings income (i.e. the bit which when added to the Non-savings income of £25,000 equals £32,400) i.e. £7,400 is taxed at 20% with the balance i.e. £7,500 - £7,400 taxed at the 40% rate.

As the total of Non-savings plus Savings income is greater than £32,400 any Dividend income added on top will be subject to the 32.5% rate.

It should thus be appreciated that there is only one amount of £2,090 of Taxable income which is taxed at 10%. Each category of Taxable income is *not* entitled to its own £2,090.

SUMMARY

- Non-savings income is taxed at 10%, 22% and 40%
- Savings income is taxed at 10%, 20% and 40%
- Dividend income is taxed at 10% and 32.5%
- Non-savings income is taxed first; then Savings income; then Dividend income
- Each category of income is added to the earlier category of income to ascertain the rates to apply
- STI equals Total income less Charges on income
- Taxable income equals STI less Personal allowance

CHAPTER 3

Personal Tax Computation

INTRODUCTION

This chapter will explain how an individual's personal income tax liability is calculated for a tax year and introduces the concepts of tax deduction at source; charges on income; and the personal allowance.

TAXABLE INCOME

Chapter 2 identified that:

STI = Total income – Charges on income
Taxable Income = STI – Personal Allowance

Each of these terms will now be looked at in turn.

Total income

Chapter 2 referred to three different categories of income, namely:

- Non-savings
- Savings
- Dividends

A person's Total income is simply the aggregate of these three categories of income for a particular tax year.

Non-Savings income comprises income from the carrying on of a trade, (i.e. trading profit), employment income and income (e.g. rent) received from a property business.

Savings income comprises interest income typically earned on cash deposits with banks and building societies.

Dividends simply refer to dividend income received from shares in UK companies.

As will be seen later in the text (see Chapters 11 and 19) income may also arise from sources outside the UK (e.g. dividends from non-UK companies; rental income from overseas owned properties).

Each type of income has its own set of rules which determines both how it is to be taxed (e.g. accruals or receipts basis) and how the appropriate amount to be taxed is to be determined (e.g. in computing the trading profit of a sole trader what expenses may be deducted; what expenses may be deducted from an employee's salary); in short, its basis of assessment.

The rules for each type of income may vary. For example, any profit from a property business (i.e. rental income less expenses) is determined by offsetting certain expenses (e.g. repairs to the property) from the rental income which accrues (i.e. rental income is calculated for a period on an accruals basis and thus the time of any actual rental receipts is irrelevant).

On the other hand dividend income from UK companies is taxed when received (i.e. the accruals basis is irrelevant).

In summary:

Type of income	Basis of assessment
Property income	Accruals basis
Trading income	Accruals basis
Interest income	Arising basis (i.e. when received or credited)
Employment income	Receipts basis (i.e. when received or credited)
Dividend income	Receipts basis (i.e. when received or credited)
Overseas income	Receipts basis (i.e. when received or credited)

More will be said later in the book about each of these income categories.

It is sufficient, at this stage, to note their existence and the above points.

Charges on Income

Having ascertained an individual's Total income for a tax year charges on income must then be deducted to arrive at STI. By deducting the charges in this manner an individual obtains tax relief for the payments.

Charges on income comprise payments which are
- interest payments on qualifying loans
- patent royalty payments

Interest on qualifying loan

Not all interest payments qualify as charges on income and thus not all interest payments can be deducted in computing STI.

To qualify the interest payments must be in respect of a borrowing which satisfies certain conditions. The main examples of a qualifying loan are:
- loan to purchase shares in an employee-controlled company
- loan to purchase an interest in a partnership

Patent royalty

All patent royalty payments qualify as charges on income. Patent royalty payments are typically payments made by someone who has been granted a licence by the owner of the patent to manufacture a particular product. The royalty payment in such a case might be, for example, 10% of gross sales.

Thus, whether the payment is interest on a qualifying loan or a patent royalty it will qualify as a charge on income.

Tax deduction at source

When an individual makes a patent royalty payment income tax at the basic rate of 22% must first be deducted from the payment.

Thus, for example, on making a patent royalty payment of say £100, income tax of £22 must be first deducted which means that the recipient only actually receives cash of £78.

However, unlike the position with respect to patent royalty payments no income tax at source is deducted form qualifying interest payments. Thus, for example, on making a qualifying interest payment of say £100 no tax at source is deducted and the recipient actually receives cash of £100.

Example 3.1

John Smith has Total Income of £39,000 (assume this income is all Non savings income) for tax year 2005/2006.

He pays interest on a qualifying loan (i.e. a charge on income) of £3,000. Remember no income tax at source is deducted when making this payment (see above).

His STI = Total income - Charges on income

STI = £39,000 - £3,000 = £36,000

Example 3.2

John Smith (as in Example 3.1) has total income of £39,000 (assume this income is all Non savings income) for tax year 2005/2006.

He pays a gross patent royalty (i.e. a charge on income) of £3,000. Although when making this payment John will deduct income tax at 22% from the gross payment, his STI remains the same.

His STI = Total income – Charges on income

STI = £39,000 - £3,000 = £36,000

Interest versus royalty payment

It will be seen from Examples 3.1 and 3.2 that STI is the same whether the charge on income is interest on a qualifying loan or a patent royalty payment. However, in Example 3.2 income tax at source of £660 (22% x £3,000) is deducted when the payment is made. This fact will somehow need to be taken into account at some point when working out John's income tax liability otherwise John's liability in Examples 3.1 and 3.2 would be different which should not be the case.

Example 3.4 (Step 7) below will illustrate how the tax deducted is taken into account.

However, as already indicated, whichever charge on income payment is made the income tax liability of John will be the same.

Personal allowance

Having subtracted any charges on income from Total income to obtain STI all that is then necessary is to deduct a Personal Allowance.

The Personal Allowance for an individual is fixed for a tax year, and for the 2005/2006 tax year it is £4,895.

Every individual is entitled to this allowance whether man, woman or child.

What the allowance represents is the amount of income to which an individual may be entitled "tax free" i.e. without being liable to income tax thereon.

It should now be possible to calculate an individual's overall income tax liability for a tax year.

However, before doing so it will be helpful to first of all look at the concept of tax deduction at source.

As was seen above, in connection with patent royalty *payments*, income tax is deducted when making such *payments*. Income tax at source is, however, also deducted from other certain types of *income* prior to it being actually received.

(Note: If an individual is aged 65 or over during a tax year then *instead of* the above personal allowance an age allowance is available. Where an individual is married then *in addition* to the above personal allowance (or in addition to the age allowance) the married man is also entitled to a married couple's allowance. These aspects are not relevant to all tax syllabuses and accordingly these issues are covered in the appendix at the end of this chapter).

Tax deduction at source ("grossing up")

The examples in Chapter 2, for the sake of simplicity, ignored the fact that some types of *income* are only received *after* income tax at source has been deducted. In other words, an individual only receives an amount of income after some income tax has been deducted from it.

However, when working out an individual's Total income any income received after income tax has been deducted must be included "gross" i.e. with the income tax deducted added back. Account must then be taken of this tax which has been deducted.

The main category of income where tax is deducted at source is:

bank/building society interest credited on cash deposits

Interest

When a person receives interest on a cash deposit with a bank and/or a building society (basically the same as a bank) income tax at source is deducted by the bank and/or building society at the rate of 20%.

Thus, when interest of, say, £100 is paid by a bank on a cash deposit the taxpayer will actually receive only £80 i.e. £100 less £20 (i.e. 20% x £100) income tax deducted at source.

When working out an individual's Total income he/she is assumed, however, to have received the gross amount of interest, in the above example, £100 (i.e. the net receipt of £80 plus the tax withheld of £20; or 80/0.8).

Another type of income where prior to receiving it tax at source is deducted is an individual's salary.

Salary

This aspect is discussed in more detail later in the book (Chapter 10). For present purposes it is sufficient to note that when an individual receives a salary from an employer, tax at source (referred to as Pay As You Earn (PAYE)) will be deducted from it. Unlike above, however, there is no single rate of tax to determine the amount of tax to be deducted; the amount deducted will in fact depend upon various factors personal to the individual (Chapter 21).

Note also that where an individual is an employee and a member of an occupational (i.e. employer) pension scheme any pension contributions made by the employee to the scheme are deductible from gross salary.

In arriving at gross salary to be included in ascertaining Total income the figure to include is salary *before* PAYE has been deducted but *after* deduction for any pension scheme contributions to an employer's pension scheme.

Dividends

When a UK company makes a dividend payment although no tax at source is actually deducted (as occurs when banks pay interest) the recipient is assumed to have received a *net* dividend to which is attached a tax credit of $1/9^{th}$ of the net dividend. The gross dividend (i.e. the net dividend plus the tax credit) is then subject to tax.

For example, when a dividend payment of say £900 is received by an individual from a company the recipient is also entitled to a tax credit of 1/9 x £900 = £100 making the gross dividend receipt of £1,000 (or 900/0.9). It is this gross figure which is included in ascertaining Total income.

The importance of the issue of tax deduction at source on certain categories of income is that in working out an individual's income tax liability it is important to include the **gross** amounts of income in the calculation of **Total income** not the net figures.

Where any tax at source has been deducted from income, the tax deducted will appear later in the calculation of an individual's income tax liability by way of a tax credit (i.e. the tax deducted at source will reduce the initially calculated income tax liability).

Let us now look at where John's income comprises Non-savings, Savings and Dividend income and some types of income need to be grossed up.

Example 3.3

John Smith has the following income for tax year 2005/2006:

Rents	£4,000
Business profits	£15,000
Bank interest (net)	£12,000
Salary (after PAYE of £2,000 has been deducted)	£13,000
Dividends (net)	£900

John is also a member of his employer's pension scheme and makes annual contributions of 5% of his salary.

The amounts of income which would be included in working out John's Total income for 2005/2006 are:

Rents		£4,000
Business profits		£15,000
Bank interest (net)	(£12,000/0.8)	£15,000
Salary	[(£13,000 + £2,000) – (5% x £15,000)]	£14,250
Dividends (net)	(£900 + 1/9 * £900)	£1,000

Notes
1. The bank interest received of £12,000 was after 20% tax had been deducted. Therefore £12,000 represents 80% of the gross amount. Thus, the gross amount will be £12,000/0.8.
2. Gross salary is simply net salary £13,000 plus PAYE deducted £2,000 i.e. £15,000 then less the pension contribution of 5% of £15,000 (i.e. £750) to give £14,250.
3. Attached to the net dividend of £900 is a tax credit of 1/9th thereof. Thus, gross dividend will be £900 plus the tax credit of 1/9th x £900 to give £1,000.

It should now be possible to calculate an individual's income tax liability for a tax year.

However, before doing so a set of pro-forma Steps is set out below which should be followed whenever working out an individual's income tax liability.

TAX COMPUTATION

First a set of rules to follow for all individual tax computations:

Step 1

Work out the various amounts of income which are taxable.

Step 2

Categorise the individual incomes into one of three categories:

- Non-Savings income (i.e. property business income, trading income and employment income)
- Savings income (i.e. interest)
- Dividend income (i.e. dividends)

Step 3

Add up the amounts under each of these three categories to give three separate sub-totals.

Step 4

Deduct from the total for Non-Savings income under Step 3 the amount of any charges on income.

If total charges on income exceed the total for Non-savings income then deduct the surplus from Savings then Dividend income.

The total of the three categories will comprise STI.

Step 5

Deduct from Non-Savings income STI (arrived at under Step 4) the personal allowance to give Non-Savings Taxable income.

If the personal allowance exceeds the total for Non-savings income STI deduct the surplus from Savings STI then Dividend STI.

(The total of the three categories gives total Taxable income.)

Step 6

Compute tax liability by applying rates of income tax to each of the three taxable income figures obtained under Step 5 for each of Non-savings income; Savings income; and Dividend income.

Step 7

Add back any income tax deducted when making any charge on income *payments* to give total income tax *liability*.

Step 8

Deduct from the total in Step 7 any income tax which may have been deducted at source from income *received* (e.g. tax on bank interest received; PAYE on salary) to get total income tax *payable*.

Example 3.4

John Smith has the following income for tax year 2005/2006:

Property business profit	£4,000
Trading profit	£15,000
Interest income (net)	£12,000
Employment income (salary as an employee after PAYE)	£13,000
Dividends (net)	£900
Charges on income (net)	£3,510
(patent royalty payments)	

John is a member of his employer's occupational pension scheme paying annual contributions of 5% of salary. PAYE of £2,000 has been deducted from John's salary.

Answer

	Non-Savings	Savings	Dividends
Step 1/2/3	£	£	£
Property business profit	4,000		
Trading profit	15,000		
Employment income	14,250		
Interest income			
(£12,000/0.8)		15,000	
Dividends			
(£900+1/9*900)			1,000
Total income	33,250	15,000	1,000
Step 4			
Less Charges on income	(4,500)		
STI	28,750	15,000	1,000
Step 5			
Less Personal allowance	(4,895)		
Taxable income	23,855	15,000	1,000

Step 6

Tax liability:

Non Savings income

2,090	@ 10%	209
21,765 (£23,855 - £2,090)	@ 22%	4,788
23,855		4,997

Savings income

Interest

8,545 (£32,400 - £23,855) @ 20%	1,709
32,400	

6,455 (£15,000 - £8,545) @ 40%		2,582
38,855		9,288
Dividends		
1,000	@ 32.5	325
39,855		
Tax liability		9,613

Step 7
Add tax deducted on making
charge on income payment
[(3,510/0.78) x 22%)]   990
Income tax liability   10,603

Step 8
Less:

Dividend tax credit	(100)	
Tax deducted re interest	(3,000)	
PAYE	(2,000)	
		(5,100)
Income tax payable		5,503

When actually working out an income tax liability the above layout should be used but do not include the references to the various "Steps" as they have been included for illustration purposes only.

Some important points to note:
- all figures included in a tax computation are *gross*
- it is necessary to keep three separate columns for each category of income
- deduct the charges on income against the Non-savings income column first
- deduct the personal allowance against the Non-savings income column first
- the personal allowance is fixed for a tax year; £4,895 for tax year 2005/2006
- the personal allowance is deducted from STI to give Taxable income
- Non-savings then Savings then Dividends are taxed in that order
- add back any tax deducted when making charges on income payments (only applies to patent royalty payments)
- deduct any tax deducted at source from *income* received
- income tax *liability* is different from income tax *payable*

Income tax liability versus income tax payable
An individual's income tax *liability* is the liability based upon aggregate income less certain deductions.

However, where some income has been received after tax at source has been deducted (e.g. bank interest) in effect this tax deducted represents a partial settlement of the individual's ultimate income tax liability on this income.

This is therefore why any tax deducted on income received must be deducted from the income tax liability calculated (see Steps 7 and 8) as only the balance is actually *payable*.

SUMMARY

The categories of income which fall within Non-Savings, Savings and Dividend Income and/or the payments which suffer deduction of tax at source need to be remembered.

The basis of assessment for each category of income is very important (as will be seen later in the book).

The pro-forma layout used to calculate an individual's income tax liability is also very important and must be remembered.

APPENDIX
AGE ALLOWANCES AND MARRIED COUPLE'S ALLOWANCE

Age Allowance

A higher rate of personal allowance (referred to as an age allowance) is available, instead of the normal personal allowance, to a taxpayer aged 65 or over *during* the tax year. If the taxpayer is in fact aged 75 or over during the tax year an even higher age allowance is available.

For 2005/06 the age allowances are:

> £7,090 aged 65 – 74
> £7,220 aged 75 or over

The above age allowances are, however, reduced if the taxpayer's STI exceeds £19,500. The reduction is given by:

> 0.5 x (STI – 19,500)

Note: in calculating STI *for this purpose only*, the gross amount of any Gift Aid payments (i.e. payments to charity; see Chapter 4) is allowed as a deduction from STI. This will reduce the amount of the above restriction thus increasing the amount of the age allowance. Gift Aid relief at the higher rate is obtained via Extended Basic Rate (see Chapter 4).

However, if applying the restriction of [0.5 x (STI – 19,500)]produces an age allowance below the normal personal allowance of £4,895 for tax year 2005/06 then the £4,895 allowance replaces the age allowance figure as reduced.

EXAMPLE A1

John Smith aged 78 has STI of £20,900 for 2005/2006.
No Gift Aid payments were made by John.
Show John's personal allowance entitlement for tax year 2005/06

Answer

Maximum age allowance for John is £7,220 based on his age of 75 in 2005/06. However STI exceeds £19,500.

Reduction of age allowance is given by:

> 0.5 x (20,900 – 19,500) = £700

Age allowance = 7,220 – 700 = £6,520

Assume John's STI had been £25,900 instead of £20,900.

Reduction of age allowance is given by:

> 0.5 x (25,900 – 19,500) = £3,200

Age allowance = 7,220 – 3,200 = £4,020

However, as this amount is less than the normal personal allowance of £4,895 John continues to be entitled to the £4,895.

Married Couples Allowance

The married couples allowance is available *in addition* to either the personal or age allowance.

It is claimable by any *married man* who is living with his wife during the tax year and where one of the spouses was 65 before 6 April 2000.

The married couples allowance for 2005/06 is:

  £5,905 where both spouses under 75 during tax year

  £5,975 where either spouse 75 or over during tax year

As with the age allowance above, the married couples allowance may be reduced where the restriction which applied to reduce the age allowance was not, itself, fully utilised. In any event the minimum married couples allowance for tax year 2005/06 is £2,280.

Unlike the personal and age allowances which reduce a person's STI to produce taxable income, relief for the married couples allowance is by way of what is referred to as a *tax reducer*. A tax reducer reduces the amount of a person's income tax liability after it has been calculated and in the case of the married couples allowance is equal to 10% of the married couples allowance.

The deduction is made *before* adding back any tax retained on any charges on income which have been paid by the person.

The married couples allowance is reduced in the year of marriage by 1/12th for each complete tax month before the wedding date (i.e. the months start on the 6th to the following 5th).

The married couples allowance is available in the tax year of separation but not after the end of the tax year in which the separation occurs.

Any unused element of the married couples allowance on the part of the husband can be transferred to the wife; in addition, if *both* spouses agree, the whole of the minimum allowance of £2,280 can be allocated to the wife *or* the wife may unilaterally claim 50% of the £2,280 i.e. £1,140.

EXAMPLE A2

John Smith a married man aged 78 (wife aged 67) has STI of £20,900 for 2005/2006.

No Gift Aid payments were made. His wife has no income.

Show John's personal/age and married couple's allowances.

Answer

Maximum age allowance for John the husband is 7,220

However, John's STI exceeds £19,500.

Reduction on age allowance therefore

$$0.5 \times (20,900 - 19,500) = £700$$

Age allowance $= 7,220 - 700$ $= £6,520$

As all the "reduction" of 700 has been used in reducing the age allowance the married couples allowance is unaffected and John is entitled to the full 5,975.

If John's STI had, however, been 25,900 not the above figure of 20,900 then:

Reduction in age allowance = $0.5 \times (25,900 - 19,500) = £3,200$

Age allowance = $7,220 - 3,200$ $= £4,020$

But minimum age allowance must be 4,895

As a consequence, the amount of the actual restriction is 7,220-4,895 = 2,325 not 3,200

Therefore the unused part of the restriction (3,200 - 2,325 = 875) is then used to reduce any married couples allowance as follows:

Married couples allowance = 5,975 – 875 = £5,100

John's income tax liability assuming the 25,900 figure for STI:

Taxable income = STI – Personal allowance = 25,900 – 4,895	=	21,005
First 2,090 of taxable income @ 10%	=	209
Next <u>18,915</u> of taxable income @ 22%	=	4,161
21,005		
Total income tax liability	=	4,370
Less		
Married couples allowance = 5,100 x 10%	=	<u>510</u>
Income tax liability		3,860

CHAPTER 4
Extended Basic Rate Band

INTRODUCTION

This chapter takes a look at the concept of the extended basic rate band which is of relevance where an individual makes either Gift Aid and/or Personal Pension payments.

What is the extended basic rate band?

The concept of the extended basic rate band refers to how income tax relief is obtained on certain payments made by an individual taxpayer.

Normally, income tax relief for a payment made is obtained by deducting the gross payment when working out an individual's Taxable income (remember in Chapter 3 where payments of patent royalties and qualifying interest payments were deducted as charges on income).

The payments to which the extended rate band concept applies are:
- Gift Aid payments and
- Personal Pension contributions.

Gift Aid payments are payments to charities.

Personal Pension contributions are, generally speaking, payments made by the self employed (i.e. those trading on their own account as sole traders) to provide for a pension; certain employees may also make such payments although in the case of employees the payments are usually made under an occupational pension scheme rather than as personal pension payments (see Chapter 22).

Tax deducted at source

Income tax at the basic rate (22% for 2005/2006) is deducted at source when making either a Gift Aid or a Personal Pension payment.

In other words, when a payment of, say, £4,000 is made (whether Gift Aid or Personal Pension) income tax at 22% (i.e. £880) is deducted. The person receiving the payment thus actually only receives £4,000 less £880 i.e. £3,120 and the person making the payment keeps the £880 (similar to the situation discussed in Chapter 3 with respect to patent royalty payments).

As a consequence of the tax deducted at source immediate tax relief at the basic rate has been obtained for the payment.

However, in working out an individual's STI *no* deduction is made in the actual computation for either the Gift Aid or Personal Pension payment (compare the situation where the patent royalty payment *was* deducted in calculating STI even though tax at source had been deducted from it; see Chapter 3).

As a consequence, if the taxpayer is a higher rate taxpayer i.e. a taxpayer who pays tax at the 40% rate, no relief at the 40% rate will have been obtained.

Extended basic rate band scheme

This higher rate tax relief is thus obtained by extending the basic rate band.

What this means is that the level of Taxable income at which income tax at the higher rate of tax (i.e. 40%) applies (currently £32,400 for 2005/2006) is increased. The increase is equal to the "gross" amount of the Gift Aid *or* Personal Pension payment (or the aggregate of both if both payments are made).

The effect of extending the basic rate band is that the 22% rate applies to this extension rather than the 40% rate which would normally apply. The effect is to produce a tax saving of 18% (i.e. 40% minus 22%) on this extra amount or extension.

Example 4.1

John Smith has Taxable Income of £35,000 and makes a Gift Aid payment of £1,560 (net). Calculate John's income tax liability.

Answer

The Gross Gift Aid payment is equal to 1,560/0.78 =2,000 (gross)

The basic rate band is thus extended by 2,000 from 32,400 to 34,400.The 40% rate will now only apply to Taxable Income above this figure.

	Taxable income £	Tax rate %	Income tax £
First	2,090	10	209
Next	30,310	22	6,668
Total	32,400		
Next	2,000	22	440
(representing extended basic rate)			
Next	600	40	240
Total	35,000		7,557

John's tax relief is therefore obtained by deducting income tax at the basic rate (22%) when actually making the payment, amounting to 22% of 2,000 (i.e. 440), and an extra 18% of tax relief is obtained by the saving of 40% minus 22% on the gross payment of 2,000 (i.e. 360) producing total tax relief of 440 + 360 i.e.800.

Example 4.2

If John's Taxable Income in the above Example was, say, £34,000 then:

	Taxable income	Tax rate	Income tax
	£	%	£
First	2,090	10	209
Next	30,310	22	6,668
Total	32,400		
Next	1,600	22	352
(representing extended basic rate)			
Total	34,000		7,229

In this case the basic rate band is only extended by 1,600 because John Smith's Taxable Income only exceeds the 32,400 by 1,600. Tax at 18% (i.e. 40% less 22%) is thus saved on 1,600 only. 22% was saved on making the 2,000 payment. Thus, total tax relief is 440 + 288 = 728.

Example 4.3

If John's Taxable Income in the above Example was, say, £32,400 then:

	Taxable income	Tax rate	Income tax
	£	%	£
First	2,090	10	209
Next	30,310	22	6,668
Total	32,400		6,877

In this case there is no extension of the basic rate band as John Smith's Taxable Income does not exceed the 32,400 and thus tax relief is only obtained at the basic rate of 22% (i.e. 22% of 2,000).

Claw back of tax deducted at source

It should be noted that where an individual's total income tax liability is less than the amount which has actually been deducted from a Gift Aid payment when it is made a partial or total claw back of any tax relief given may occur i.e. some or all of the tax deducted when the payment was made may need to be given back to the tax authorities.

On the other hand, with respect to Personal Pension payments, no such claw back occurs in such circumstances.

Example 4.4

John Smith's income tax liability for 2005/2006 is £500. John made a Gift Aid payment during the tax year of £2,340 (net).

On making the payment John will have deducted tax at source of 22% x £3,000 = £660 and thus will have received tax relief of £660.

In this case John's actual income tax liability will be £160 (i.e. £660 - £500).

Example 4.5

John Smith has the following income for 2005/2006:
- Business profits £30,000
- Salary £20,000
- Net dividends £6,750
- Building Society interest £3,000 (net)

John makes the following payments:
- Gross charges on income of £2,000 (assume interest on qualifying loan)
- Gift Aid payment of £780 (net)

Calculate John's income tax liability and his income tax payable for 2005/2006.

Answer

	Non Savings	Savings	Dividends	Total
Trading profit	30,000			
Employment income	20,000			
B/S interest				
(3,000/0.8)		3,750		
Dividends				
(6,750 plus 1/9 x 6,750)			7,500	
	———	———	———	
Totals	50,000	3,750	7,500	
Less: Charges	(2,000)			
STI	48,000	3,750	7,500	59,250
Less: PA	(4,895)	-	-	
Taxable income	43,105	3,750	7,500	54,355

Income tax calculation

Non savings

£2,090 @ 10%	209
£30,310 @ 22%	6,668
£32,400	
£1,000 @ 22%	220
(EBR due to the Gift Aid payment)	

£9,705 @ 40%	<u>3,882</u>
£43,105	10,979
Savings	
£3,750 @ 40%	1,500
Dividends	
£7,500 @ 32.5%	<u>2,438</u>
Tax liability	14,917
Less	
Tax credit on divs	(750)
Tax deducted on B/S interest	<u>(750)</u>
Tax payable	13,417

The Gift Aid scheme applies to any charitable donation whether one off or regular payments (unless covered by the payroll giving scheme).

As already stated relief at the taxpayer's highest rate of income tax is available.

In order for the charity to be able to recover from the tax authorities the income tax which has been deducted by the donor at source the donor must be UK resident and must give an appropriate declaration to the charity concerned providing his/her name and address, charity's name, description of donation made and a statement that the gift is made under the Gift Aid scheme.

SUMMARY

Where an individual makes either Gift Aid or Personal Pension payments neither payment is deducted in working out an individual's Taxable income.

Tax relief at the higher rate of tax (i.e. the 40% rate) is obtained by simply extending the basic rate band by the gross amount of the Gift Aid and/or Personal Pension payment, basic rate income tax relief having been obtained by deducting tax at source.

If an individual makes both types of payment then the basic rate band is extended by the aggregate amount of both payments.

Tax deducted at source when making a Gift Aid payment may be clawed back; this is not the case for Personal Pension payments where any tax deducted is retained by the individual.

CHAPTER 5

Income from a property business

INTRODUCTION

This chapter will identify the key issues associated with the taxation of income which is generated from land situated in the UK for income tax purposes; basically rental income.

The end of the chapter will consider the position of rental income received by companies.

Description

Income tax is levied on the profits of a property business which means a business designed to generate income from land.

Whilst property business income primarily consists of rental income it may also consist of the receipt of what are called premiums.

A premium is simply a "one-off" lump sum of cash which the person renting the property (i.e. the tenant) pays to the person from whom the property is being rented (i.e. the landlord) and which is normally payable in addition to any rent which is payable. It is normally payable only in respect of commercial (e.g. offices) rather than residential properties.

Basis of assessment and expenses

The profits of a property business are calculated in the same way as profits of a trade (see Chapter 6).

The amount assessable is therefore the aggregate property income less expenses for the tax year under consideration.

Accruals basis

Income

The accruals basis is applied in ascertaining the amount of rental income to be assessed for a tax year. Therefore the actual date of payment or receipt of rent is irrelevant.

Expenses

Expenses are also deductible on an accruals basis.

Expenses which *are* deductible are those allowable under the normal rules for trades/businesses (see Chapter 6)

e.g. the expenses must have been wholly and exclusively incurred for the purpose of the business (and thus not for private purposes) and would typically include:

- insurance of the property
- estate agents fees (e.g. for finding tenants)

- repairs (e.g. redecorating; repairing the roof, broken windows etc)
- interest on loans borrowed for the purchase/improvement of the property
- specific (but not general) provision for bad debts
- bad debts written off.

Examples of expenditure which is *not* deductible would include:

- capital expenditure e.g. expenditure on fitting a new and improved roof rather than simply repairing it; having to incur expenditure on a newly acquired property *before* it could be let out eg having to solve a major problem of rising damp (in this case the income is treated as capital expenditure not revenue expenditure and thus not deductible)
- general provisions (rather than specific provisions which would be allowable) for bad debts;
- expenditure incurred for private purposes (e.g. landlord lives in a flat above a flat which he rents out. If the whole of building was redecorated some part of this cost would be disallowed as relating to the landlord's private flat. The percentage of cost allowed would need to be agreed with the tax authorities).
- depreciation of assets (e.g. furniture in furnished letting)

Capital allowances

Whilst capital expenditure is not a deductible expense in computing the profits of a property business capital allowances (a form of tax allowed depreciation on capital assets purchased; see Chapter 7) are sometimes available.

However, in the case of a *furnished* (not unfurnished) property letting capital allowances are not available but a deduction is still permitted on one of two bases:

- *renewals basis* i.e. although there is no tax relief for the initial cost of furniture the whole of the subsequent cost of replacement (not improvement) furniture is deductible as a revenue expense in the tax year of replacement; *or*
- 10% *wear and tear* allowance per tax year i.e. a deduction equal to 10% of gross rent *or* 10% of rent less tenant costs paid by the landlord but normally the tenant's burden (i.e. water rates and council tax).

Example 5.1

John Smith owns a furnished flat which he lets to a tenant for an annual rent of £8,400 payable monthly in advance. However, the rent due for February, March and April 2006 was not paid until later in 2006.

Calculate John's property business profit assessment for 2005/2006.

Answer

John is assessed on his property business profit on an accruals basis.

For tax year 2005/2006 he is assessed on 12 x £700 = £8,400

The fact that three months worth of rent was not paid until later in 2006 i.e. in the next tax year (i.e. 2006/07) is irrelevant as property income is taxed on an accruals and not receipts basis.

Example 5.2

John Smith owns a furnished flat which he lets out on a regular basis. The flat was let out for the whole of the tax year 2005/2006.

The annual rent of £6,750 is payable monthly in advance.

Expenses incurred by John during the tax year are as follows:

	£
Flat buildings insurance	375
Repairs (i.e. painting/decorating and roof repair)	500
Estate agent commissions	1,000
Water rates	250
Council tax	775
Structural repairs	4,250

Calculate John's property business profit assessment for 2005/2006.

Answer

	£	£
Gross rents		6,750
Less: Expenses:		
Insurance	375	
Repairs	500	
Commissions	1,000	
Water rates	250	
Council tax	775	(2,900)
Wear and tear allowance		
(10% x (6750 – (250 + 775)))		(573)
		3,277

Notes

1. Structural repairs are capital and therefore not deductible (only revenue expenses are deductible)
2. Water rates and Council tax are liabilities of the tenant not the landlord, John Smith. However, as they are in fact paid by John this has to be taken into account when working out his "wear and tear" allowance; if the tenant had in fact paid both these items then John's "wear and tear" allowance would have been 10% x 6,750 i.e. £675.
3. Gross rent is assessable on an accruals basis and therefore whether all of the rent is actually paid in 2005/2006 is irrelevant (see Example 5.1 above).

More than one property

Where more than one property is owned the property business profit is simply the aggregate of the profit arising on each property treated as part of a single property business producing one single profit/loss figure.

This means that any loss which might arise on one property is automatically offset against the profit on any other property.

Example 5.3

John Smith rents out a number of furnished properties. For 2005/2006 his income and expenses for each property are as follows:

	Prty 1	Prty 2	Prty 3	Prty 4	Prty 5
Gross rent	4,000	7,000	2,500	4,250	1,600
Expenses	1,000	1,250	4,000	6,000	4,600

Calculate John's property business profit assessment for 2005/2006.

Answer

	Prty 1	Prty 2	Prty 3	Prty 4	Prty 5
Gross rent	4,000	7,000	2,500	4,250	1,600
Less:					
Expenses	1,000	1,250	4,000	6,000	4,600
Profit/loss	3,000	5,750	(1,500)	(1,750)	(3,000)

Assessment = 3,000 + 5,750 + (1,500) + (1,750) + (3,000) = 2,500

Note

The property business profit assessment is simply the total for all the properties thus enabling profits and losses to be automatically offset.

Premiums received for grant of short lease

As indicated earlier, the profits from a property business include not only rental income but premiums (i.e. a cash sum payable by tenant to landlord normally on commencement of a lease). However, only premiums paid in respect of short leases (i.e. of 50 years or less) are taxable.

For tax purposes a premium is effectively treated as if it was rental income for the landlord.

Basis of assessment

Unlike rent, however, which is assessed on an accruals basis a premium is assessed in the tax year in which the lease is granted.

Taxable element of premium

Only a part of the premium is assessable.

The taxable element of the premium is worked out according to the formula:

Amount assessable =

[Premium – 2% x Premium x (duration of lease – 1)]

(note: premiums for an *assignment* i.e. where entire property interest is sold are treated differently to the above and are not examinable)

Example 5.4

John Smith received a premium of £10,000 on 1st June 2005 when he let out a furnished house under a 10 year lease which he owned. A monthly rent of £500 payable on 1st of each month is also chargeable.

Calculate John Smith's property business profit assessment for 2005/2006.

Answer

Property business income comprises both the rent (on an accruals basis) and a proportion of the premium (in tax year of granting of lease) is taxable.

Taxable element of premium = $10,000 - [2\% \times 10,000 \times (10 - 1)] = 8,200$

Rents accrued from 1.6.05 to 5.4.06 = $500 \times 10 = 5,000$

(effectively the first five days of April 2006 are ignored; rent paid on 1st April 2006 brought into assessment in 2006/07 not 2005/2006)

Assessment = 8,200 + 5,000 = 13,200 for tax year 2005/06

Grant of a sub-lease

Where a tenant grants a sub-lease to a sub-tenant any premium paid by the subtenant to the tenant is assessed on the grantor tenant as above.

However, if that tenant had paid a premium on receiving his own lease then a measure of relief from assessment on the sub-lease premium is available. The relief is:

$$\frac{\text{Duration of sublease}}{\text{Duration of headlease}} \quad \text{x} \quad \text{Taxable premium for headlease}$$

Example 5.5

A grants a lease to B for 40 years on 1.3.1993 with a premium of £16,000 paid by B to A.

B grants a sub-lease to C on 1.6.2005 for 10 years with C paying B a premium of £30,000.

How is B taxed for 2005/2006?

Answer

Taxable element of Premium received by B on sub-lease =

$30,000 - [2\% \times 30,000 \times (10 - 1)]$	=	24,600

Less:

Allowance for premium paid by B to A =

$[16,000 - [2\% \times 16,000 \times (40 - 1)]] \times 10/40$	=	(880)
Premium taxable on B for 2005/2006	=	23,720

Trading expense deduction

The *receipt* of a premium, as indicated above, is taxable as part of the profits from a property business.

However, a deduction is also available to the payor of the premium as a trading expense if the payor is carrying on a trade (see Chapter 6) and the property is used in the trade.

The amount allowable/deductible is equal to the amount assessable on the landlord per the above formula divided by the number of years of the lease. This amount is then deductible for each year for the life of the lease.

Furnished Holiday Accommodation

A property business may include or consist of the commercial letting of furnished holiday accommodation.

Where the property business includes both furnished holiday lettings and other lettings (i.e. non-holiday lettings) two separate calculations are carried out keeping the holiday letting profits separate from the profits arising from the other properties. This is because the profit from furnished holiday lettings is treated differently for tax purposes (see below).

Accommodation is qualifying holiday accommodation if:
- it is available for commercial letting to the public for ≥ 140 days in the tax year *and* is so let in this period for ≥ 70 days *and*
- if not more than 155 days comprise periods of occupation of > 31 days during which the accommodation is in the same occupation.

Income from furnished holiday accommodation gives rise to the following:
- income regarded as earned income (useful re personal pension contributions; see Chapter 22)

- losses treated as trading losses (this is not the case for losses arising on other property lettings) therefore may be relieved as such (e.g. use can be made of sections 380 and 385; see Chapter 8)
- capital gains tax rollover and business taper relief may apply (see Chapters 12 and 14)
- capital allowances permitted (see Chapter 7)

None of the above four points apply to rental income arising from property which does not qualify as income from furnished holiday accommodation.

If a taxpayer owns two or more properties each of which satisfies the 140 day condition but which do not all satisfy the 70 day condition these properties will be regarded as satisfying the 70 day rule if their average number of days let is at least 70 days.

In applying this rule it is possible to include only those properties where the average meets the 70 day test.

Example 5.6

John Smith owns six flats which he lets out furnished. None of the properties are ever occupied for more than 31 days by the same person. However, some of the properties are more attractive than the others and so the actual lettings vary as amongst the flats.

For the tax year 2005/2006 the following actual lettings arise:

Flat One	90 days
Flat Two	60 days
Flat Three	75 days
Flat Four	62 days
Flat Five	80 days
Flat Six	40 days

Except for Flat Three all flats were available for letting for at least 140 days.

Calculate whether each flat can qualify as furnished holiday lettings.

Answer

Flat Three cannot qualify as furnished holday accommodation as the basic 140 day condition is not satisfied.

Flats Two and Four do satisfy the 140 day condition but are each not actually let for the minimum 70 days.

Flats One and Five are each let for the minimum 70 days.

By averaging the number of letting days amongst these four flats (ignoring Flats Three and Six) produces an average number of days of 292/4 = 73 days. Therefore John could claim to average these four flats which would mean each flat will then be regarded as a furnished holiday letting.

> Flat Six has been excluded as its inclusion with all or any of the other flats does not enable it to meet the 70 day average. Flat Six will not therefore be treated as a furnished holiday letting.

Rent-a-Room Scheme

Gross rents up to £4,250 for 2005/2006 are exempt from income tax if they relate to the letting of furnished accommodation which is a part of a main residence.

However, up to £4,250 the taxpayer can instead ignore the above exemption and calculate the property income assessment under the normal rules.

If gross rents exceed £4,250 the normal rules apply with no exemptions; however, the taxpayer may elect to be assessed instead on the excess of gross rents over £4,250 with no expense deductions.

Example 5.7

John Smith rents out a room in his house for £4,000 for the tax year 2005/2006. His allowable expenses are £1,000.

As the rent is below £4,250 it will be exempt. It would not make sense for John to claim to be assessed on £4,000 less £1,000 i.e. £3,000 under the normal rules.

If however, he let the room for £5,500 with expenses of £2,000 it would not make sense to be assessed under the normal rules on £5,500 less £2,000 i.e. £3,500. In this case an election to be taxed on the excess of £5,500 over £4,250 should be made.

Property business losses

Any loss arising from a property business can only be carried forward to be offset against future property business profits (unless, as indicated above, the loss arises from furnished holiday accommodation lettings).

Companies

It may be appropriate to read this section after having studied Chapter 16.

The tax treatment of rents whether received by an individual or company is very similar and is as described above.

However, there are some differences. For a company in receipt of rental income and/or premiums note the following:
1. relief for interest on loans re purchase/improvement of property (see below);
2. the basis period for assessment is the *accounting period* of the company not the *tax year* which applies for an individual;
   (However, for a self employed individual who prepares his business accounts to say 30 June each year and pays out rent for a property used

in his trade then any deduction will need to be time apportioned as normal; see Chapter 6);

3. for a company any losses arising from a property business are off-settable against total profits (before charges on income) of the same accounting period (see Chapter 17); and/or group relievable (see Chapter 18); any surplus loss then remaining being eligible to be carried forward for offset against future profits (before charges on income) arising from the property business of the company.

Interest paid and received: Companies only (see Chapter 16)
The loan relationship rules
Where loans have been entered into for the purpose of trade (e.g. to provide working capital or to buy plant and machinery) the interest thereon will be deductible on an accruals basis in computing the company's trading profit.

In other cases (e.g. interest re loans related to property) any interest payable by the company must be netted off against any interest receivable and the balance falls to be charged according to the loan relationship rules. An accruals basis is adopted.

In other words for a company any interest payable on loans to buy and/or improve property for letting is not deducted in arriving at the profits of the property business (as is the case for individuals; see above) but is treated under the loan relationship rules as an expense thereof.

SUMMARY

*   Rental income and premiums from land in the UK less expenses is taxed as property business profit

*   Rental income is taxed on an accruals basis

*   A premium is taxed in the tax year of grant of the lease (must be 50 years or less)

*   Rental income and expenses of more than one property are simply aggregated to produce one property business profit assessment

*   Rental income from furnished holiday accommodation is also taxed as property income but is not aggregated with rental income from non-furnished holiday accommodation

*   Losses (other than in connection with furnished holiday lettings) arising from a property business can only be relieved by carrying forward for offset against future profits of the property business.

CHAPTER 6

Trading profits

INTRODUCTION

This chapter will look at how business profits of a sole trader are computed for tax purposes and then assessed for income tax purposes.

Sole trader versus company

A sole trader is someone who carries out a business in his own name. In other words no company is involved.

For example, John Smith may carry out his tax consultancy business under the name of "John Smith" or he may use what is referred to as a trade name such as "The London Tax Consultancy". In either case no company is involved.

As a consequence, any profits made from the business are business profits of John Smith and are subject to income tax.

Accounts profit versus Taxable profit

As with all businesses it becomes necessary to compute the profit arising from a sole trader business. Normal accountancy principles will apply in calculating the accounts profit.

However, for income tax purposes the rules which apply may not be the same as those which apply for accountancy purposes which means that the accounts profit for a period is likely to be different from the taxable profit for the period.

Where there is a tax rule which is different from the accountancy rule the tax rule prevails. An example would be client entertaining expenditure. In determining a sole trader's account's profit for a period the costs of entertaining clients of the business would be deducted. However, for tax purposes such costs are *not* deductible. It thus becomes necessary in this case to add-back these costs to the accounts profit in arriving at the correct taxable profit of the business for the relevant period.

As will be seen below other adjustments to the accounts profit to obtain taxable profit are also necessary.

Nevertheless, the starting point in ascertaining the taxable profit for a period is the accounts profit i.e. the net profit as shown by the accounts.

Allowable expenses for tax purposes

In principle for an expense to be allowable in computing a sole trader's taxable business profit it must:

be wholly and exclusively incurred for the purpose of the business.

In other words if an expense has a dual private and business purpose it is not a tax deductible business expense. Thus a travel expense which was incurred by a sole trader for business and holiday purposes would not be deductible.

In practice it may, however, be possible to dissect an expense into its business and non-business elements. In this case the business element would be deductible even though technically the cost does not satisfy the "wholly and exclusively" test. For example, where a sole trader uses a motor car for business and private purposes it is often possible to agree with the tax authorities an appropriate percentage split between business and private usage so that an appropriate percentage of the costs of running the car can be deducted in computing taxable profit.

In addition, an expense must also meet various other requirements if it is to be deductible. In particular, the expense concerned must not be capital as opposed to revenue in nature and must basically be an expense which is expended in earning the profits of the business.

Period of Account

The period over which accounts are prepared for a sole trader is referred to as a *period of account* (companies are taxed on profits of an *accounting period*, rather than *periods of account*, which for tax purposes cannot be longer than 12 months; see Chapter 16).

A period of account for a sole trader may, for tax purposes, be longer or shorter or equal to 12 months.

Adjustment of accounts net profit

To work out the taxable profit for a period of account there are *four* types of adjustment which need to be made to the corresponding net profit of the accounts.

Two adjustments involve *adding-back* items to the net profit per the accounts and two adjustments involve *deducting* items from the net profit shown in the accounts.

Adding back items
- *expenditure* shown in accounts but not deductible for tax purposes
- *income* assessable as trading income but not shown in the accounts

Deduction items
- *expenditure* not shown in the accounts but deductible in arriving at trading profit
- *income* shown in the accounts but not assessable as trading income

Typically, most adjustments will arise from the need to add back expenses which have been deducted in arriving at net profit for accounts purposes which for tax purposes are not in fact, for various reasons, tax deductible.

Adding back

Expenditure shown in the accounts but not deductible for tax purposes

Political donations: (although trade subscriptions are generally deductible e.g. an accountant's subscription to the ACCA; and small donations to a local charity are normally deductible; note, however, if the payment to charity constitutes a Gift Aid payment then the payment is a charge on income and thus not a deductible trade expense (see Chapter 4)).

Fines and/or penalties: e.g. fine for breach of health regulations; car park fine for sole trader; (however, car park fine paid by sole trader on behalf of employee whilst on employer's business is usually allowable). Fines would cover illegal payments and payments for bribery.

Client entertaining: (although employee entertaining is deductible).

Gifts to clients: (for a gift to a client to be deductible the gift must cost less than £50 per client per year, the gift must carry a conspicuous advertisement for the business *and* the gift must not be of food, drink or tobacco (although gifts to employees are normally deductible if reasonable and not excessive)).

Capital improvements: a capital improvement could be the purchase of a capital asset (e.g. a piece of equipment or machinery or building; note that in such cases capital allowances may be available; see Chapter 7). Alternatively if, for example, the roof of a factory was in need of repair then the expenditure to repair it would be deductible. However, if in repairing the roof it was substantially improved at the same time then such expenditure is likely to be regarded as capital and therefore not deductible. By statutue the cost of registering patents and trade marks, although capital, are deductible as are the incidental costs of obtaining loan finance.

Depreciation: the depreciation of a capital asset is not deductible. However, instead, capital allowances may be permitted (see Chapter 7).

Legal and professional fees: e.g. accountants' fees incurred in relation to capital or non-trading item acquisitions (e.g. fees associated with acquiring a piece of capital plant or machinery or the granting of a lease); however, legal and professional fees charged in relation to deductible items of expenditure (e.g. legal fees for the collection of trade debts) are deductible; accountants' fees for the preparation of a sole trader's accounts and tax computation are also deductible; similarly, legal costs associated with the *renewal* of a lease of 50 years or less are deductible.

General provisions of any sort: e.g. general provisions for bad trade debts (*specific* provisions for *specific* bad trade debts are deductible; a bad trade debt written off is also deductible). Normally, in any question it will be movements of the provision which will be either deductible or taxable depending upon whether the resultant provision is specific or general.

Salary or interest on capital paid to the sole trader: (a salary which is reasonably paid to the sole trader's wife, who is an employee, is deductible).

Private expenses of the sole trader: e.g. payments by the business of his private car expenses and/or his flat rental payments (such payments on behalf of employees are deductible. However, see Chapter 10 for impact on employee's tax position).

Interest payable on loans not incurred for trade purposes e.g. a loan which the sole trader used to buy a property for renting to third parties (see Chapter 5).

Expenditure incurred more than seven years prior to the commencement of trading: (expenditure incurred within seven years of the commencement of the sole trader's trade is deductible if it would have been deductible if it had been incurred after such commencement; it is assumed to have been incurred on the first day of actual trade).

A proportion of any lease payments paid in relation to an expensive motor car, i.e. one with a retail price of more than £12,000 (unless it is a low CO_2 emissions vehicle). The allowable proportion is determined as:

$$\text{annual leasing charge} \quad \times \quad \frac{12,000 + \frac{1}{2}(\text{retail price when new} - 12,000)}{\text{Retail price when new}}$$

There is, however, no restriction for low emission motor cars.

Educational/training courses for the sole trader where the course is in relation to the sole trader acquiring new skills or knowledge (if the course merely updates existing skills or knowledge the cost will be deductible; educational courses for employees are deductible).

Expansionary removal costs (removal costs simply to other similar premises would be deductible).

Income assessable as trading income but not shown in the accounts

The only item relevant here is the taking of stock in trade from the business by the owner/sole trader for personal consumption and either not paying for the stock or paying less than their full value.

For example, a wine trader may take some of his stock of wine for his personal consumption without paying for it.

In such cases the full market value of the items taken (basically, their selling price) must be added to the net profit as shown by the accounts (i.e. simply increases income by this amount) less any amount actually paid by the owner (which will generally be zero).

Deducting items

Income shown in the accounts but not assessable as trading income

This refers to any item of *non-trading* income.

Typically such items would include:
- interest income, rental income and dividend income
- capital profits
  (e.g. profit on sale of fixed assets normally a capital gains tax not income tax issue)

Expenditure not shown in the accounts but deductible in arriving at trading profit

Two types of expense fall into this category:
- capital allowances (see Chapter 7) which may be claimed on items of plant and machinery and on industrial buildings
- a part of any premium which may be payable under a lease of 50 years or shorter (see Chapter 5).

Thus, to work out a sole trader's taxable profit for a period of account requires that the net profit shown in the accounts for that period be adjusted for each of the above four potential adjustments. In all cases all types of adjustment will not always be necessary.

Remember the only point of this exercise is to arrive at the taxable trading profit of the sole trader for the period of account. The fact that, for example, bank interest is added back does not mean that such interest is not liable to income tax but merely that it is not liable to tax as trading profit.

The following somewhat long example highlights many of the issues just raised.

Example 6.1

John Smith started trading as a wine merchant on 1 April 2001, preparing annual accounts to 31 March each year. His accounts for the year ended 31 March 2006 show the following:

	£
INCOME	
Gross profit	250,000
Bank interest received	8,000
Dividends received	3,500
Rental income	4,000
Profit on sale of capital items	2,500
	268,000
EXPENSES	
Salaries: staff	65,000
wife	25,000

Shop premises:		
	repairs and maintenance	6,600
	rent & business rates	7,500
	council tax	850
	water rates	225
	buildings insurance	1,500
	gas and electricity	2,600
	telephone	1,275
Motor expenses		9,000
Depreciation		12,700
Professional charges		1,000
Advertising, promotion and gifts		7,600
Sundry expenses		12,000
		(152,850)
Net profit		115,150

Notes

1. John's wife only works part-time for the business and if John was to employ someone other than his wife he would only need to pay a salary of £15,000.
2. John and his wife occupy a flat above the shop. It has been agreed that this flat represents 40% of the overall premises (i.e. flat plus shop). Business rates are £2,500.
3. Repairs and maintenance of the premises include £1,600 of improvements and the redecoration of John's flat at a cost of £750.
4. The telephone charge of £1,275 includes a fixed line rental of £250 and private business calls of £400.
5. John is leasing his car which new has a retail price of £25,000. The car is not a low CO_2 emissions car. His private use has been agreed as 40%. The leasing cost included is £3,000. The balance of £6,000 represents normal running costs.
6. Professional charges include legal fees of £375 in connection with a new 5 year lease; accountancy fees of £500 and £125 for legal fees in connection with pursuing a trade debt.
7. The gifts amounted in total to £1,200 and consisted of food hampers for clients.
8. Sundry expenses included client entertaining of £5,000; a donation to a local charity of £250; car park fines of £250 for John and £150 for his wife. The balance of the expenses is in connection with printing costs for business cards, stationary and invoices plus postage costs.

9. Over the Christmas period John took wine for his family consumption which had cost him £800. His normal gross profit percentage on sales is 60%.

Calculate John's adjusted trading profit for the year ended 31st March 2006.

Answer

John

Year ended 31 March 2006

		£	£
		–	+
Net profit per accounts			115,150
Bank interest		8,000	
Dividends		3,500	
Rents		4,000	
Capital profit		2,500	
Wages: wife	(25,000 – 15,000)		10,000
Premises (private use element)			
repairs & maintenance	(1,600 + 750)		2,350
rent & rates	40% x (7,500 – 2,500)		2,000
council tax			850
water rates	40% x 225		90
insurance	40% x 1,500		600
gas and electricity	40% x 2,600		1,040
telephone	(250 + 400)		650
Motoring:leasing costs	(3,000 – 1,332)		1,668
normal running costs (40% × 6,000)			2,400
Depreciation			12,700
Professional charges			375
Advertising, gifts etc			1,200
Sundry expenses	(5,000 + 250)		5,250
Goods for own use	(800/0.4)		2,000
Adjusted trading profit [115,150 - 18,000 + 43,173]			**140,323**

Notes

1. Wife's salary exceeds a normal arm's length amount by 10,000 which is therefore added back.

2. Repairs and maintenance include improvements of 1,600 which are not repairs but capital and are therefore not deductible. The repairs attributable to the private flat are not business expenses and so not deductible.

3. Only 60% of the premises costs are deductible. All the council tax has been added back is this is a personal cost of John and not a business cost.
4. The telephone line rental is all added back as this cannot be split into business and private elements. The telephone call costs can however be so split; only the business-call costs are deductible.
5. Only a part of the car leasing cost is deductible calculated as follows:

$$[3{,}000 \times \frac{[12{,}000 + 0.5 \times (25{,}000 - 12{,}000)]}{25{,}000}] \times 60\% \quad = 1{,}332$$

6. Legal charges in connection with a new lease are capital and therefore not deductible.
7. The gifts comprise food and are therefore not deductible.
8. Client entertaining and car park fines for John are not deductible.
9. Goods taken for own use must be treated as if sold at their normal market prices.

Basis of assessment

Having worked out the taxable profit for a period of account it is then necessary to determine the amount of that taxable profit which falls liable to income tax for a particular tax year or year of assessment. This requires a set of rules. These rules determine the basis period for the relevant tax year.

For example, John Smith produces his accounts for the twelve months to 30th June each year. For the year to 30th June 2005 how much of these profits fall liable to income tax for the tax year 2005/2006? To answer this requires a set of rules.

The normal rule

A sole trader is assessed on the taxable trading profit of the 12 months to the account date (i.e. the date to which accounts have been prepared) falling in the relevant tax year.

Thus, for John Smith in the above example, for the tax year 2005/2006 the taxable trading profit is the profit for the twelve months ended 30th June 2005. The basis period is the period 1st July 2004 to 30th June 2005.

If John prepared his accounts to 30th September 2005 then the taxable trading profit for the tax year 2005/2006 would be the taxable profit for the twelve months ended 30th September 2005. The basis period is the period 1st October 2004 to 30th September 2005.

This rule is known as the current year basis (CYB).

Tax year of starting to trade

A different rule applies for the tax year in which an individual starts to trade.

The taxable profit for the tax year in which a sole trader starts to trade is the taxable profit from the date of commencement of the trade to the end of that first tax year (i.e. 5th April).

If John Smith starts to trade on 1st July 2002 then the first tax year is 2002/03. His taxable profit for the tax year 2002/03 will be the taxable profit for the basis period 1st July 2002 to 5th April 2003.

Example 6.2

John Smith prepares his first set of accounts to 31st December 2006. He started to trade on 1st August 2005.

Therefore for the tax year 2005/2006 the tax year in which John started to trade his taxable profit is for the basis period 1st August 2005 to 5th April 2006.

Example 6.3

John Smith prepared his first set of accounts to 31st June 2006. He started to trade on 1st October 2005.

Therefore for the tax year 2005/2006 the tax year in which John started to trade his taxable profit is for the basis period 1st October 2005 to 5th April 2006.

Second tax year of trade

For the second tax year the amount of the taxable profit depends upon:

- whether or not there is an account date in the second tax year to which the accounts have been prepared
- whether the period from the date of commencement of trading to the account date in the second tax year is twelve months, shorter or longer

Taking each option in turn:

No account date in the second tax year
The taxable profit is simply the taxable profit for the *tax year itself* (i.e. 6th April to following 5th April)

Account date in the second tax year and period from date of commencement of trading to account date is twelve months or less

The taxable profit is the taxable profit for the *first twelve months of trading.*

Account date in second tax year and period from date of commencement of trading to account date more than twelve months

The taxable profit is the taxable profit for the period of *twelve months to the account date.*

Example 6.4

John Smith started to trade on 1st January 2005. He prepared his first set of accounts as follows:

(a) 30th June 2006

(b) 31st December 2005

(c) 30th June 2005

(d) 31st March 2006

What periods for tax years 2004/2005 and 2005/06 are taxable?

Answer

In each of the above four options (a) to (d) the *first* tax year is **2004/2005** i.e. the tax year in which John started to trade.

Therefore the taxable profit for the tax year 2004/2005 is for the period 1st January 2005 (i.e. the date the trade started) to 5th April 2005 (i.e. the end of that tax year in which the trade started).

(a) 2005/06 is the second tax year of trade. In this case there is no account date in 2005/06.Therefore taxable profit for tax year 2005/06 is for the period 6th April 2005 to 5th April 2006.

(b) 2005/06 is the second tax year of trade.

In this case there is an account date in the tax year and the period from commencement to this date is twelve months exactly.

Therefore taxable profit for tax year 2005/06 is for the period 1st January 2005 to 31st December 2005

(c) 2005/06 is the second tax year of trade.

In this case there is an account date in the tax year and the period from commencement to this date is less than twelve months.

Therefore taxable profit for tax year 2005/06 is for the period 1st January 2005 to 31st December 2005

(d) 2005/06 is the second tax year of trade.

In this case there is an account date in the tax year and the period from commencement to this date is more than twelve months.

Therefore taxable profit for tax year 2005/06 is for the period 1st April 2005 to 31st March 2006.

Third tax year of trade

The taxable profit is the taxable profit for the twelve months ended on the account date in this tax year.

Example 6.5

John Smith started to trade on 1st January 2005. He prepared his accounts as follows:

(a) to 30th June 2006 and 30th June each year thereafter.

(b) to 31st December 2005 and 31st December each year thereafter

(c) to 30th June 2005 and 30th June each year thereafter

(d) to 31st March 2006 and 31st March each year thereafter

What period for the third tax year 2006/07 is taxable?

Answer

The taxable profit for the tax year 2006/07 the third tax year of trading is:

(a) the twelve months to 30th June 2006

(b) the twelve months to 31st December 2006

(c) the twelve months to 30th June 2006

(d) the twelve months to 31st March 2007

The various periods referred to in the above examples are normally referred to as base or basis periods.

Overlap profit

It may have become clear from the examples above that in most cases some taxable profit is in fact taxed twice. Such profits are referred to as *overlap profits*.

Example 6.6

John Smith started to trade on 1st July 2004. He prepares his accounts to 30th June each year.

What are the base periods for the first three tax years and identify the overlap profits?

Answer

2004/2005

Taxable profit for period 1st July 2004 to 5th April 2005.

2005/06

Taxable profit for period 1st July 2004 to 30th June 2005.

2006/07

Taxable profit for period 1st July 2005 to 30th June 2006.

The taxable profit attributable to the period 1st July 2004 to 5th April 2005 is taxed twice and is thus the overlap profit. This profit is taxed in the tax years 2004/2005 *and* 2005/06.

INCOME TAX

Overlap profit relief

There is no relief for such overlap profit until either the sole trader changes his accounting date in the future and/or ceases to trade (see Example 6.9 below).

At both these times some relief may be available. This relief is obtained by deducting the amount of the overlap profit from the taxable profit of the tax year of cessation or accounting date change.

Taxable profit allocated to base periods

Having ascertained the base periods for the relevant tax years all that is then required is to work out the actual amount of taxable profits allocated thereto.

Example 6.7

John Smith prepares his accounts to 31st December each year. He started to trade on 1st September 2002 and prepared his first set of accounts to 31st December 2003.

His adjusted profits (i.e. his taxable trading profits) are as follows:
1st September 2002 to 31st December 2003   £160,000
1st January 2004   to 31st December 2004   £320,000
1st January 2005   to 31st December 2005   £64,000

What is John Smith's taxable trading profit for each tax year?

Answer

2002/03

Tax year in which trade started.
Taxable profit is for period 1st September 2002 to 5th April 2003
i.e. £160,000 x 7/16 = £70,000

Note:

1st September 2002 to 5th April 2003 is 7 months; the first 5 days of April are ignored Period 1st September 2002 to 31st December 2003 is 16 months over which taxable profit is £160,000.
Hence, for 1st September 2002 to 5th April 2003 taxable profit allocated to this period is going to be =
7/16 x £160,000 = £70,000

2003/04

Second tax year of trading.

Taxable profit is for period 1st January 2003 to 31st December 2003 (i.e. 12 months to account date 31.12.03 as there *is* an account date (31.12.03) in second tax year but first set of accounts for period in excess of 12 months).
i.e. £160,000 x 12/16 = £120,000

2004/05

Third tax year of trading.

Taxable profit is for period 1st January 2004 to 31st December 2004
i.e. £320,000

2005/06

Fourth tax year of trading.

Taxable profit is for period 1st January 2005 to 31st December 2005
i.e. £64,000

Cessation of trading

This occurs when the sole trader no longer continues to trade.

Basis of assessment

In the tax year in which the trade ceases the taxable trading profit for that tax year is the taxable profit for the period from the end of the base period of the tax year prior to the tax year of cessation to the date of cessation.

Example 6.8

John Smith has been trading for a number of years. He prepares his accounts to 30th November each year. He ceased to trade on 30th June 2005.

What is the taxable profit for the tax year 2005/2006?

Answer

The tax year of cessation is 2005/2006.

The date of cessation is 30th June 2005.

The tax year prior to the tax year of cessation is therefore 2004/05.

The base period for 2004/05 is the period 1st December 2003 to 30th November 2004.

The end of the base period for this tax year is therefore 30th November 2004.

Therefore for the tax year 2005/2006 the taxable profit is for the period 1st December 2004 to 30th June 2005.

Example 6.9

John Smith has been trading for a number of years. He prepares his accounts to 30th November each year. He ceased to trade on 31st December 2005. He has overlap profits of £50,000. His taxable profits for his last three tax years of trading are as follows:

1st December 2003 to 30th November 2004: £400,000

1st December 2004 to 30th November 2005: £500,000

1st December 2005 to 31st December 2005: £100,000

What is the assessment for the tax year of cessation?

Answer

The tax year of cessation is 2005/2006.

The tax year prior to cessation is 2004/05.
The base period for 2004/05 is the period 1st December 2003 to 30th November 2004

The taxable profit for the tax year 2005/2006 (the tax year of cessation) is therefore for the period
1st December 2004 to 31st December 2005
i.e. £500,000 + £100,000 = £600,000

However, relief for the overlap profit is available in the tax year of cessation. Therefore the final assessment for 2005/2006 is
£600,000 - £50,000 = £550,000

Change of accounting date

A sole trader may decide for various reasons to change his accounting date.

When this occurs new rules are used to determine the relevant base period for the tax year of the change. The tax year of the change is the tax year in which accounts are first made up to the new accounts date or the tax year in which the accounts have not been made up to the old date.

Any change of accounting date in the first three tax years applies automatically.

Otherwise, for a change of accounting date to be valid:

- the change of accounting date must be notified to the Inland Revenue by 31st January following the tax year in which the change is made
- the first accounts to the new date must not exceed 18 months in length
- there must not have been a change of accounting date within the previous five tax years (this condition does not apply if the change is made for genuine commercial reasons).

When a change of accounting date occurs four possibilities arise:

- two accounts dates arise in same tax year
- no accounts date occurs in the tax year

- one set of accounts cover a period of ≥12 months
- one set of accounts cover a period of < 12 months

Two account dates in tax year
Base period starts at the end of the base period for tax year prior to tax year of change of accounting date and ends on the new accounts date.

Example 6.10

John Smith prepares his accounts to the 30th September each year the last being to 30th September 2005. He then changed his accounting date and prepared his next set of accounts to 31st March 2006.

The tax year of change is 2005/2006.

There are two account dates in this tax year i.e. 30.9.05 and 31.03.06

Therefore base period for tax year 2005/2006 is 1st October 2004 to 31st March 2006.

No account date in tax year
A date has to be manufactured.

This is done by deducting 12 months from the new account date and the base period is then the 12 months to this new manufactured date.

Example 6.11

John Smith prepares his accounts to 31st March each year the last being to 31st March 2005. He then changed his accounting date to 30th April and prepared his next set of accounts to 30th April 2006.

The tax year of change is 2005/2006.

However, there is no date to which accounts have been prepared in this tax year.

Therefore, it is necessary to manufacture an accounts date by taking off 12 months from the new date of 30th April 2006 to give 30th April 2005.

Therefore base period for tax year 2005/2006 is 1st May 2004 to 30th April 2005.

One set of accounts covering a period of ≥ 12 month accounts
Base period is the period beginning at the end of the base period for the prior tax year to the new account date.

Example 6.12

John Smith prepares his accounts to 30th June each year the last being to 30th June 2004. He then changed his accounting date to 30th September and prepared his next set of accounts to 30th September 2005.

The tax year of change is 2005/2006.

The set of accounts from 1st July 2004 to 30th September 2005 is more than 12 months.

Therefore base period for tax year 2005/2006 is 1st July 2004 to 30th September 2005.

One set of accounts covering a period of <12 months accounts
Base period is the 12 months to the new accounts date.

Example 6.13

John Smith prepares his accounts to 30th June each year the last being to 30th June 2004. He then changed his accounting date to 31st May and prepared his next set of accounts to 31st May 2005.

The tax year of change is 2005/2006.

The set of accounts from 1st July 2004 to 31st May 2005 is less than 12 months.

Therefore base period for tax year 2005/2006 is 1st June 2004 to 31st May 2005.

Overlap profits
As was indicated earlier in the chapter overlap profits (i.e. those profits taxed twice) which arise when a sole trader starts to trade (see Example 6.6 above) may be relievable when the sole trader changes his accounting date.

However, for this to occur the change of accounting date must give rise to a base period of in excess of 12 months. If the change of date gives rise to a base period of 12 months or less no relief for earlier overlap profits can be given.

Thus, relief for earlier overlap profits will be available when:
• two account dates occur in the tax year of the change (Example 6.10 above), or
• one set of accounts of in excess of 12 months are prepared (Example 6.12 above).

The amount of overlap relief available is calculated as follows:

$$\frac{\text{Overlap profits b/f from earlier years of trading}}{\text{Length of period over which Overlap profits arose accounting}} \quad \times \quad \text{(Length of first set of accounts to new date } minus \text{ 12)}$$

Example 6.14

John Smith prepares his accounts to the 30th September each year the last being to 30th September 2005. He then changed his accounting date and prepared his next set of accounts to 31st December 2005.

The tax year of change is 2005/2006.

There are two account dates in this tax year i.e. 30.9.05 and 31.12.05

Therefore base period for tax year 2005/2006 is 1st October 2004 to 31st December 2005 i.e. 15 months long.

Assume overlap profits b/f are £50,000 and that they arose over an overlap period of five months.

Therefore overlap relief available is

$$\frac{£50,000}{5} \times (15 - 12) = £30,000$$

In other words relief of three months worth of overlap profits is available (the three months being the excess over 12 months of the new set of accounts).

Example 6.15

John Smith prepares his accounts to 30th June each year the last being to 30th June 2004. He then changed his accounting date to 30th October and prepared his next set of accounts to 30th October 2005.

The tax year of change is 2005/2006.

The set of accounts from 1st July 2004 to 30th October 2005 is more than 12 months.

Therefore base period for tax year 2005/2006 is 1st July 2004 to 30th October 2005 i.e. 16 months long.

Assume overlap profits b/f are £50,000 and that they arose over an overlap period of five months.

Therefore overlap relief available is

$$\frac{£50,000}{5} \times (16 - 12) = £40,000$$

In other words relief of four months worth of overlap profits is available (the four months being the excess over 12 months of the new set of accounts).

Valid and invalid accounting date changes

Any changes of accounting date in the first three tax years of trading result in above new bases applying automatically.

At any other time certain conditions must be satisfied:

- period of account resulting from change must be ≤ 18 months in length
- no previous change of accounting date must have occurred in prior five tax years
- notification to Inland Revenue by 31st January of tax year following change must be given.

SUMMARY

The starting point for working out a sole trader's taxable profit for a period of account is the accounts profit prepared according to normal accountancy principles.

Adjustments are necessary to the accounts profit because in certain cases there is a clash between the rules for tax and those for accountancy; where this arises the tax rules prevail.

The date to which a sole trader prepares his accounts will affect the base periods for each tax year. In particular the extent of any overlap profits will be affected by the date to which the first set of accounts are prepared. The rules for determining the appropriate base period for a tax year are extremely important.

In any computation before the taxable profits for a tax year can be determined it is necessary to convert the accounts profits to the corresponding taxable profits for the relevant period of account.

CHAPTER 7

Capital Allowances: Income Tax

INTRODUCTION
This chapter will look at the tax equivalent of the accountant's depreciation i.e. capital allowances.

As indicated in Chapter 6 depreciation charged in a sole trader's accounts is not a tax deductible item in computing taxable trading profit. Instead, capital allowances are utilised which are treated as a trading expense and are deductible in computing the taxable trading profit.

Trading expense
Capital allowances are treated as a trading expense when computing a sole trader's taxable trading profit.

Chargeable period
Capital allowances are computed for a chargeable period which, for income tax purposes, is any period of account (assuming such period is 18 months or shorter).

Capital items
Capital allowances are available for:
- plant and machinery; and
- industrial buildings.

Plant and machinery (P & M)
P & M is basically items or apparatus used by a sole trader in carrying out his business. Such apparatus is of a permanent nature and thus does not include the sole trader's stock in trade which is bought and sold as quickly as possible.

P & M includes:
- motor vehicles
- office furniture
- fixtures and fittings
- moveable partitions (often seen in offices)
- light fittings
- computer software
- fire regulation expenditure
- thermal insulation expenditure in industrial buildings
- air conditioning equipment

Items which do not qualify as P & M include:
- football stand

- canopy over a petrol station forecourt
- false ceilings used to hide electrical wiring

Types of allowance

Capital allowances are granted to a sole trader who incurs capital expenditure on P & M which is used for the purposes of his trade.

There are two types of capital allowance:
- first year allowance
- writing down allowance

First year allowance (FYA)

A 40% (or possibly 50%, see below) or a 100% FYA may generally be available.

40% capital allowance

A FYA is available at the rate of 40% of the relevant expenditure incurred in the period of account on the P & M.

This applies irrespective of the length of the period of account and irrespective of the point within the period when the expenditure is actually incurred.

However, it applies only where the business is a small or medium (not large) sized business. (For examination purposes it is not necessary to know what determines whether a business is small, medium or large; the question will indicate).

50% capital allowance

For capital expenditure incurred by small unincorporated businesses between 6th April 2004 and 5th April 2005 the 40% FYA is increased to 50%. For companies the time limits are 1st April 2004 to 31st March 2005. However, it only applies to small (not medium or large) sized businesses.

Computations

The Finance Act 2004 introduced the 50% FYA referred to above.

When carrying out capital allowance computations the exact date of the incurrance of the expenditure is important as this will determine the rate of capital allowance which will apply.

In particular, extra care needs to be taken if a sole trader's period of account straddles the 6th April 2004 or 5th April 2005 dates. For example, John Smith's period of account may be 1st July 2003 to 30th June 2004. In this case, whether the expenditure is before or on or after 6th April 2004 will determine which of the 40% or 50% FYA rates applies. The same issue would also apply, for example, to the period of account 1st July 2004 to 30th June 2005.

100% capital allowance

A 100% FYA is available in only limited circumstances. It applies to any motor car where the CO_2 emission rate does not exceed 120g/km (referred to as a *low emission car*); the business may be *small, medium or large*.

The 100% allowance also applied to expenditure (incurred before 31st March 2004) on information and communication technology equipment (e.g. computers). However, this specific allowance is no longer examinable.

No FYAs

No FYA is available on expenditure incurred on motor cars (other than expenditure on a low emission car).

FYAs can be claimed in full or some or all of it may be disclaimed (i.e. not claimed).

Where any part of a FYA is not claimed this does not mean that the part not claimed is lost. As will be seen below, the part not claimed simply increases the amount of any subsequent writing down allowance.

Example 7.1

John Smith a sole trader has been trading for a number of years and prepares his accounts to the 30th June each year. In the year to 30th June 2005 John purchased a piece of P & M at a cost of £30,000 on which:
a.   40% FYA is available
b.   50% FYA is available
c.   100% FYA is available.

John is a small sized business. John's taxable trading profit *before* capital allowances for the period to 30th June 2005 is £400,000.

Calculate the capital allowances to which John is entitled and the resulting taxable profit under (a), (b) and (c) for tax year 2005/2006.

Answer

	(a)	(b)	(c)
Period 1st July 2004 to 30th June 2005			
Cost of P & M	30,000	30,000	30,000
Less:			
(a) FYA 40% x 30,000 =	(12,000)		
(b) FYA 50% x 30,000 =		(15,000)	
(c) FYA 100% x 30,000 =			(30,000)
Tax written down value as at			
30th June 2005:	18,000	15,000	Nil

Tax year 2005/2006

Base period is the period of account 1st July 2004 to 30th June 2005 (i.e. the CYB basis; see Chapter 6).

Taxable profit (pre CAs)	400,000	400,000	400,000
Less:			
FYA	(12,000)	(15,000)	(30,000)
Taxable profit	388,000	385,000	370,000

Notes

1. After capital allowances have been claimed for a period of account the amount of expenditure not yet written off is referred to as the asset's *tax written down value*. Thus, in the above as at 30th June 2005 the P & M under (a) had a value for tax purposes or tax written down value of £18,000. This figure of £18,000 only has relevance for tax purposes. It does not mean that the P & M is actually worth this amount were it to be sold.

2. John will be assessed on taxable trading profits for the tax year 2005/06 based on the taxable profit of the base period 1st July 2004 to 30th June 2005 i.e. £388,000 for (a); £385,000 for (b) and £370,000 for (c).

3. The date within the period of account 1st July 2004 to 30th June 2005 when the expenditure is incurred will determine whether a 40% or 50% FYA applies.

Writing down allowance (WDA)

A WDA of 25% *per annum* is available for *each* of the periods of account *following* the period of account in which the expenditure was first incurred on the P & M and in which a FYA may have been claimed.

A WDA, unlike a FYA, is an allowance *per annum* and therefore depends upon the length of the period of account. If the period of account is shorter or longer than 12 months the WDA is then adjusted either down or up respectively (e.g. period of account is 9 months. Therefore WDA will be (25% x 9/12) of the relevant cost).

The WDA for each period of account for a single piece of P & M is based on the asset's *tax written down* value (i.e. original cost less allowances claimed) at the end of the previous period of account and is thus calculated on what is referred to as a *reducing balance basis*.

Thus, for each successive period of account the amount of WDA will in principle reduce.

Example 7.2

John Smith prepares his business accounts to 31st December each year. In the year to 31st December 2003 John incurs capital expenditure of £100,000 on P & M (not motor cars). John's business is a medium sized business.

Calculate John's capital allowances for years ended 31st December 2003, 2004 and 2005.

Answer

As John's business is medium sized and the P & M purchased does not include any motor cars then the FYA can only be 40% not 50% or 100%.

Year ended 31.12.03

Capital expenditure	100,000
Less:	
FYA 40%	(40,000)
Tax written down value (TWDV)	60,000

Year ended 31.12.04

Tax written down value b/f	60,000
Less:	
WDA 25% p.a	(15,000)
TWDV	45,000

Year ended 31.12.05

Tax written down value b/f	45,000
Less:	
WDA 25% p.a	(11,250)
TWDV	33,750

Notes

1. The WDA for each period of account is reduced as it is based on a reducing tax written down value.
2. As John's business is a medium-sized business, the 50% FYA cannot apply.
3. As John's business is a medium-sized business, the 100% FYA can only apply if the expenditure had been incurred on low emission cars.

FYA versus WDA

It is not possible for a FYA *and* a WDA to be claimed for the same period of account in respect of the same amount of expenditure.

Normally, therefore, a FYA is claimed in the period of account in which the expenditure is first incurred and a WDA is then claimed for each succeeding period of account (see Example 7.2 above).

Example 7.3

John Smith a sole trader prepares his accounts to the 30th June each year. In the year to 30th June 2005 John purchases a piece of P & M at a cost of £30,000 on which:

(a) 40% FYA is available

(b) 50% FYA is available

(c) 100% FYA is available.

John is a small sized business.

Calculate the capital allowances to which John is entitled.

Answer

	(a)	(b)	(c)
Period 1st July 2004 to 30th June 2005			
Cost of P & M	30,000	30,000	30,000
Less:			
(a) FYA 40% x 30,000 =	(12,000)		
(b) FYA 50% x 30,000 =		(15,000)	
(c) FYA 100% x 30,000 =			(30,000)
Tax written down value as at 30th June 2005	18,000	15,000	Nil
Period 1st July 2005 to 30th June 2006			
Tax written down value as at 30th June 2005	18,000	15,000	Nil
Less:			
WDA at 25% p.a	(4,500)	(3,750)	Nil
Tax written down value at 30th June 2006	13,500	11,250	Nil
Period 1st July 2006 to 30th June 2007			
Tax written down value as at 30th June 2006	13,500	11,250	Nil
Less:			
WDA at 25% p.a	(3,375)	(2,813)	Nil
Tax written down value at 30th June 2007	10,125	8,437	Nil

Notes

1. The tax written down value of the P & M asset as at 30th June 2005 after FYA has been claimed is then used as the starting point for the calculation of the WDA for the next period of account i.e. for the period 1st July 2005 to 30th June 2006 etc.

2. FYA was available in the first period of account in which the P & M was bought. Thereafter only a WDA is available on a reducing balance basis.

3. If the expenditure had been incurred in the period 1st July 2004 to 5th April 2005 the FYA would be 50% (i.e. (b) above). If it had been incurred in the period 6th April 2005 to 30th June 2005 the FYA would be 40% (i.e. (a) above).

4. If John's business had been a medium-sized business the FYA, irrespective of date of incurrence of expenditure, could not be 50%.

5. Where a 100% FYA was available (as in (c) above) no subsequent WDA can arise.

Pooled assets

Although a FYA has been calculated for each separate item of P & M in the above examples this does not in fact occur where WDAs are being calculated.

After a FYA has been calculated for a single item of P & M and the original cost of the P & M has been reduced by this FYA for a period of account, the balance of the expenditure (i.e. original cost less FYA) on this item of P & M is then aggregated with the expenditure not yet written off for all other items of P & M i.e. pooled.

The WDA for the next period of account is then calculated on the total value of the pool.

The value of the pool of P & M expenditure may be increased when items of P & M are purchased and decreased when items of P & M are sold.

The WDA for any period of account is calculated on the balance of the pool i.e. after taking into account asset purchases and sales.

In other words in the period of account in which an asset is first purchased a FYA will normally be claimed and for this initial period the asset does not form part of the pool. After claiming the FYA on the asset just purchased the tax written down value of the asset (i.e. purchase price minus FYA) is then included in the pool for the next chargeable period in respect of which a WDA will then be claimed.

Example 7.4

John Smith has P & M with a pooled TWDV as at 31st December 2004, the date to which his accounts are prepared, of £140,000.

In January 2005 he sells some P & M for £20,000 and in March 2005 buys some P & M for £15,000 (on which a FYA of 40% may be claimed).

Show John's capital allowances position.

Answer

Period 1st January 2005 to 31st December 2005

TWDV as at 1.1.05	140,000
Sale Jan 2005	(20,000)
	120,000
WDA 25% p.a	(30,000)
	90,000

Additions FYA

Purchase March 2005	15,000	
Less:		
FYA 40%	(6,000)	
		9,000
TWDV as at 31.12.05		99,000

Period 1st January 2006 to 31st December 2006

TWDV as at 1.1.06	99,000
Less:	
WDA 25% p.a	(24,750)
TWDV as at 31.12.06	74,250

Notes

1. Sales of P & M reduce the size of the P & M pool.
2. Sales are removed from the pool *before* calculating the WDA for that period of account.
3. Where a purchase of P & M qualifies for a FYA then the FYA is computed for the period of account in which the P & M is purchased. At this point the P & M is not pooled. Any expenditure remaining after the FYA is then pooled. Thus, in the above example the £15,000 P & M purchase was reduced by a FYA of £6,000 down to £9,000 and it was this £9,000 which was then pooled.

Example 7.5

Using the figures from Example 7.4

John Smith has P & M with a pooled TWDV as at 31st December 2004, the date to which his accounts are prepared, of £140,000.

In January 2005 he sells some P & M for £20,000 and in March 2005 buys some P & M for £15,000 (on which a FYA of 40% may be claimed).

In addition, he buys some P & M in July 2005 for £40,000 on which no FYA is available.

Show John's capital allowances position.

Answer

Period 1st January 2005 to 31st December 2005

Additions no FYA

TWDV as at 1.1.05	140,000
Sale Jan 2005	(20,000)
Purchase July 2005	40,000
	160,000
WDA 25% p.a	(40,000)
	120,000

> **Additions FYA**
>
> | | | |
> |---|---|---|
> | Purchase March 2005 | 15,000 | |
> | Less: | | |
> | FYA 40% | (6,000) | |
> | | | 9,000 |
> | TWDV as at 31.12.05 | | 129,000 |
>
> **Period 1st January 2006 to 31st December 2006**
>
> | | |
> |---|---|
> | TWDV as at 1.1.06 | 129,000 |
> | Less: | |
> | WDA 25% p.a | (32,250) |
> | TWDV as at 31.12.06 | 96,750 |
>
> **Note**
>
> In this case as compared to Example 7.4 John purchased an additional piece of P & M in July 2005 in respect of which no FYA could be claimed. In this case a WDA can be claimed instead in the period of account of purchase i.e. 1st January 2005 to 31st December 2005. However, this WDA is not claimed separately for this individual purchase. The P & M cost is simply added to the pool i.e. the tax written down value of £140,000 at the beginning of the period of account.

Not all P & M purchased is added to the pool.

Non-pooled assets

There are, however, some assets which do not form part of the pool of P&M.

These assets are:

- expensive motor cars
- assets with some private use
- short-life assets
- long-life assets

In each of these cases each asset is treated separately and all allowances are computed separately.

Expensive motor cars

An expensive motor car is one costing more than £12,000.

Not only do such cars not join the pool but the maximum WDA for any period of account is £3,000 per annum, irrespective of the cost of the car.

This restriction does not apply to vans and lorries which do join the general pool of P&M irrespective of their cost (and on which FYAs may be claimed).

The restriction does not apply to low CO_2 emission cars which get a 100% FYA irrespective of cost (see above).

Note that if there is more than one expensive car each car is treated separately i.e. expensive cars are themselves not pooled together. (See Example 7.6 below).

Assets with private use

Any asset which is used partly for business and partly for private purposes by the owner (i.e. the sole trader) of the business is not pooled.

Capital allowances are computed individually for each such asset. However, although the capital allowances computation is carried out as normal the amount of allowance which can actually be treated as a tax deductible item is reduced by the private percentage usage i.e. only the percentage usage attributable to business can be deducted as trading expense.

If the asset which is used partly privately is used by an employee of the business (i.e. not the owner) no such restriction of allowances occurs.

Note that if there is more than one asset used privately each asset is treated separately i.e. privately used assets are not pooled together.

(See Example 7.6 below).

Short-life assets

An asset may be treated as a short-life asset, and is likely to be so treated, where it is anticipated that it is likely to be sold or scrapped within four years of the end of the period of account in which it was purchased for less than its tax written down value at that time.

The advantage of short life asset treatment is that a balancing allowance (see below) will arise on sale which would not be the case if the asset had simply been added to the general pool.

If the asset is not in fact sold by the end of the period of account four years after the end of the period when it was purchased its tax written down value is at that time (i.e. end of four years) transferred to the general pool at the commencement of the next period of account.

Note that if there is more than short life asset each asset is treated separately i.e. short life assets are not pooled together.

Long-life assets

Such an asset is defined as one with a working life of 25 years or more measured from the date the asset is first brought into use.

No FYA is claimable on long-life assets.

The WDA is 6% per annum but in the case of long-life assets a separate pool of such assets is created in the same manner as applies for the general pool of P & M i.e. they are not treated on an individual basis as applies for motor cars, assets used privately and short-life assets (see above).

For these provisions to apply the business concerned must spend more than the equivalent of £100,000 per annum on such assets (otherwise these assets are put in the general pool of P & M and 25% WDAs will be available).

Sales of assets
Balancing allowance/Balancing charge
Capital allowances are available on P&M purchased. In the year of purchase a FYA will normally be available and thereafter a WDA will be available.

If the asset is not sold or scrapped eventually its original cost will be totally written down to zero.

If, however, a piece of P & M is sold then in the period of account in which the sale occurs no FYA or WDA can be claimed. The effect of such a sale depends upon whether the asset is in the general pool or is one of the four categories of asset described above.

In all cases, however, on the sale the amount brought into account is:

the lower of the actual sale proceeds or the asset's original cost.

General pool
The sale of an asset out of the general pool simply means that the sale proceeds reduce the size of the pool i.e. the pool will decrease by the amount of sale proceeds. No balancing allowance or balancing charge will explicitly arise as it will implicitly be taken into account (see below).

Motor cars/Assets with private use/Short life assets
In each of these three cases the sale of the asset will precipitate a balancing allowance or balancing charge depending upon whether the sale proceeds are respectively less than or more than the tax written down value of the asset at the time of sale.

Remember in the period of sale no FYA or WDAs may be claimed on that asset.

Long-life assets pool
The sale of an asset out of the long-life asset pool simply means that the sale proceeds reduce the size of the pool i.e. the pool will decrease by the amount of sale proceeds. No balancing allowance or balancing charge will explicitly arise (see below).

Balancing allowance/Balancing charge
In the period of account in which a balancing allowance occurs it is treated as a trading expense in computing taxable trading profit and thus reduces taxable trading profit in the same way as does a FYA and WDA.

A balancing charge, however, is treated as taxable trading income and thus increases taxable trading profit.

Note that where an asset is sold the amount brought into account is the lower of original cost and sale proceeds. This is because it is not possible to claw back more allowances than have been given for the asset.

Example 7.6

John Smith prepares his accounts to 30th June each year. He started to trade on 1st October 2004. His first accounts were prepared to 30th June 2005. His tax adjusted profits *before* deducting capital allowances are as follows:

Period of account 1st October 2004 to 30th June 2005   £100,000
Period of account 1st July 2005 to 30th June 2006   £350,000
Period of account 1st July 2006 to 30th June 2007   £500,000

John purchased the following items of P & M:

1st October 2004	office furniture	£15,000
1st November 2004	car for himself (10% private use)	£16,000
31st May 2005	low emission car for his secretary	£10,000
25th June 2005	office furniture	£17,000

John sold the car he had bought for himself on 31st December 2006 for £7,000.

Calculate John's taxable trading profit for the first three tax years of trading assuming he is a medium sized business.

Answer

Capital allowances computation

Period 1.10.04 to 30.6.05	*FYA*	*General Pool*	*Expensive car*	*Allowances Claimed*
Additions no FYA				
1.11.04 Car (himself)			16,000	
WDA 25% x 9/12			(2,250) [1]	2,025
Additions FYA				
1.10.04 Furniture	15,000			
FYA 40%	(6,000)			6,000
		9,000 [2]		
25.6.05 Furniture	17,000			
FYA 40%	(6,800)			6,800
		10,200 [2]		
31.5.05 Car (secretary)	10,000			
FYA 100%	(10,000) [3]			10,000
		Nil		
TWDV at 30.6.05		19,200	13,750	**24,825**
Period 1.7.05 to 30.6.06	*FYA*	*General Pool*	*Expensive car*	*Allowances Claimed*
TWDV b/f		19,200	13,750	
WDA 25%		(4,800)	(3,000)	**7,500**
TWDV at 30.6.06		14,400	10,750	

Period 1.7.06 to 30.6.07

TWDV b/f	14,400	10,750	
Sale of car		(7,000)	
Balancing allowance		3,750 (4)	3,375
WDA 25%	(3,600)		3,600
TWDV at 30.6.07	10,800		**6,975**

Notes

1. There is a restriction on the amount of WDA for an expensive car (i.e. a car costing more than £12,000). The maximum WDA is £3,000 per annum. Thus, in the above case where the period of account is 9 months the WDA is [9/12 x £3,000] = £2,250.

   However, 10% of the car is used privately. Thus, only 90% of the available WDA can be claimed as a trading expense i.e. 90% x £2,250 = £2,025.

2. Before being pooled, the cost of each item of furniture is first reduced in the period of purchase by FYAs. The furniture purchased on 25th June 2005 would have qualified for a 50% (not 40%) FYA if John's business had been small not medium sized.

3. Unlike motor cars in general, low emission cars are entitled to a 100% FYA.

4. When the car is sold, in this case for less than its TWDV at that time, a balancing allowance arises. However, again only 90% of the car is used for business and thus only 90% of the balancing allowance can be claimed.

5. The final column headed "Allowances Claimed" represents the amount of the allowances for each period of account which can be claimed as trading expenses in computing taxable trading profit.

6. Note the order and layout: *"Additions no FYA"* computed before *"Additions FYA"*.

The taxable trading profits *after* capital allowances for each period of account are thus:

1st October 2004 to 30th June 2005	£100,000 less £24,825	= £75,175
1st July 2005 to 30th June 2006	£350,000 less £7,500	= £342,500
1st July 2006 to 30th June 2007	£500,000 less £6,975	= £493,025

Applying the base period rules discussed in Chapter 6 gives:

Tax year 2004/2005

Basis period 1st October 2004 to 5th April 2005

Taxable trading income:

6/9 x £75,175   = **£50,117**

> **Tax year 2005/2006**
> Basis period 1st October 2004 to 30th September 2005
> Taxable trading income:
> £75,175 + 3/12 x £342,500 =   **£160,800**
>
> **Tax year 2006/2007**
> Basis period 1st July 2005 to 30th June 2006
> Taxable trading income =   **£342,500**

Hire purchase and leasing

Hire purchase

An asset bought on hire purchase is treated as if it had been purchased outright for cash. As a consequence, capital allowances are available based on the cash price.

Leased assets

Under a lease the lessee merely hires the asset over the leased period. The hire charge is treated as a normal trading expense/deduction.

However, where the asset concerned is an expensive motor car (i.e. one with a retail price of over £12,000) a restriction is placed on the amount of the leasing costs which is eligible for treatment as a deductible trading expense (see Chapter 6).

Industrial buildings

Capital allowances are available for capital expenditure incurred on the construction and/or purchase of certain buildings and are referred to as *industrial buildings allowances (IBA)*.

Qualifying buildings

The buildings on which IBAs may be claimed are industrial buildings and hotels.

An industrial building, for example, includes a factory which is used for manufacturing purposes and any ancillary buildings used for storing the finished goods manufactured and/or raw materials.

Any buildings which provide for the employees of the above buildings will also qualify for IBAs (e.g. staff canteen; sports pavillion).

A drawing office (but not other types of office; see below) attached to an industrial building will also qualify for IBAs.

Non-qualifying buildings

However, other types of office (e.g. administrative offices) do not qualify for IBAs; nor do shops, showrooms or residential properties (see below where the 25% test is satisfied).

Industrial use at end of period of account

IBAs, as is the case with P & M, are calculated for periods of account and thus the amount of the IBA will depend upon the length of the period of account not the length of ownership of the building within the period.

However, it must be noted that for an IBA to be available for a period of account the building must be in industrial use on the last day of the period of account.

Non-industrial use at end of period of account

Where a building is not in industrial use on the last day of a period of account a notional allowance applies.

A notional allowance is one which reduces the tax written down value of the building for tax purposes for the period of account but which cannot be claimed by the trader as a deductible trading expense. It thus represents no more than a notional deduction.

First year allowance (FYA)

There is no first year IBAs.

Writing down allowances (WDA)

A WDA of 4% per annum is available for *each* period of account *including* the period of account in which the expenditure is first incurred (as no FYA is available) on the industrial building assuming at the end of each period of account the building is in industrial use.

A WDA is an allowance per annum and therefore depends upon the length of the period of account.

The WDA for industrial buildings, unlike the WDA for P & M, is a fixed 4% per annum of the original qualifying cost of the building; it is not calculated on a reducing balance basis but on a straight line basis.

In addition there is no pooling. IBAs are calculated separately for each building.

Example 7.7

John Smith prepares his accounts to 31st March each year and on 1st July 2002 purchases a new industrial building for £200,000 using it for industrial purposes immediately. On 1st April 2004 John began to use the building for a non-industrial purpose until 31st March 2005 immediately after which it reverted to industrial use.

Calculate John's IBA position.

Answer

Period ended 31st March 2003

Cost	200,000
Less:	
WDA 4% p.a	(8,000)
TWDV	192,000

Period ended 31st March 2004

TWDV	192,000
Less:	
WDA 4% p.a	(8,000)
TWDV	184,000

Period ended 31st March 2005

TWDV	184,000
Less:	
Notional WDA 4% p.a	(8,000)
TWDV	176,000

Period ended 31st March 2006

TWDV	176,000
Less:	
WDA 4% p.a	(8,000)
TWDV	168,000

Notes

1. John Smith in computing his taxable trading profit will be able to claim as a trading expense a WDA of £8,000 for each of the above periods of account except for the period ended 31st March 2005.

2. For the period ended 31st March 2005 the building was not in industrial use by John on the last day of that period i.e. 31st March 2005. Thus, John cannot claim a WDA for this period. However, whilst no WDA can be claimed by John the TWDV of the building is still reduced by a *notional* WDA.

Qualifying versus non-qualifying expenditure

It is often the case that a building may be used partly for industrial purposes and partly for non-industrial purposes; in such cases so long as the cost of the non-industrial element does not exceed 25% of the total cost of the whole building IBAs on the full cost will be available. Otherwise the IBA is restricted to the cost of the qualifying element of the building.

Example 7.8

John Smith incurs capital expenditure of £150,000 on the construction of an industrial building. £15,000 relates to administrative offices.

On what expenditure can John claim IBAs?

Answer

As the expenditure in connection with the non-qualifying offices is only 10% of total cost i.e. £15,000/£150,000 and thus less than the 25% limit, the whole of the £150,000 including the £15,000 is eligible for IBAs.

Had the figure for offices been £50,000, i.e. more than 25% of the £150,000, then only £100,000 of expenditure is eligible for IBAs.

Example 7.9

John Smith prepares his accounts to 31st March 2006.
He purchased two new industrial buildings (B1 and B2) on 1st December 2005 for a cost of £200,000 and £300,000 respectively and brought both into industrial use immediately.
Calculate John's IBAs.

Answer

Period ended 31st March 2006

	B1	B2
Cost	200,000	300,000
Less:		
WDA 4% p.a.	(8,000)	(12,000)
TWDV	192,000	288,000

Period ended 31st March 2007

	B1	B2
TWDV	192,000	288,000
Less:		
WDA 4% p.a.	(8,000)	(12,000)
TWDV	184,000	276,000

Note: no pooling of the two buildings B1 and B2; only 4% p.a. WDAs available

---

Tax life of building

The tax life of an industrial building is 25 years (hence the 4% WDA) measured from the date when the building is first brought into use irrespective of whether such usage is for industrial or non-industrial purposes.

Balancing adjustments (i.e. balancing allowances/charges) will only occur if and when an industrial building is sold within its tax life.

Qualifying expenditure

IBAs are based upon the cost of an industrial building. Cost for this purpose depends upon how the "cost" is incurred and whether the building purchased is a new or used second-hand building.

New building

In the case of a new building *cost* is:

- cost of construction of the building if constructed by the user of the building; or
- price paid for the building if bought unused from a builder; or
- lower of cost of construction and price paid for building if bought unused from someone other than the builder.

In each of the above three situations "cost" excludes the cost of land and any cost attributable to non-industrial use where such usage exceeds 25% of the total cost (excluding the land value).

However, "cost" does include the cost of any site preparation (e.g. drainage installation; ground clearance and levelling) and professional fees associated with the construction of the building (e.g. architect's and surveyor's fees; note legal fees re purchase are not included as part of "cost"). Landscaping costs are excluded.

Example 7.10

John Smith incurs £225,000 on the construction of an industrial building.

He then sells the building unused to Bill Brown for £275,000 (excluding land cost) for use in his trade.

What is the amount of expenditure on which Bill Brown can claim IBAs?

Answer

Bill Brown's IBAs will be based on:
- £275,000 if John Smith is a builder
- the lower of £225,000 and £275,000 if John Smith is not a builder

---

Example 7.11

John Smith arranges for an industrial building to be constructed for use in his trade at a construction cost of £650,000. He could have bought a similar industrial building unused from a builder for £675,000 (excluding land cost).

What is the amount of expenditure on which John can claim IBAs?

Answer

£650,000 if John arranges for construction of the building
£675,000 if purchased unused from the builder

Example 7.12

John Smith incurred expenditure on a new industrial building of £400,000 broken down as follows for use in his trade:

Purchase price of land	£100,000
Levelling land	£10,000
Building infrastructure	£290,000

(£290,000 includes:

drawing office	£5,000
canteen	£3,000
general offices	£25,000)

Show the expenditure in respect of which John may claim IBAs.

Answer

Total expenditure	400,000
Less:	
Cost of land	(100,000)
Potential Qualifying expenditure	300,000

Included in the above 300,000 expenditure is 25,000 attributable to the general offices which in principle is not eligible for IBAs. However, if the 25,000 is not more than 25% of the total cost of the building (excluding land) then it will be deemed to qualify for IBAs. Thus:

25,000/300,000 = 8.33% which is less than 25%

Therefore the whole of the £300,000 expenditure qualifies for IBAs.

Note: the cost of land should always be deducted from total cost *before* applying the 25% test.

Second hand used building

The WDAs available to the purchaser of a second hand used industrial building depend upon the vendor's position at the date of sale and invariably will not be the normal 4% per annum WDA.

The buyer simply takes over the vendor's IBA position.

Thus, the WDA for the buyer is calculated as follows:

WDA = Residue of expenditure after sale
Tax life remaining for building

Residue of expenditure after sale =

TWDV prior to sale (+ Balancing charge *or* - Balancing allowance on sale)

(TWDV means tax written down value)

In effect the WDA calculated for the buyer is based on the *lower* of original cost and price paid by the buyer.

Remember that in the period of account of sale no WDAs are available; only a balancing charge or a balancing allowance can arise (this is also the case for plant and machinery which is not included in the general pool).

Example 7.13

John Smith a sole trader makes up his accounts to 31st March each year. On 1st March 1999 John began to use an industrial building which had cost him £60,000. On 1st February 2006 John sold the factory for £55,200 to Bill Brown another sole trader who makes up his accounts to 30th June each year. Bill begins to use the building for industrial purposes immediately.

Calculate the IBA position for both John and Bill.

Answer

John Smith

Period 1st April 1998 to 31st March 1999

Cost	60,000
Less:	
WDA 4%	(2,400)
TWDV	57,600

John will also be entitled to a WDA for each of the periods ended 31st March 2000 to 31st March 2005 inclusive i.e. 6 years at 4% per annum (i.e. 2,400) equals 14,400.

Thus 7 years of WDAs are available in total to John prior to sale (i.e. 7 x 2,400 = 16,800).

Thus TWDV as at 31st March 2005 is 60,000 – 16,800 = 43,200

Period ended 31st March 2006

TWDV as at 31.3.05	43,200
Sale proceeds	55,200
Balancing charge	12,000

In the period ended 31st March 2006 when John sold the building he was not entitled to a WDA. In this period either a balancing allowance or balancing charge will arise (in this case a balancing charge as sale proceeds exceed the TWDV at the date of sale). The 12,000 will be treated as taxable trading income on the part of John for the period ended 31st March 2006.

Bill Brown

Period ended 30th June 2006

$$WDA = \frac{\text{Residue after sale}}{\text{Tax life remaining}} = \frac{\text{TWDV before sale + Balancing charge}}{\text{Tax life remaining}}$$

$$= \frac{43,200 + 12,000}{19 \text{ years 1 month}} = 2,892.63$$

Therefore Bill Brown is entitled to a WDA of 2,892.63 for the remaining tax life of the building.

The position for the buyer and seller also depends upon whether the building has been in continual industrial use since purchase or whether at some time non-industrial use occurred.

Also, as indicated above, where an industrial building is sold for more than original cost (the examinations exclude the position of a sale for less than original cost for part non-industrial use buildings) then the balancing charge will be equal to the actual IBAs given and claimed (i.e. those allowances which have been treated as tax deductible trading expenses) which will therefore exclude notional IBAs.

Example 7.14

This example continues Example 7.7.

John Smith prepares his accounts to 31st March each year and on 1st July 2002 purchases a new industrial building for £200,000 using it for industrial purposes immediately. On 1st April 2004 John began to use the building for a non-industrial purpose until 31st March 2005 immediately after which it reverted to industrial use.

Assume John now sells the building on 1st July 2006 for £225,000 (i.e. more than cost) to Bill Brown.

Calculate John's IBAs.

Answer

John

Period ended 31st March 2007

TWDV as at 1st April 2006	168,000
Sale proceeds	(200,000) (see Note below)
Balancing charge	32,000
Less:	
Notional allowances	(8,000)
Actual Balancing charge	24,000

Notes

1. "Sale proceeds" (whether on sale of industrial buildings *or* plant and machinery) should always be taken to be the *lower* of the sale proceeds and original cost; any sale proceeds over original cost will be taxed as a capital gain (see Chapter 12). In this example therefore "sale proceeds" will be the lower of 225,000 and 200,000. This also ensures that the correct amount of allowances is clawed back.

2. There can be no claw back of *notional* allowances as these were never claimed as tax deductible trading expenses in the first instance. Thus, 8,000 of notional allowances (for the period ended 31st March 2005) are not clawed back.

3. The buyer's WDA is then based on the figure of 168,000 + 24,000 = 192,000.

SUMMARY

The following key points should be noted:

Plant and machinery

- FYAs and WDAs are computed for periods of account
- a FYA *and* a WDA cannot be claimed for the same asset for the same period of account
- FYA may be 40%, 50% or 100%
- WDA is 25% per annum on a reducing balance basis
- not all P & M is pooled
- acquisitions increase the general pool whereas sales decrease the general pool
- some allowances depend upon whether the business is small, medium or large
- expensive cars have a WDA cap of £3,000 per annum

Industrial buildings

- no FYA on industrial buildings
- WDA is 4% per annum on a straight line basis

- no pooling of IBAs
- an industrial building's life for IBA purposes starts when it is first brought into use whether industrial or non-industrial
- WDAs dependent upon whether industrial building is a new or second hand
- WDAs on a new industrial building depend on whether constructed or purchased and if the latter from whom purchased
- notional allowances may arise where an industrial building not in use on the last day of a chargeable period for industrial purposes
- no WDAs in chargeable period of sale; only a balancing allowance or charge
- in ascertaining balancing allowance or charge on a sale the lower of sale proceeds and original cost is used
- cost of land is never eligible for IBAs
- no IBAs on offices (other than drawing offices) unless the 25% limit satisfied.

CHAPTER 8

Sole Trader and Business Losses

INTRODUCTION

Sole traders as well as making trading profits may also make trading losses. This chapter looks at how a sole trader may utilise such losses if they arise.

Trading losses

There are various ways in which a sole trader on making a trading loss for a period of account can use it. Three of these are of general application with the other uses only being available in certain situations.

Thus a trading loss can be:

- carried forward and offset against future trading profits (section 385)
- offset against STI of the tax year of the trading loss (section 380)
- offset against net chargeable gains of tax year of trading loss (section 72)

Trading loss relief is also available in specific situations as follows:

- in the early years of trade may be offset against STI of more than one tax year (section 381)
- on cessation may be offset against more than one previous tax year's trading profits (section 388)
- on incorporation of a sole trader-ship may be offset against future income received from the company (section 386)

It is usual to refer to the possible use of trading losses by referring to the appropriate section numbers. Each of the above section numbers refer to sections of the Income and Corporation Taxes Act 1988 (as amended) except for section 72 which is section 72 of Finance Act 1991.

If the relevant conditions for a particular relief are satisfied a taxpayer can select one or more of the various reliefs to use as appropriate.

However, irrespective of which section is to be used, trading losses must be offset in the order in which they occur. In other words, earlier trading losses must be offset before later trading losses.

Where for a period of account a trading loss arises the assessment for the relevant tax year is treated as "nil" (see Example 8.1 below).

Trading loss carry forward (section 385)

Any trading loss of a period of account can be carried forward indefinitely for offset against future trading profits. The trading loss must be used against future trading profits as soon as possible.

Section 385 does not permit the trading loss to be carried back; only forward and it can only be offset against trading profits.

Example 8.1

John Smith has been trading for a number of years and prepares his accounts to 31st December each year. He has the following results:

Year ended 31.12.03 trading loss   £10,000
Year ended 31.12.04 trading profit   £3,000
Year ended 31.12.05 trading profit   £6,000

How can John use section 385 relief.

Answer

	Tax year 2003/04	Tax year 2004/05	Tax year 2005/06
Trading profit/loss	nil	3,000	6,000
Less:			
Section 385	nil	(3,000)	(6,000)
Net trading profit/loss	nil	nil	nil

Note

The trading loss for y/e 31.12.03 has been used first against the trading profit for y/e 31.12.04 and second against trading profit for y/e 31.12.05. After such offset there is still an unrelieved trading loss of 10,000 less (3,000 + 6,000) i.e. 1,000 for John to carry forward for offset against future trading profits under section 385. As John has been trading for a number of years the CYB basis applies to determine the basis periods for each tax year (see Chapter 6).

It is important to note the layout which should be used (i.e. tax years across the page). Where a trading loss occurs (e.g. in y/e 31.12.03 above), the assessment for the tax year for which this period of account is the basis period (i.e. 2003/04) is "nil" and hence "nil" appears under "Tax year 2003/04". The trading loss amount itself of £10,000 for y/e 31.12.03 only appears when it is being utilised against other trading profits (i.e. for tax years 2004/05 and 2005/6).

Trading loss offset against STI (section 380)

A trading loss for a period of account can be offset against the STI of the tax year for which the period of account is the basis period and/or the STI of the immediately preceding tax year.

The taxpayer can choose which option to adopt. However, whichever option is chosen the trading loss must be offset to the maximum possible extent in the tax year of relief against that year's STI.

There are effectively four possible options under this section:

- trading loss offset *only* against STI of tax year of loss
- trading loss offset *only* against STI of tax year prior to tax year of loss
- trading loss offset against STI of tax year of loss *and* then STI of prior tax year
- trading loss offset against STI of prior tax tear *and* STI of tax year of loss

The taxpayer can choose any of these four options.

Remember STI is Total income less Charges on income (see Chapter 2).

Where STI for a tax year exceeds the trading loss then the trading loss should be deducted against non-savings, then savings then dividend income for the relevant tax year.

Where a trading loss arises in two succeeding tax years the trading loss from the earlier tax year must be offset before the later trading loss may be offset.

Example 8.2

John Smith has been trading for a number of years and prepares his accounts to 31st December each year and has the following results:

Year ended 31.12.03 trading profit   £34,000
Year ended 31.12.04 trading loss   £48,000
Year ended 31.12.05 trading profit   £60,000

John also has other income for 2003/04 and 2004/05 of £5,000 and £6,000 respectively and charges on income of £2,800 and £2,500 respectively.

How can John use section 380 relief?

Answer

	2003/04	2004/05	2005/06
Trading profit/loss	34,000	nil	60,000
Less:			
Section 385 relief	nil	nil	nil
Net trading profit/loss	34,000	nil	60,000
Other income	5,000	6,000	nil
Total income	39,000	6,000	60,000
Less:			
Charges on income	(2,800)	(2,500)	nil
STI	36,200	3,500	60,000
Less:			
Section 380 relief	(36,200)	nil	nil
	nil	3,500	60,000
Less:			

Personal allowance	nil	(3,500)	(4,895)
Taxable income	nil	nil	55,105

Notes

1. The trading loss for y/e 31.12.04 is a trading loss for tax year 2004/05. Any of the four options described above may be chosen.

2. It can be seen however that to offset any part of the trading loss in tax year 2004/05 would not make sense as Taxable income for that year is in any event "nil" even without using the trading loss due to the personal allowance. Therefore under section 380 the only option which makes sense is to offset the 2004/05 trading loss against STI of the prior tax year 2003/04 namely 36,200.

3. After this offset 48,000 - 36,200 = 11,800 of trading loss remains unrelieved. This can then be carried forward under section 385 against future *trading profits* (not STI) of future tax years (i.e. in this example 2005/06). This offset is not shown above. Had it been shown Taxable income for 2005/06 would be 43,305 after the full 11,800 had been offset against the 60,000 followed by the 4,895 personal allowance.

Generally speaking, the most tax efficient way to utilise section 380 relief is to offset the trading loss against the prior tax year's STI and then if any unused trading loss still arises to offset it then against the STI of the tax year of the loss. In other words, generally speaking the sooner tax relief can be obtained the better.

Trading loss offset against capital gains (s72 FA 1991)

It may make sense to return to study this part after a study of capital gains in Chapter 12 has been undertaken.

This relief is a little unusual as it permits an *income* loss to be offset against a *capital* gain. Normally, income losses may only be offset against income and capital losses only against capital gains.

Before the section can be used for a particular tax year section 380 for that tax year must have been applied.

The trading loss for the tax year thus needs to be first offset against STI of the same tax year and assuming a part of the trading loss still remains unrelieved this surplus may then be offset against any capital gains less capital losses of the same tax year.

However, although the trading loss is offset against current tax year net gains the actual amount of the surplus trading loss available for relief is in fact the *lower* of the unrelieved trading loss and net capital gains less capital losses brought forward.

The loss relief is therefore given before taper relief.

Example 8.3

John Smith has the following amounts arising for 2005/06:

Trading loss	£30,000
Statutory total income (STI)	£20,000
Capital gain	£35,000
Capital loss	£16,000
Unrelieved capital loss b/f from earlier years	£10,000

The annual exemption for 2005/06 is £8,500.

Calculate for 2005/06:

(a) the s380 loss relief against STI, and

(b) the additional loss relief against chargeable gains.

Answer

(a) Income tax computation, 2005/06

STI	20,000
Less: S380 loss relief	(20,000)
Taxable income	nil

Therefore unrelieved trading loss for 2005/06 is 30,000 minus 20,000 = 10,000.

(b) CGT computation, 2005/06

Current year gain		35,000
Less: current year capital loss		(16,000)
		19,000
Less: s72 FA 91 trading loss relief –*lower* of:		
(i) Unrelieved trading loss after s380 relief	10,000	
(ii) Net current year gains	19,000	
Less: b/f capital loss	(10,000)	
	9,000	(9,000)
		10,000
Less capital loss b/f		(1,500)
		8,500
Less: annual exemption		(8,500)
Taxable amount		nil

Notes

1. Before section 72 relief could be claimed for the tax year of the trading loss (i.e. 2005/06) the 30,000 trading loss had to be relieved under section 380 against STI for tax year 2005/06.

2. As a surplus trading loss of 10,000 arose even after section 380 relief then section 72 could be claimed.

3. The amount of the surplus trading loss of 10,000 which was available to be offset against net current tax year capital gains (i.e. 19,000) is the *smaller* of the surplus trading loss (i.e. 10,000) and net current tax year capital gains (i.e. 19,000) less any current capital losses brought forward (i.e. 10,000) i.e. 9,000.

    Thus, in this case 9,000 of the surplus trading loss of 10,000 was available for offset against the 19,000 net capital gains for the tax year 2005/06.

4. Having offset the trading loss against net capital gains under section 72 the resulting 10,000 of net capital gains still remaining can then be reduced by using a part of the capital loss brought forward of 1,500.

5. The amount used under point 4 above is restricted such as to leave into CGT charge the annual exemption for 2005/06 i.e. 8,500 (see Chapter 12). The final chargeable gains amount is then "nil".

6. 8,500 of the capital loss b/f (i.e. 10,000 - 1,500) can then be carried forward for offset against future capital gains. 1,000 of the trading loss (i.e. 10,000 - 9,000) can be carried forward for offset under section 385.

Trading losses offset in early years of trade (section 381)

In the early years of a sole trader's trade, trading losses are in particular likely to arise.

As a consequence special loss relief is available in the first four tax years of the trade.

Any trading loss arising in the first four tax years of a trade may be offset against STI of the three tax years immediately preceding the tax year of the trading loss beginning with the earliest and ending with the latest tax year (i.e. the so-called First in First Out (FIFO) basis).

Although section 381 only applies in these particular circumstances a sole trader may still choose to utilise either sections 380, 385 and/or section 72 if preferred. Generally speaking, however, in these circumstances section 381 is likely to give maximum tax relief soonest.

A typical scenario might be where an employee decides to leave his employment and set up his own sole trader business. Under section 381 any early tax year trading losses might be carried back and offset against earlier tax year's STI, which will of course include the person's salary. It may then be possible to obtain a tax refund for some or all those earlier tax years.

Example 8.4

John Smith started in business on 1ˢᵗ July 2003 and prepares his accounts to 30ᵗʰ June each year. His results are as follows:

y/e 30ᵗʰ June 2004   Trading loss   £24,000
y/e 30ᵗʰ June 2005   Trading profit   £2,500

Prior to setting up his own business John was an employee and received the following salaries:

2002/03   £5,868
2001/02   £11,050
2000/01   £9,520

John also receives each tax year other income of £4,500.

Show John's tax position if section 381 is claimed.

Answer

First it is necessary to calculate John's trading profit/loss for each tax year. This simply involves using the basis period rules discussed in Chapter 6.

First tax year is 2003/04 and produces trading loss of 9/12 x 24,000 = 18,000

Second tax year is 2004/05 and produces trading loss of 24,000 - 18,000 = 6,000

Remember that if a trading loss arises in the first period of trading, relief for the loss cannot be given twice (i.e. overlap profits are possible but not overlap losses). Thus, for 2004/05 the normal basis period of 1.7.03 to 30.6.04, which gives a trading loss of 24,000, needs to be reduced by the trading loss of 18,000 (for 1.7.03 to 5.4.04) for the tax year 2003/04.

	2000/01	2001/02	2002/03	2003/04	2004/05	2005/06
Trading income	nil	nil	nil	nil	nil	2,500
Salaries	9,520	11,050	5,868	nil	nil	nil
Other income	4,500	4,500	4,500	4,500	4,500	4,500
STI	14,020	15,550	10,368	4,500	4,500	7,000
Less:						
Section 381 relief	(14,020)	(3,980)	nil	nil	nil	nil
Section 381 relief		(6,000)				
Revised STI	nil	5,570	10,368	4,500	4,500	7,000
Less:						
Personal allowance	(4,895)	(4,895)	(4,895)	(4,895)	(4,895)	(4,895)
Taxable income	nil	675	5,473	nil	nil	2,105

Notes

1. The trading loss of 2003/04 must be considered first i.e. before the later trading loss of 2004/05.

2. Under section 381 this loss may be carried back three preceding tax years to 2000/01 and offset against that tax year's STI. In this case it is

possible to relieve 14,020 of the 18,000 leaving 3,980 to be then offset against STI for tax year 2001/02.

3. The trading loss of 6,000 for 2004/05 can similarly be carried back under section 381 to the preceding three tax years and thus in this case to 2001/02 where the remaining STI after relief for the 3,980 i.e. 11,570 (i.e. 15,550 - 3,980) can be offset by the 6,000.

4. Note, however, that the use of the 2003/04 trading loss in 2000/001 resulted in a loss of the personal allowance for that tax year.

How would the above position compare if John had instead decided to utilise section 380 relief rather than section 381 relief?

	2000/01	2001/02	2002/03	2003/04	2004/05	2005/06
Trading income	nil	nil	nil	nil	nil	2,500
Less:						
Section 385	-	-	-	-	-	(2,500)
Salaries	9,520	11,050	5,868	nil	nil	nil
Other income	4,500	4,500	4,500	4,500	4,500	4,500
STI	14,020	15,550	10,368	4,500	4,500	4,500
Less:						
Section 380 relief	nil	nil	(10,368)	(4,500)	(4,500)	nil
Revised STI	14,020	15,550	nil	nil	nil	4,500
Less:						
Personal allowance	(4,895)	(4,895)	(4,895)	(4,895)	(4,895)	(4,895)
Taxable income	9,125	10,655	nil	nil	nil	nil

Notes

1. Under section 380 the trading loss of 2003/04 of 18,000 has been offset against the previous tax year's (i.e. 2002/03) STI reducing it to nil. The balance (i.e. 18,000 - 10,368) 7,632 has then been offset against STI for 2003/04 under section 380 reducing STI to nil and leaving 7,632 - 4,500 i.e. 3,132 of 2003/04 trading loss which can only now be carried forward under section 385.

2. The trading loss of 2004/05 of £6,000 has been used under section 380 to offset the STI for that tax year. Of the 2004/05 loss of 6,000 this claim has used 4,500 leaving 1,500 to be carried forward under section 385.

3. In 2005/06 the 2,500 offset under section 385 is out of 3,132 carried forward from 2003/04 (see Note 1 above) not out of the 2004/05 1,500 available for carry forward.

Comparing the Taxable income figures under each option shows that earlier tax relief is obtained using section 381 i.e. 2000/01 and 2001/2 figures for Taxable income are lower and therefore less tax would be paid for those tax years.

Trading losses in closing year (s388: terminal loss relief)

Terminal loss relief only arises when a sole trader ceases to trade.

A terminal loss is a trading loss of the last twelve months of trading.

Under section 388 such a loss may be offset against any trading profit of the last tax year in which the trade ceases and any trading profits of the preceding three tax years (taking the later tax years first; i.e. a LIFO basis approach).

The terminal loss is a trading loss of the last twelve months of trading less any part of which may have been relieved first under section 380. The terminal loss is calculated by adding together the following components:

(i) actual trading loss from 6th April to date of cessation

(ii) actual trading loss incurred from a date 12 months before date of cessation to following 5th April.

If either (i) or (ii) produces a profit then it is assumed to be nil for the purpose of calculating the terminal loss.

Any overlap profits still unrelieved are added to the amount under (i) above.

Remember from Chapter 6 that on a sole trader's cessation the basis period for the final tax year is from the end of the basis period of the immediately preceding tax year prior to cessation to the date of cessation.

Example 8.5

John Smith prepares his accounts to 30th June each year. John ceased to trade on 31st May 2006. His trading profits and losses are as follows:

30th June 2003 Trading profit £70,000
30th June 2004 Trading profit £36,000
30th June 2005 Trading profit £12,000

Period ended 31st May 2006 produced a trading loss of £44,000.

Assume overlap profits unrelieved of £15,000.

Show John's position assuming a section 388 claim is made.

Answer

Terminal loss is the trading loss for the 12 month period 1.6.05 to 31.5.06 (date of cessation).

This period is split:

6.4.06 to 31.5.06 Trading loss for this period = [2/11 x (44,000)] (8,000)
Overlap profits unrelieved   (15,000)
                                                        (23,000)

1.6.05 to 5.4.06

Trading loss for this period [9/11 x (44,000) + 1/12 x 12,000]   (35,000)

Therefore terminal loss   (58,000)

	2003/2004	2004/05	2005/06	2006/07
Trading profit	70,000	36,000	12,000	nil
Less:				
Section 388 relief	(10,000)	(36,000)	(12,000)	nil
Trading profit	60,000	nil	nil	nil

Notes

1. For the tax year of cessation i.e. 2006/07 a trading loss of 44,000 arose plus unrelieved overlap profits of 15,000 i.e. 59,000.
2. Of this 59,000 some 58,000 has been relieved under section 388. Thus, 1,000 of trading loss (i.e. 59,000 - 58,000) remains unrelieved for tax year 2006/07. This could be relieved under section 380 if John had any other income for this tax year.
3. The terminal loss has been relieved first against the trading profit for tax year 2005/06 then carried back to 2004/2005 and then to 2003/04.

Trading loss relief on incorporation of a sole trader-ship (section 386)

It is not unusual for a sole trader after having traded for a while to contemplate converting the sole-tradership into a limited company.

This can be carried out relatively tax efficiently assuming certain conditions are satisfied.

Subject to the satisfaction of certain conditions, unrelieved accumulated trading losses arising at the date of incorporation from the sole-tradership may be carried forward for offset against the first *available income* of the former proprietor which he receives from the company.

Available income refers to salary, directors' fees and dividends.

The trading losses unrelieved and carried forward are offset first against earned income (i.e. salaries and directors' fees) and then against unearned income (i.e. dividends).

Example 8.6

On the advice of his accountant John Smith transferred his sole trader business to a limited company, JS Ltd, on 1st July 2005. The consideration for the transfer was an issue of ordinary shares. As at the date of the transfer of the business John had unrelieved trading losses of £55,000. John's salary from the company is £16,000 per annum and net dividends of £900 per annum are received in December each year.

Show how John will obtain relief under s386 for the trading losses from his business.

Answer

	2005/06	2006/07	2007/08	2008/09
Employment income	12,000	16,000	16,000	16,000
S386 loss relief	(12,000)	(16,000)	(16,000)	(8,000)
Dividends	1,000	1,000	1,000	1,000
S386 loss relief	(1,000)	(1,000)	(1,000)	nil
STI	nil	nil	nil	8,000

Notes

1. The trading loss of 55,000 has been offset in each tax year, commencing with tax year 2005/06, first against the salary John draws and then against any dividends received.
2. The salary of 12,000 for 2005/06 arises because John only worked for JS Ltd in that tax year for nine months i.e. 1.7.05 to 5.4.06 giving 9/12 x 16,000 = 12,000.
3. The trading loss of 55,000 is exhausted in tax year 2008/09.
4. Dividends are gross i.e. [900 + 1/9 x 900].

SUMMARY

Utilising trading losses in the most tax efficient manner can be difficult.

However, irrespective of which section is to be used trading losses must be offset in the order in which they occur. Thus, earlier trading losses are dealt with before later trading losses.

Assuming that none of the special circumstances arise (e.g. trade cessation; incorporation; etc) then, generally speaking, trading losses of a tax year should be offset under section 380 against the prior tax year's STI and any surplus loss remaining unrelieved should then be offset under section 380 against current tax year STI. Any remaining unrelieved trading loss can then be carried forward under section 385 for offset against future trading profits.

CHAPTER 9

Partnerships

INTRODUCTION

This chapter will examine how partners in partnerships are taxed.

General

The first thing to note is that a partnership is not a separate taxpayer. Whereas a company is a taxpayer in its own right separate from its shareholders, directors and employees a partnership is not.

As a consequence it is the individual partners and not the partnership itself who are taxed.

Basis of assessment

Although a partnership is not a separate taxpayer an overall partnership trading profit is computed for a period of account adopting the same rules as apply to a sole trader (see Chapter 6).

This overall partnership trading profit is then allocated amongst the partners according to the profit sharing ratios laid down in the partnership deed and each partner is then subject to income tax accordingly.

Each partner at this point is treated exactly as if he was in fact a sole trader. Thus all the normal rules relating to identifying the basis periods of assessment for a tax year apply (see Chapter 6). In addition, all the ways in which a sole trader may offset a trading loss (e.g. section 380; 385 etc; see Chapter 8) also apply to an individual partner.

Methods by which partners are remunerated

Each partner in a partnership is entitled to a share of the partnership profit for a period of account.

Pending the final determination of the partnership profit for a period of account each partner will typically receive drawings throughout this period. These drawings are in effect an advance against his final profit share once determined. Although technically these advance amounts are clearly an advance against any ultimate profit share, in questions on partnerships such amounts are commonly referred to as salaries (these amounts are not however salaries in the employment income sense; see Chapter 10).

It is also not unusual for a partner to receive interest on any capital which he will typically have contributed to the partnership on becoming a partner.

Thus in sharing out any partnership profit for a period of account any interest paid on capital during that period of account and any "salaries" already paid again during that period of account must be taken into consideration.

Example 9.1

John, Jack and James are partners in a partnership which began trading on 1st January 2003. They share profits in the ratios of 3:2:1. They each contributed capital as follows and each receives interest thereon at 5%:

John	£50,000
Jack	£45,000
James	£30,000

Each partner is to receive a salary of £25,000 per annum.

The partnership accounts are prepared to 31st December each year and the adjusted taxable trading profits for the partnership are as follows:

Year ended 31st December 2003   £125,000
Year ended 31st December 2004   £200,000

Calculate each partner's trading profit assessment for the tax years 2002/2003, 2003/04, and 2004/2005.

Answer

	John	Jack	James	Total
Period of account:				
1.1.03 to 31.12.03:				
Salary	25,000	25,000	25,000	75,000
Interest on capital:				
5% of £50,000	2,500			2,500
5% of £45,000		2,250		2,250
5% of £30,000			1,500	1,500
Balance of profit share				
3:2:1	21,875	14,583	7,292	*43,750*
Total	49,375	41,833	33,792	125,000
Period of account:				
1.1.04 to 31.12.04:				
Salary	25,000	25,000	25,000	75,000
Interest on capital:				
5% of £50,000	2,500			2,500
5% of £45,000		2,250		2,250
5% of £30,000			1,500	1,500
Balance of profit share				
3:2:1	59,375	39,583	19,792	*118,750*
Total	86,875	66,833	46,292	200,000

Notes

1. The steps in the calculation for each period of account are as follows:
    First, salary and interest on capital are calculated for each partner and then aggregated;
    Second, the total balance of profit share (the figure in bold italics above i.e. *43,750*) is calculated by taking the total salaries plus total interest on capital from the trading profit figure for that period of account (i.e. for 1.1.03 to 31.12.03 125,000 – (75,000 + 2,500 + 2,250 + 1,500) = 43,750
    Third, this total balance profit share figure (i.e. 43,750) is then divided according to the profit share ratios (i.e. 3:2:1) to give the figures in italics *21,875 14,583 and 7,292* for John, Jack and James respectively.
2. The above steps are then repeated for each subsequent period of account.

It now becomes necessary to work out each partner's individual trading profit assessment for each tax year.

Remember that to do this the normal sole trader basis period rules apply. Thus:

Name of partner	Tax year	Basis period	Assessment
John	2002/03	1.1.03 to 5.4.03	3/12 x 49,375 = 12,344
	2003/04	1.1.03 to 31.12.03	49,375
	2004/05	1.1.04 to 31.12.04	86,875
Jack	2002/03	1.1.03 to 5.4.03	3/12 x 41,833 = 10,458
	2003/04	1.1.03 to 31.12.03	41,833
	2004/05	1.1.04 to 31.12.04	66,833
James	2002/03	1.1.03 to 5.4.03	3/12 x 33,792 = 8,448
	2003/04	1.1.03 to 31.12.03	33,792
	2004/05	1.1.04 to 31.12.04	46,292

Notes

1. As the partnership started to trade on 1.1.03 then the tax year 2002/03 is the first tax year of trading and thus the opening basis period rules apply.
2. Each partner is treated as a sole trader and his assessments computed accordingly.
3. Overlap profits also arise for each partner. The overlap period is in each case the period 1.1.03 to 5.4.03.

Changes during a period of account

It may be that either or all of salaries, interest on capital and balance of profit shares may change during a period of account. In this case then, of course, account needs to be taken of such changes. Nevertheless, the above approach is still adopted.

Example 9.2

John and James have been in partnership for a number of years preparing their partnership accounts to 30th September each year. For the year ended 30th September 2005 the partnership adjusted taxable trading profit is £60,000.

Effective 1st July 2005 John and James agreed to change their profit shares and the salaries each received. Prior to 30th June 2005 the salaries for John and James were £15,000 p.a. and £20,000 p.a. respectively and from 1st July 2005 were changed to £18,000 p.a. and £25,000 p.a.

Profit shares were changed from 3:2 to 2:1.

Show the allocations for the period of account 1.10.04 to 30.9.05.

Answer

	John	James	Total
Period of account			
1.10.04 to 30.9.05			
Split:			
1.10.04 to 30.6.05			
Salary			
9/12 x 15,000	11,250		11,250
9/12 x 20,000		15,000	15,000
Balance of profit share			
3:2	*11,250*	*7,500*	*18,750*
Total (9/12 x 60,000)	22,500	22,500	45,000
1.7.05 to 30.9.05			
Salary			
3/12 x 18,000	4,500		4,500
3/12 x 25,000		6,250	6,250
Balance of profit share			
2:1	*2,833*	*1,417*	*4,250*
Total (3/12 x 60,000)	7,333	7,667	15,000
Total	29,833	30,167	60,000

Notes

1. As the profit share ratios change *during* (and not at the end of a period of account) it is necessary to split the period of account (i.e. 1.10.04 to 30.9.05) into separate time periods; one period from the start of the period of account to the date of the changes (i.e. 1.10.04 to 30.6.05) and

one from that date to the end of the period of account (i.e. 1.7.05 to 30.9.05). The adjusted profit for the period of account is then split into these two periods (i.e. 45,000 and 15,000 each respectively 9/12ths and 3/12ths of 60,000).

2. The salaries etc for each partner have also changed and account needs to be taken of these changes also.

3. A simple time apportionment approach is taken.

4. Also note that interest on capital is not always paid.

Changes in the partnership

Typically during the lifetime of a partnership some partners will leave the partnership and new partners will join.

For those who leave they will be treated as ceasing to trade. Similarly, for those who join they will be treated as commencing to trade.

The partners who simply continue to trade both before and after such changes there are no tax effects upon them; they will simply continue to be assessed on the relevant basis.

In other words, for any partnership it may be that for a particular tax year some partners (i.e. those just joining) will be assessed using the commencement rules; some will be assessed using the cessation rules (i.e. those leaving); whilst the remaining partners will be assessed on the usual CYB basis (see Chapter 6).

Example 9.3

John and Jack have been in partnership since they started trading on 1st July 2002. The partnership accounts are prepared to 30th June each year. On 1st July 2003 James joins the partnership. On 1st July 2005 Jack leaves the partnership leaving John and James.

For simplicity, assume that profits are always shared equally and that no salaries or interest on capital are paid.

Adjusted profits are:

Year ended 30.6.03	£50,000
Year ended 30.6.04	£60,000
Year ended 30.6.05	£120,000
Year ended 30.6.06	£200,000

Show the assessments for each partner for the relevant tax years.

Answer

Period of account	John	Jack	James	Total
1.7.02 to 30.6.03				
Profit share				
1:1	25,000	25,000	nil	50,000

Period of account
1.7.03 to 30.6.04
Profit share
1:1:1   20,000   20,000   20,000   60,000

Period of account
1.7.04 to 30.6.05
Profit share
1:1:1   40,000   40,000   40,000   120,000

Period of account
1.7.05 to 30.6.06
Profit share
1:1   100,000   Nil   100,000   200,000

Name of partner	Tax year	Basis period		Assessment
John	2002/03	1.7.02 to 5.4.03	9/12 x 25,000 =	18,750
	2003/04	1.7.02 to 30.6.03		25,000
	2004/05	1.7.03 to 30.6.04		20,000
	2005/06	1.7.04 to 30.6.05		40,000
	2006/07	1.7.05 to 30.6.06		100,000
Jack	2002/03	1.7.02 to 5.4.03	9/12 x 25,000 =	18,750
	2003/04	1.7.02 to 30.6.03		25,000
	2004/05	1.7.03 to 30.6.04		20,000
	2005/06	1.7.04 to 30.6.05	40,000	
		Less: Overlap relief	(18,750)	
				21,250
	2006/07			Nil
James	2002/03			Nil
	2003/04	1.7.03 to 5.4.04	9/12 x 20,000	15,000
	2004/05	1.7.03 to 30.6.04		20,000
	2005/06	1.7.04 to 30.6.05		40,000
	2006/07	1.7.05 to 30.6.06		100,000

Note

The opening tax year basis rules applied to John and Jack for tax year 2002/03 but to 2003/04 for James. For tax year 2005/06 when Jack left the partnership the cessation basis rules applied to Jack for that tax year. This happened to be the same basis period as for John and James for 2005/06 because Jack left on the last day of the period of account. However, unlike John and James, Jack is able to obtain relief for his overlap profits of 18,750 in the tax year of cessation.

Capital allowances

As in the case of the sole trader, capital allowances are treated as a tax deuctible trading expense.

It may be, however, that some assets are owned by the partnership as a whole, for example office equipment and furniture (both qualifying as plant and machinery for capital allowance purposes; see Chapter 7) whereas some assets are owned by the individual partners, for example motor cars.

In such cases capital allowances are computed on all assets for the relevant period of account of the partnership as normal but their deduction is:

- against partnership profits as a whole, i.e. *before* allocating profits amongst the partners, for partnership assets but
- against individual partner profits for individually owned assets

---

Example 9.4

John and James are in partnership which owns all the assets except for two cars which they each own individually.

For the year ended 31st December 2005 partnership adjusted trading profit *pre* capital allowance deductions was £175,000. John and James share profits 3:2 respectively. John's salary is £20,000 p.a. and that of James £25,000 p.a.

The partnership assets have a tax written down value as at 1st January 2005 of £60,000.

John's car has a tax written down value at this time of £20,000 and James' £10,000.

John uses his car 70% for business; James uses his car 60% for business.

Calculate John and James' profit allocations.

Answer

Capital allowances for period of account 1.1.05 to 31.12.05.

	General Pool	Expensive cars		CA Claimed
		John	James	
TWDV 1.1.05	60,000	20,000	10,000	
WDA (25% p.a.)	(15,000)	(3,000)	(2,500)	15,000
				3,000 x 70%
				2,500 x 60%
TWDV 31.12.05	45,000	17,000	7,500	

Therefore partnership adjusted taxable trading profit for ear ended 31.12.05 is:

	John	James	Total
Trading profit pre CAs	175,000		
Less CAs	(15,000)		
Trading profit post CAs	160,000		

Partnership Profit Allocation for Period of account 1.1.05 to 31.12.05

	John	James	Total
Salary	20,000	25,000	45,000
Balance of profit share			
3:2	69,000	46,000	115,000
Total	89,000	71,000	160,000
Less:			
CAs	(2,100)	(1,500)	
Profit share	86,900	69,500	

Notes

1. In calculating the partnership profit available for sharing out between the two partners only capital allowances on partnership assets are deducted (i.e. 15,000).
2. Once the partnership profits are allocated to each partner then each partner may deduct capital allowances on privately owned assets.
3. Note that only the business proportion of the capital allowances for the cars may be deducted (e.g. for James 60% of 2,500 i.e. 1,500).
4. Note also that maximum WDA for expensive cars is 3,000 p.a. (this applies to John's car).

Trading losses

Trading losses are allocated to individual partners in exactly the same manner in which partnership profits are allocated.

Once allocated each partner may then utilise any of the loss reliefs available to the sole trader (see Chapter 8).

Thus, sections 380 and 381 may be used in the early tax years of trading; section 385 may be used; and in the event of a cessation (e.g. a partner leaving the partnership) section 388 may be invoked.

Limited liability partnerships

Such partnerships are a relatively new vehicle.

The basic concept is that under such partnerships each partner's liability to contribute to, for example, third parties claims against the partnership and partnership losses is limited by agreement. Generally, a partner's exposure to such items is unlimited.

For tax purposes the partner's tax liabilities are as discussed above. However, the one difference is in connection with losses.

The amount of any trading loss which may be offset against a partner's other income is limited to the amount of capital the partner has contributed to the partnership.

SUMMARY

The key issue to note in connection with partnerships is that the partnership as a whole is not itself taxed. Only the individual partners are taxed on their share of the partnership profit.

To ascertain a partner's share of the partnership profit requires of course that the partnership's overall profit be computed. This is done exactly as is done for a sole trader.

One slight difference in this regard concerns capital allowances. Partnership owned assets and partner owned assets are entitled to the same amount of capital allowances but their deduction occurs at different points in the computations.

Trading losses are available to each partner as they are to a sole trader.

CHAPTER 10

Employee Taxation

INTRODUCTION

This chapter will look at all aspects associated with the taxation of employees including the taxation of benefits provided by an employer to an employee (e.g. a company car).

General

Prior to 6th April 2003 employees were taxed under Schedule E Cases I, II or III.

However, effective 6th April 2003 Schedule E has been abolished. From this date earnings of employees are taxed under the Income Tax (Earnings and Pensions) Act 2003 (ITEPA 2003).

It is now no longer appropriate to refer to "Schedule E income" but to either "employment income" or "income taxable under ITEPA 2003".

Whilst the relevant legislative provisions have changed the underlying manner in which employees are taxed the position post 6th April 2003 is still basically the same as it was prior to 6th April 2003.

The new legislation has, however, introduced a number of new terms including the terms "general earnings", "specific employment income", "net taxable earnings" and "net taxable specific income".

Employed or self-employed

Whether an individual is an employee (i.e. works for an employer under a contract of employment) or is self-employed (i.e. works for himself/herself in his/her own business) is important because the tax treatments are different in each case.

An employee is taxed under ITEPA 2003 whereas a self employed person is taxed under the provisions of ITTOIA 2005 (see Chapter 6).

The basic division between the two is that an employee has a contract *of* service whereas a self employed person has contracts *for* services.

Although there are no exact rules for determining whether an individual is self employed or an employee factors which would be taken into account would include:

- control over how the work is to be done
- whether the performer of the services needs to provide his own equipment
- whether he hires his own helpers
- who bears the financial risk

- the degree of management exercised
- the extent to which participation in profits arising occurs
- whether work is carried out for only one client/customer
- method of payment for work done
- holiday entitlement

As indicated above usually no one single factor determines the issue. Basically, all factors are reviewed and then a decision is taken.

Some of the differences between the self employed and an employee are:

- a self-employed person is liable to income tax under the provisions of ITTOIA 2005 and is required to make two payments on account of the tax year's liability and a balancing payment (see Chapter 21) whereas an employee pays income tax on earnings each month (or week) under the so-called Pay As You Earn Regulations i.e. self employed income tax payments are made later;
- the expense rules (i.e. those expenses which are tax deductible) for an employee are more rigorous than for the self-employed i.e. more difficult to satisfy; and
- a self-employed person pays Class 2 and 4 National Insurance Contributions (NIC) whereas an employee pays Class 1; the latter is greater than the former (see Chapter 20).

Employment income

An individual is liable under ITEPA 2003 on general earnings and specific employment income which together are referred to as employment income.

General earnings include salary, wages, tips/gratuities and so-called money's worth (i.e. something capable of being converted into money) plus amounts treated as earnings (i.e. benefits under the benefits code; see below).

Basis of assessment

Receipt of money earnings

General earnings consisting of money earnings are taxable when received not when earned even if they are not for that tax year. Receipt occurs at the earlier of the following times:

- when payment is made of or on account of earnings or
- when a person becomes entitled to payment.

For directors, receipt occurs at the date when a sum is credited in the company's accounts or records (e.g. crediting the director's account will constitute receipt) if this is earlier.

Receipt of non-money earnings

Benefits (other than non-cash vouchers)

General earnings not consisting of money are to be treated as received in the tax year in respect of which they are treated as earnings for that tax year. This rule applies to the provision of:

- cash vouchers
- credit tokens
- living accommodation
- cars, vans and related benefits and
- loans
- use of asset without transfer
- transfer of used asset

Non-cash vouchers

- For non-cash vouchers receipt occurs:
- in tax year in which cost of provision is incurred or
- if later, tax year in which voucher received by employee

Other

Otherwise receipt occurs when the benefit is provided to the employee.

Benefits code

In addition to receiving a salary an employee may also receive what are called benefits. Benefits refer to items such as a company car; an interest free loan; provision of accommodation; etc.

Although these are not rewards in the form of monetary consideration they are invariably provided in return for work done or services provided by the employee. They are therefore in principle subject to income tax just as is an employee's salary.

The legislation lays down how specific benefits are to be valued.

However, not all benefits are subject to income tax (i.e. some benefits are exempt from income tax; see below).

Under the new benefits code the approach taken (which is different to that pre 6th April 2003) is that *all* employees are subject to the code except those parts which are specifically stated as not applying to employees in excluded employment.

Excluded employment/lower paid employees

An employee is in excluded employment if he is a lower paid employee.

A lower paid employee is one whose earnings for the tax year are less than £8,500 (pro rated for less than a complete tax year). A director cannot be a lower paid employee unless the certain conditions are satisfied (see below).

In ascertaining whether the £8,500 amount is attained it is to be *assumed* that the employee is *not* a lower paid employee (i.e. is not in excluded employment). This assumption is necessary as lower paid employees are not subject to income tax on all benefits (which would mean that any such benefit would be included with a nil value).

In ascertaining whether the £8,500 is equalled or exceeded the computation is carried out *before* deducting any allowable expenses except for deductions for contributions to an approved pension scheme and/or payments made under the payroll charity giving scheme.

In general, a *director* will be categorised as lower paid if he:
- earns less than £8,500 a year, *and*
- owns 5% or less of the ordinary share capital of the company, *and*
- works full time for the company (or the company is a charity)

Example 10.1

John Smith receives a salary of £7,000 per annum for the tax year 2005/06.

In addition John receives the following benefits:
- a company car which has a taxable value of £1,200
- an interest free loan which has taxable value of £550
- use of a hi-fi set which has a taxable value of £400

John also contributes 5% of his salary to an approved company pension scheme.

Is John in excluded employment ie is he a lower paid employee?

Answer
To work out whether John is a lower paid employee requires the assumption that he is and thus any benefits are valued on this basis (i.e. not valued as if he were a lower paid employee). Thus:

Salary	7,000
Company car	1,200
Loan	550
Hi-fi set	400
	9,150
Less:	
5% x 7,000	(350)
Total earnings	8,800 per annum

John is not therefore a lower paid employee.

Approach to use when working out the value of a benefit
When working out the value of a benefit for a tax year the general approach is:

- STEP 1

Work out the value of the benefit for the whole tax year according to the relevant provision

- STEP 2

Reduce the value in Step 1 to the extent that the benefit is not available for any part of the tax year

(e.g. because it was provided part way through tax year)

- STEP 3

Deduct from the value arrived at in Step 2 any employee contributions towards the benefit.

(e.g. because the employee may contribute to the cost of the benefit)

Benefits Taxable on All Employees

General rule

The general rule for valuing a non-monetary benefit is that the benefit must be capable of conversion into cash. If the benefit cannot be so converted then it is not taxable as a benefit (unless the benefit is that of a non-lower employee).

Assuming, however, that it is convertible into cash then the measure of the benefit is its *second hand value*.

Example 10.2

JS Ltd buys a made-to measure suit for its employee John Smith. The cost of the suit to the employer is £500 (i.e. this is the purchase price for the employer).

However, John's taxable benefit is its second hand value e.g. only £150.

In other words, the cost to the employer of providing a benefit may be different from the benefit's second hand value as is the case in this example.

If the employee is *not* a lower paid employee the measure of the benefit is the *cost* to the employer not its second hand value. Thus, in Example 10.2 if John Smith had not been a lower paid employee the benefit would have been £500 (not £150).

This general rule does not apply, however, where a benefit is taxed according to its own specific rule (e.g. company cars; accommodation; etc see below).

Specific benefits

Specific benefits which are taxable in the hands of *all* employees (i.e. lower paid employees and other employees (normally referred to as higher paid employees)) and which are *not* subject to the above general rule are:

- vouchers and credit tokens
- living accommodation

Vouchers and credit tokens

Non Cash vouchers (i.e. one exchangeable for goods or services but not cash) give a benefit equivalent to the expense incurred by the employer in providing the vouchers (i.e. not on its exchange value).

Exceptions:

- Vouchers or goods received from third parties are not taxable provided the value does not exceed £150 inclusive of VAT; the person providing the benefit is not connected with the employer and the voucher is not linked to current or past services.
- Vouchers exchangeable for sporting activities are not chargeable when made available to all employees.
- Vouchers for car parking near employer premises are exempt.
- First 15p of luncheon vouchers are exempt (excess taxable).

Cash vouchers (i.e. a voucher which can be exchanged for cash) give rise to a benefit equal to its exchange value.

Credit tokens (e.g. a company credit card) give rise to a benefit equal to the cost to the employer of providing the goods, services etc obtained using the credit token.

Living accommodation

The measure of the benefit of the provision of living accommodation depends upon whether the accommodation is job or non job related.

Not job related accommodation

The benefit for the provision of accommodation comprises two parts:

the *greater* of the:

- annual rateable value of the accommodation *and*
- the rent paid by employer

plus an additional charge where the cost of providing the accommodation exceeds £75,000. The additional charge is:

(Cost of provision - £75,000) x appropriate percentage.

The *appropriate percentage* is the official interest rate applying to beneficial loans at the beginning of the relevant fiscal year for which the benefit is being valued (currently 5% for tax year 2005/2006).

Cost of provision versus market value

"Market value" is substituted for "cost of provision" if the property has been owned by the employer for more than six years *at the date of taking up occupation by the employee.*

Improvement expenditure incurred on the property *prior to the beginning of a fiscal year* increases cost or market value as appropriate for that tax year.

Note, however, that unless cost of the accommodation is £75,000 or greater at the beginning of the relevant tax year market value cannot apply. Thus, if cost of providing the accommodation is less than £75,000 no additional charge can apply even if market value exceeds this cost.

Deductions from the additional charge occur for bona fide business use of the accommodation and/or for rent paid by the employee that exceeds the benefit under the normal charge (i.e. any rent paid by employee is first offset against the basic charge f and then against the additional charge).

Example 10.3

(a) John Smith is provided with a house on 6th April 2005 which was purchased by his employer, JS plc, for £550,000 in January 2002. The annual value of the house is £2,000 and John pays rent of £500 a month to the company.

Calculate John Smith's assessable benefit for 2005/06, assuming the official rate of interest is 5.0%.

Answer

Benefit equals:

Annual value	2,000
Additional benefit 5% x (550,000 – 75,000)	23,750
	25,750
Less: Employee contribution (i.e. 500 x 12)	(6,000)
	19,750

Assuming the house had in fact been purchased prior to 6th April 1999 then market value at 6th April 2005 would be substituted for cost of the accommodation.

(b) JS Ltd purchased a flat in 1996 for £100,000. Expenditure was subsequently incurred by JS Ltd on property improvements of £60,000 in 2002 and a further £50,000 in December 2005. JS Ltd made the property available to an employee, John Smith, on 6th April 2004.

The market value of the property was £250,000 on 6th April 2004 and £300,000 on 6th April 2005.

Annual rateable value of the property is £3,000.

Calculate John Smith's assessable benefit for 2005/06, assuming the official rate of interest is 5.0%.

Answer

Benefit equals:

Annual value	3,000
Additional benefit 5% x (250,000 – 75,000)	8,750
	11,750
Less: Contribution by employee	nil
	11,750

Notes

1. *Additional benefit:* At date of first occupation by John the flat has been owned by JS Ltd for more than six years after purchase; therefore market value is substituted for cost i.e. 250,000 is used to determine the benefit.
2. The improvements in December 2005 (i.e. tax year 2005/2006) will not affect the computation of the benefit for the tax year 2005/06 but will affect the benefit for the tax year 2006/07.
3. For tax year 2006/07 the additional charge will be based upon market value i.e. 250,000 plus 50,000 i.e. 300,000.

Job related accommodation

No benefit arises if the occupation of the property is 'job related' i.e.

- where it is necessary for the employee to reside there to perform his or her duties e.g. a caretaker, *or*
- where it is customary to occupy it for the better performance of his or her duties; *or*
  (these two exceptions do not apply to directors, other than full time working directors who do not own more than 5% of the employing company's ordinary share capital (i.e. have a material interest))
- if it is provided for the employee's personal security.

Benefits taxable only on non lower paid (ie higher paid) employees

The following benefits are taxable only on those employees who are not lower paid:

- accommodation expenses
- motor cars
- motor car fuel
- own car use
- beneficial loans
- use of assets (and purchase/gift following use)

Specific rules apply to each of the above benefits as will be seen below.

Ancillary expenses connected with living accommodation

Although the provision of accommodation is a benefit whether the employee is a lower paid employee or not this is not the case with respect to expenses associated with the accommodation.

Only those employees who are *not* lower paid are taxable on such expenses.

Ancillary expenses of accommodation include:
- heating
- lighting
- cleaning
- repair and maintenance
- provision of furniture (at 20% of cost)

Telephone costs (i.e. calls and line rental) are *not* regarded as "ancillary expenses" although they are treated as a benefit and taxable.

Where the accommodation is "job related" the amount of the "ancillary expenses" which are treated as a benefit are normally restricted to 10% of "net earnings" i.e. salary plus benefits (other than ancillary benefits in question) less certain expenses (primarily, pension contributions to approved pension schemes and any own car mileage allowance expense claims). Note also that there is no assessment on council tax or rates paid by an employer where the accommodation is job related.

The 10% restriction does not apply to directors, other than to full time working directors with no material interest.

Example 10.4

John Smith's employer JS Ltd provides him with accommodation which cost £70,000 and has an annual rateable value of £1,000. In addition to providing the accommodation JS Ltd also bears the costs of the accommodation during tax year 2005/06 as follows:

Electricity	1,340
Gas	1,200
Cleaning and maintenance	2,500
Telephone	850
Structural repairs	3,000

It has been agreed with the tax authorities that 70% of the telephone call charges relate to business use. The line rental included in the telephone costs is £50.

Calculate the assessable benefit for 2005/06.

Answer

Benefits are taxable as follows:

Ancillary expenses:

Electricity	1,340
Gas	1,200
Cleaning and maintenance	2,500
	5,040

Telephone: line rental		50
Call costs	800	
Less: business calls	(560)	
	240	
	5,330	

Notes

1. The accommodation benefit itself would simply be £1,000.
2. Ancillary expenses exclude telephone costs.
3. Line rental cannot be split into business and private elements; as a consequence all the line rental cost is taxable.
4. Structural repairs are not taxable as they are the liability of the landlord and not the employee occupying the property.
5. If the accommodation had been job-related and John's salary had been £35,000 then the expenses benefit would have been the lower of 5,040 (total ancillary expenses) or [[10% of (35,000 + 290)] plus 290] i.e. [3529 + 290] = 3,819.

Use of assets made available for private use

This benefit arises where an employee is permitted the use of an asset without title to the asset being transferred to the employee from the employer. In other words the asset continues to belong to the employer.

The measure of the benefit is the higher of:

- the annual value of the use of the asset; and
- the annual amount of the sums paid by the employer as rent and/or hire charge

The annual value is equal to 20% of the asset's market value at the date it is first provided to the employee.

The benefit is reduced by private contributions after any time apportionment where the asset is provided for part of tax year only.

(Note that where a computer is provided for use by an employee and computers are generally available to all employees, the first £500 per annum of benefit is exempt; however, any excess amount is taxable as a benefit).

Example 10.5

John Smith is provided by his employer with a hi-fi set for his use. It is provided on 6th April 2005 at which time its market value is £7,000.

Calculate the benefit to John for the tax year 2005/06.

Answer

The benefit = 20% x 7,000 = 1,400

Gift of asset following use

If an asset owned by the employer and previously made available to an employee for use is subsequently transferred to an employee the benefit arising from the transfer of title of the asset from employer to employee is the *greater* of:

- market value of the asset at the date of transference; and
- market value of the asset when first made available for the employee's use less the aggregate of the use benefits assessed on the employee

Effective from 6th April 2005 the above does not apply to a gift of a computer following its use by an employee if the cost of the computer was £2,500 or less. In such cases at the date of the gift the benefit is simply taken to be the former of the above two tests ie simply its market value at the date of the gift. Where the cost exceeds £2,500 then the above rules will continue to apply as normal.

Example 10.6

John Smith has been using an asset (not a computer costing £2,500 or less) provided by his employer from 6th April 2003 until 6th October 2005. At 6th October 2005 John was given the asset by his employer when its market value at that date was £2,750.

On 6th April 2003 the market value of the asset was £6,000.

Calculate John's benefit for each relevant tax year.

Answer
The use benefit will be as follows:

2003/04	20% x 6,000 =	1,200
2004/05	20% x 6,000 =	1,200
2005/06	20% x 6,000 x 6/12 =	600

On 6th October 2005 John purchased a previously used asset:
The benefit of the purchase will be the greater of:
1. 2,750 (i.e. market value of asset at date of purchase) and
2. 6,000 – [1,200 + 1,200 + 600] (i.e. market value when first made available less use benefit) = 3,000

Therefore John will be assessed on the benefits as follows:

2003/04	1,200	
2004/05	1,200	
2005/06	600 + 3,000 =	3,600

Motor cars

Motor cars are probably one of the most popular benefits provided to employees.

INCOME TAX

Not only is the provision of a car (a so-called company car) a taxable benefit but where any fuel (i.e. petrol and/or diesel) is paid for by the employer this fuel is treated as an additional benefit (see below).

Where a company car is made available to an employee and is available for private use by the employee (which invariably will be the case) the benefit is as follows:

(List price – Capital contribution by employee) x % (based upon CO_2 emissions)

List price includes the cost of the car, delivery charges (excluding road fund licence) and standard accessories fitted at the time of purchase (this may not be the actual price paid by the employer when purchasing the car) and is capped at £80,000 (i.e. the maximum list price used to work out the benefit cannot exceed this figure). Optional accessories fitted at the time of delivery are added to the list price.

Capital contribution by the employee applies where the employee himself contributes to the purchase price of the car (this figure is capped at £5,000).

% refers to the % which is determined according to the CO_2 emissions of the car. Up to 140 grams per kilometre of CO_2 emissions the % is 15%. For each complete 5g/km above 140 g/km the % increases by 1% (a cap of 35% applies).

The above CO_2 rule also applies to diesel cars but in this case the % worked out as above is then increased by 3% (but again subject to a maximum of 35%).

Where any accessory is added after delivery of the car has been taken, for the tax year in which they are fitted (and of course subsequent tax years) the list price is increased by the cost of such items except that any individual accessory fitted at a cost of below £100 is ignored.

The benefit calculated as above is regarded as taking into account various costs such as road tax, repairs and maintenance, insurance etc. (other than car fuel which as commented above is taxed as a benefit separately).

Example 10.7

John Smith is provided with a company car by this employer on 6th April 2005. The car has a CO_2 emission of 238g/km and a list price of £25,000. John would like to know the likely benefit if the car is petrol and if it is diesel.

Answer

% which applies to the list price is = 15% + [[238 – 140]/5] x 1% = 15% + 19% =34%

Assuming the car is a diesel car then the benefit is as above i.e. 34% but plus 3% i.e. 37% capped at 35%.

Note: in working out the % any % is rounded *down* not up i.e. in the above [238 – 145]/5 = 19.6 which is rounded down to 19%.

Example 10.8

John Smith is provided with a petrol company car by this employer on 6th October 2005. The car has a CO_2 emission of 197 g/km and a list price of £25,000.

Accessories after John took delivery were fitted in December 2005 at individual costs of £250, £300 and £65 and at a cost individually of £150 in December 2006.

John would like to know the likely benefit of the car.

Answer

For the tax year 2005/06 the benefit is = [15% + [[197 – 140]/5] x 1%] x [25,000 + 250 + 300]

$$= [15\% + 11\%] \times [25,550]$$
$$= 6,643$$

However, the car was only available to John for six months of this tax year.

Therefore the benefit = 6/12 x 6,643 = 3,322 for 2005/06.

Note: the accessory fitted after delivery of £65 in 2005/06 is below the £100 threshold and thus ignored; the accessory fitted in 2006/07 tax year of £150 will be taken into account for 2006/07 and later tax years but not 2005/06.

Example 10.9

John is employed by JS Ltd. The company provided him with a company car with CO_2 emissions of 215g/km. The list price of the car was £30,000.

John provided a capital contribution of £6,000. John's total mileage for the tax year 2005/06 is 12,500 miles of which 9,000 miles were on business.

Car tax, repairs and maintenance and car insurance paid by the employer for the tax year 2005/06 amounted to £2,750.

Calculate John's benefit for 2005/06.

Answer

The benefit = [15% + [[215 – 140]/5] x 1%] x [30,000 – 5,000]

$$= [15\% + 15\%] \times 25,000$$
$$= 7,500$$

Note: John's capital contribution is capped at £5,000. The various expenses of the car are ignored as it is assumed (other than fuel) that such expenses are included in the benefit calculation already. Car mileage is also totally irrelevant.

Pool cars

There is no benefit for an employee provided with the use of a pool car.

A pool car is a car which:

- is used by more than one employee or director, *and*
- there is no (or merely incidental) private use, *and*
- the car is not kept at the home of the employee overnight.

Classic Cars

These are cars which are:

- older than 15 years at the end of the tax year *and*
- have a market value at the end of the tax year exceeding £15,000 (which also exceeds original list price)

In this case the benefit is based on the *market value* of the car rather than on its list price where market value is greater than list price.

Vans

Vans are treated differently and more favourably than motor cars.

Effective 6th April 2005, the rules have been modified from those which applied prior to this date.

The benefit for 2005/06 is £500 if the age of the van is less than 4 years old at the end of that tax year; otherwise the benefit is £350.

However, the benefit is nil where the van is made available to the employee mainly for use on the employee's business travel and private use by the employee is forbidden although travel from home to work is acceptable.

Car and van fuel benefit

Car

A car fuel benefit arises where any private fuel is made available to an employee with a company car by reason of his or her employment.

From 6th April 2003 the car fuel benefit is based upon CO_2 emissions as is the basic car benefit itself (see above). The same percentage figure will be used for both purposes (i.e. car benefit and fuel). A three per cent supplement will apply where diesel fuel is provided. The minimum and maximum percentages are 15% and 35%.

To calculate the benefit on the provision of fuel the relevant percentage figure will be multiplied against a set figure for the year. For the year 2005/06 the set figure is £14,400.

Thus the minimum and maximum car fuel benefits are £2,160 (15% of £14,400) and £5,040 (35% of £14,400) respectively.

Unlike the general rule for benefits under which an employee's contributions reduce the value of any benefit, where an employee makes any contributions towards car fuel costs these contributions do *not* reduce the benefit *unless* the employee contributes the full cost of his private fuel usage in which case no fuel benefit arises.

Van

For the tax year 2005/06 there is no fuel benefit.

Example 10.10

John Smith is given a petrol driven company car for the tax year 2005/06. The car has CO_2 emissions of 190g/km.

John's employer pays for all the running expenses of the car including fuel for private purposes.

Calculate John's car fuel benefit for the tax year 2005/06.

Answer

% used to calculate the company car tax benefit itself for 2005/06 is:
$[[15\% + [(190 - 140)/5 \times 1\%]] = 25\%$.

The fuel scale charge for 2005/06 will therefore be:
$14,400 \times 25\% = 3,600$.

As with other benefits the benefit is reduced on a time basis if the car is unavailable for use.

Had the car been diesel then the % applicable would have been (25% + 3%) i.e. 28%.

Example 10.11

John Smith is employed by JS Ltd. The company provided him with a diesel company car with a 1,800 cc engine size and CO_2 emissions of 205 g/km.

The list price of the car is £25,000. All car fuel is paid for by John's employer.

John's business mileage for the tax year 2005/06 was 20,000 miles and running costs of the car for this period (excluding car fuel costs) were £1,650.

Calculate John's benefits for the tax year 2005/06.

Answer

Car benefit
Benefit = $[[15\% + [205 - 140]/5]] \times 25,000 = 7,000$

Fuel benefit
Benefit = $28\% \times 14,400 = 4,032$

Total benefit = 7,000 + 4,032 = 11,032

Salary Sacrifice re cars

Where an employee is offered a choice of additional salary *or* a company car he will be assessable on whichever is taken; in other words on the car if taken calculated as above or simply the cash if taken.

INCOME TAX

Car park space and chauffeur

The provision of a personal chauffeur is a taxable benefit but the provision of a car park space at or close to the workplace is not a taxable benefit.

Own car: approved mileage allowance payments

A company car is a car owned by an employer and made available to an employee. Any benefit associated therewith is calculated as described above.

However, in some cases although no company car is provided to an employee by an employer the employee may use his own car to travel on business.

Where this occurs the employee may be reimbursed by his employer without such reimbursement falling to be treated as a taxable benefit *if* the amounts paid by the employer to the employee are no greater than the approved mileage allowances provided by statute.

The approved mileage allowances are as follows:
- 40p per business mile for the first 10,000 business miles
- 25p per business mile for business mileage above 10,000 business miles

Where the payment by the employer is *less* than the above allowances the difference may be claimed by the employee as additional tax deductible expenses against his employment income.

If the allowances paid by the employer *exceed* these allowances then the excess is taxable on the employee as a benefit.

It is to be noted that such allowances are designed to cover all costs of use of a car on business. Thus, it is not possible for an employee to deduct any additional costs of running the car (e.g. car insurance; repairs and maintenance; etc) although capital allowances may be available (see Chapter 7).

Example 10.12

John Smith uses his car on business as his employer does not provide its employees with company cars.

During the tax year 2005/06 John travelled 22,000 miles of which 12,000 miles were on business.

John's employer pays a flat business mileage allowance of 50p per mile.

Calculate John's tax position in respect of such an allowance.

Answer

Approved mileage allowance = 10,000 x 40p + 2,000 x 25p	= 4,500
Employer payment = 12,000 x 50p	= 6,000
John will therefore be treated as receiving a benefit of 6,000 - 4,500 = 1,500	

If instead John's employer had provided payment of 10p per mile then of the approved amount calculated above of 4,500 John will have received only 12,000 x 10p i.e. 1,200.

Thus, John will not have received any taxable benefit and will in fact be able to claim an expense deduction against his employment income of 4,500 - 1,200 i.e. 3,300

Beneficial loans

Interest free or cheap loans to employees are taxable as a benefit.

Loans which are caught are those where the interest paid by the employee in a tax year is less than that which should have been paid according to the official rate of interest (fixed at 5% per annum for tax year 2005/06).

Where, however, at no time during a tax year do all such loans exceed £5,000 no benefit is deemed to arise.

The measure of the benefit is calculated either using the normal (or averaging) *or* alternative method and is basically the difference between the interest actually paid and that given using the official rate.

The latter (i.e. alternative) method gives a more accurate figure and may be used if either the employee or the Inland Revenue so elect.

Example 10.13

John Smith an employee borrows on 6th April 2005 from his employer £10,000 for a family holiday. His employer charges interest at the rate of 3% per annum. The loan is still outstanding at 5th April 2006.

Calculate John's benefit for the tax year 2005/06.

Answer
Benefit =
[[Amount outstanding at 6.4.05 + Amount outstanding at 5.4.06]/2]x [5% - 3%]
= [[10,000 + 10,000]/2] x 2% = 200

If John repaid £4,000 on 5th December 2005 then his benefit under the average method would be:

[[10,000 + [10,000 - 4,000]/2] x 2% = 160 (see Example 10.15).

Example 10.14

John Smith an employee borrows on 6th October 2005 from his employer £10,000 for a family holiday. His employer charges interest at the rate of 3% per annum. The loan is still outstanding at 5th April 2006.

Calculate John's benefit for the tax year 2005/06.

Answer

Benefit = [[Amount outstanding at 6.10.05 + Amount outstanding at

5.4.06]/2] x [5% - 3%] x 6/12

= [[10,000 + 10,000]/2] x 2% x6/12 = 100

Note: as the loan is only outstanding for six months i.e. 6th October to 5th April in 2005/06 then interest is calculated only for this period; hence the use of 6/12ths.

Example 10.15

John Smith an employee borrows on 6th April 2005 from his employer £10,000 for a family holiday. His employer charges interest at the rate of 3% per annum. On 6th December 2005 John repaid £4,000.

Calculate John's benefit for the tax year 2005/06.

Answer

As per example 10.13 using the average method produces a benefit of 160.

Under the alternative method the benefit would be:

10,000 x [5% - 3%] x 8/12 + 6,000 x [5% - 3%] x 4/12 = 133 + 40 = 173

In this case the Inland Revenue would elect to tax John on the benefit as calculated under the alternative method as of course this provides them with a greater income tax liability.

Note: under the alternative method interest is calculated only on the exact amount of loan outstanding. Thus in the above 10,000 was outstanding from 6.4.05 to 5.12.05 (i.e. eight months) and then after John's repayment of 4,000 only 6,000 was then outstanding from 6.12.05 to 5.4.06 (i.e. four months).

Loan written off
Where a loan is written off either in whole or in part the amount so written off is treated as a taxable benefit.

Employment related benefits
In addition to all of the above there is a general provision which basically taxes all benefits not taxed elsewhere in the legislation (this is referred to as a residual liability).

Such benefits are, however, still only taxable on non lower paid employees.

Employment related benefits are those benefits (other than those already specifically taxed under their own rules discussed above) which are provided by reason of the employee's employment whether they are *convertible into cash or not*.

The measure of an employment related benefit is the *cost to the employer* of providing it. This overrides the normal rule (see above) which taxes such a benefit on the basis of its second hand value (which generally speaking will be lower; see Example 10.2 above).

Lump sum payments on termination or variation of employment

Such payments may be tax free, partially taxable or fully taxable.

Where a payment is made in connection with a person leaving an employment and is taxable it is taxable in the year of *receipt* not the year of leaving.

Example 10.16

John Smith has his contract of employment terminated on 31st December 2005. He receives a compensation payment on 30th June 2006.

If the compensation payment is subject to income tax it will be liable in the tax year of receipt i.e. 2006/07 not in the tax year in which John's contract was terminated i.e. 2005/06.

Tax free payments

Where a lump sum payment is made:
- under an approved pension scheme and/or
- made on account of injury, accidental death or disability
- it is exempt from income tax.

Taxable payments
Contractual entitlement

Payments to which an employee is contractually entitled (i.e. are provided for in his contract of employment) are generally taxable in full e.g. terminal bonuses.

If a contract of employment provides for an employer to make a payment in lieu of notice (i.e. a payment made by the employer where the employer has not given the employee the required period of notice specified in his contract of employment) then such a payment would be fully taxed.

Where no such payment in lieu provision is in the employment contract, such a payment would be tax free.

Partially tax free payments
Redundancy payments and ex gratia payments

Payments which are made at the discretion of the employer (so called ex gratia payments; i.e. employer not legally required to make such payments) to compensate an employee for loss of employment are exempt up to £30,000; any excess is taxable.

Any statutory redundancy payment (a statutory redundancy payment is a payment which is legally required to made by the employer by law when an employee is made redundant) made to an employee counts as part of the above tax free £30,000.

An ex gratia payment can include cash payments and/or benefits in kind (e.g. keeping company car or being allowed to use it for, say, one year after termination of the employment).

Where a termination package is partially exempt and exceeds £30,000 then this exempt amount is allocated first against earlier payments and benefits and, in any particular tax year, is allocated against cash payments before non-cash benefits (e.g. company car).

Other amounts

The cost of the provision for counselling and help in finding an employee new employment (or self employment) is not a taxable benefit.

The continued use of a mobile phone would not be taxable (the provision of a mobile is in any event a tax free benefit; see below) and the continued use of a computer (if within the £500 per annum annual limit; only excess over £500 p.a. taxable) would similarly not be taxable.

A departing employee may be paid an amount in return for agreeing to limit his/her future activities; this amount is fully taxable.

Taxability

Any part of the termination payment which is taxable is treated as the highest part of an individual's income above non-savings, savings and dividend income.

Example 10.17

John Smith on being made redundant in February 2006 receives compensation for loss of employment of £42,000 which includes a statutory redundancy payment of £4,000. His other income for 2005/06 is a salary of £25,000 from which PAYE of £3,500 had been deducted.

In 2005/06 John receives bank interest of £1,600 (net).

Calculate John's tax position for 2005/06.

Answer

Using the pro-forma of Chapter 3:

	Non savings	Savings	Dividends	Compensation
Salary	25,000			
Bank interest (gross)		2,000		
Compensation				
(42,000 - 30,000)	——	——		12,000
STI	25,000	2,000		12,000
Less: PA	(4,895)	——		——
Taxable income	20,105	2,000		12,000

Calculate income tax liability as normal taking non savings income first followed by, savings, dividends and then compensation:

TI	Rate	Tax	
2,090	10%	209	
18,015	22%	3,963	
20,105			
2,000	20%	400	
22,105			
10,295	22%	2,265	
32,400			
1,705	40%	682	
34,105			7,519
Less: Tax deducted at source:			
Bank interest		(400)	
PAYE		(3,500)	
			(3,900)
Tax payable			3,619

Deductible Expenses for Employment Income

In arriving at the net taxable earnings or net taxable specific income of an employee certain deductions may be made.

General rule

The general rule is that an employee may deduct an expense if the expense has been incurred *wholly, exclusively and necessarily in* the performance of his employment duties.

Thus, for example no deduction is allowed for expenses which have not been incurred *in* the performance of the duties but in order to carry the duties out e.g. payment of a fee to an employment agency used to find a job; similarly the costs of newspapers could not be deducted from a journalist's salary as the reading of such newspapers merely prepared the journalist to carry out his duties.

The need to meet the wholly, exclusively and necessarily test has resulted in very few expenses being eligible for deduction mainly on the grounds that very few expenses are actually necessarily incurred. By necessary is meant that the duties of the employment require that the expenses be incurred; it is not sufficient that the expenses are incurred due to the personal choice of the employee and/or because the employer requires the employee to incur the expense.

By way of example, the expense incurred by a bank manager who was required by his employer to join a London club was not able to deduct the expense against his earnings. The reason was that the expense had not been incurred *necessarily.*

Similarly the wholly and exclusively part of the test requires that the expense be incurred solely for business purposes. As a consequence, if the expense has been incurred partly for business and partly for private purposes then no part of it will be deductible by the employee. In some situations, however, where it is possible to split an expense into a business and private element the former will be deductible. This will generally not be possible or very often is likely to prove very difficult.

Business entertainment expenses are specifically denied as a deductible expense for an employee. In other words an employee cannot deduct expenses he may incur himself on business entertaining.

However, the more likely situation would be where an employer reimburses the employee for such expenses. In this situation the reimbursement is basically taxable on the employee but in this case the employee is allowed a deduction for the expenses.

Travel expenses

Travel expenses are allowed as a deduction if the employee is required to incur the expenses in the course of his employment and the expenses are necessarily incurred on travelling in the performance of his employment duties.

Thus, travel expenses incurred in travelling from home to work are not incurred in the performance of the employee's duties and are therefore not deductible. However, where an employee travels for example from one office of his employer to another office such travel expenses are deductible. Travelling sales employees will also be able to deduct their travel expenses as they travel from customer to customer typically but not always by car.

It must be appreciated that any deductible travel expenses must be reasonable; what is reasonable will be determined according to the surrounding facts.

Where an employee uses his own car to travel on business the above rules on deductibility do not apply if the employee receives approved mileage allowance payments (see above) from his employer or if the employee is entitled to receive such allowance payments from his employer.

Benefits code expenses

Where an employee is taxed on benefits under the benefits code a deduction is available for the amount of the expense if had the employee incurred the expense himself it would have been deductible under the *general rule* above.

Overseas travel expenses

Part UK and part Overseas

Where an employment is partly carried out in the UK and partly overseas expenditure incurred on all business journeys (including travel outside the UK) reimbursed by the employer or paid for by the employer is deductible. *However, no deduction is available if the employee bears the cost without reimbursement.*

Wholly overseas

Where an employee is wholly employed abroad travel expenses and reimbursements of them are not excluded from being taxed. However, a deduction is available for the costs of:

- the initial travel abroad to take up the employment and for the return journey at the end of the employment on business *whether the cost is ultimately borne by employer or employee,* and
- any related subsistence.

Where employee spends 60 or more continuous days outside the UK expenses of travel of the spouse and children under 18 are not taxable if met by the employer (limited to two trips in year of assessment). *No deduction is available however if the employee bears the cost.*

Any number of trips made by the employee between his place of work and the UK can be paid for by the employer without such payments being taxed as earnings. *If the employee pays the costs without reimbursement he cannot deduct them.*

The cost of medical insurance and/or medical treatment outside UK where treatment arises because employee is performing his job outside UK is exempt (note: cost of providing medical insurance within UK is taxable for higher paid employee).

Where the trip involves both business and private elements, there will normally be an apportionment.

Specifically authorised deductible expenditure

Certain expenditure if incurred by an employee is specifically authorised as deductible.

Such expenditures are:

- contributions to an approved company pension scheme
- fees and subscriptions to prescribed professional bodies
- payments to charity under a payroll deduction scheme operated by an employer
- mileage allowance relief.

Reimbursed expenditure (other than business entertainment expenses)

Where expenses are reimbursed by the employer to the employee or the employee receives a round sum expense allowance the employee will be taxed thereon subject to a claim for any allowable expenses (not applicable to the lower paid).

However, an exemption for round sum allowances or reimbursement of actual expenses incurred applies in connection with incidental overnight expenses up to the maximum of £5 per night in UK (£10 non-UK). If these maxima are exceeded no part of the exemption applies.

Miscellaneous exempt benefits

The main exempt benefits are:

- use of a mobile phone
- free or subsidised canteen meals if available to all employees
- use of computer if annual *benefit* is less than £500 per annum (excess is taxable)
- employer contributions to approved pension plan
- provision of car park space at or near place of work (or reimbursement to employee of costs in paying for such a car park place)
- certain gifts and entertainment (entertaining provided by third parties not a benefit; gifts from a third party up to £250 in a tax year exempt; no benefit re provision by employer of parties etc if cost to employer per employee does not exceed £150/year)
- stress counselling and outplacement counselling for redundant employees
- provision of in-house sports and recreational facilities
- the first £8,000 of removal expenses (excess taxable)
- the first 15p per day of luncheon vouchers
- job related accommodation
- cheap loans up to £5,000 in a tax year

SUMMARY

An employee is subject to income tax on salary plus any benefits.

Different benefits are taxed differently and a lower paid employee is not taxed on all benefits as is the case for a non lower paid employee (subject to certain exempt benefits).

Expenses may be deducted in arriving at an employee's taxable earnings although generally speaking expense deductions are somewhat limited.

CHAPTER 11

Personal Tax: Overseas Aspects

INTRODUCTION
This chapter takes a brief look at some aspects of the taxation of non-UK source income referred to as *relevant foreign income* for UK resident individuals and introduces the concept of double taxation relief.

Residence and Ordinary Residence
Both these concepts have a material bearing on an individual's income and capital gains tax liabilities.

Residence
An individual is resident in the UK for UK tax purposes if:
- physically present in UK for 183 days or more in a tax year; or
- averages 91 days or more in any tax year measured over a four year period (in which case residence starts from the commencement of the fifth tax year).

Days of arrival and departure are ignored for these tests.

Ordinary residence
An individual will be ordinary resident if he is habitually resident which, in general, means physical presence in the UK on average for 91 days per tax year averaged over a four year period (in which case residence starts form the commencement of the fifth tax year).

Note that an individual can be resident but not ordinarily resident and vice versa.

Complete tax year
Strictly an individual is resident and/or ordinarily resident for a complete tax year.

However, by concession a tax year may be split where:
- an individual comes to the UK for permanent residence or to work in UK for at least two years
- leaves the UK for permanent residence abroad or to spend at least three years abroad
- an individual leaves the UK to take up full time employment abroad and the employment spans a complete tax year and return visits to the UK are less than 183 days in any tax year and are less than 91 days per tax year averaged over four years.

Coming to UK
An individual coming to the UK with the intention of remaining for three years or more will be treated as resident from the date of arrival.

So will someone who comes to the UK to work for at least two years.

Similarly ordinary residence status will apply from the date of arrival in the former case but only in the latter case if the work is for at least three years (thus if work is for less than three years ordinary resident status commences at commencement of tax year after the third anniversary of their arrival).

Leaving the UK

Leaving for permanent residence abroad (i.e. for at least three tax years) or for full time employment overseas (spanning a complete tax year) or for self employment full time abroad (spanning a complete tax year) gives rise to non-residence and non-ordinary residence status.

For an individual who has been resident or ordinary resident in the UK for any part of at least four of the previous seven tax years and who becomes not resident and not ordinarily resident for less than five years will still be liable to capital gains tax on assets owned before leaving the UK (for capital gains tax an individual is liable if either resident *or* ordinarily resident; see Chapter 12).

All gains made in the year of departure will be taxed in that year. Gains made during the period of absence will be taxed in the year when the person resumes UK residence and losses will be allowed on a similar basis. Taper relief, however, will be computed only up to date of actual sale of asset.

Gains on assets acquired whilst abroad are exempt if sold between tax year of departure and tax year of return (losses not allowable).

Domicile

A person's domicile is where he has his permanent home.

A child acquires the domicile of his father at birth (domicile of origin) unless illegitimate when he acquires his mother's domicile at birth.

An individual can only for UK tax purposes have one domicile.

Nationality and/or residence are irrelevant in determining domicile status.

Until aged 16 if the father/mother's domicile changes so does the child's; this is known as a domicile of dependency.

At 16 a child then can acquire a domicile of choice which is independent of his father/mother's domicile. This is not easy to do and requires that all links with the former country of domicile are severed and new links are set up in the newly chosen country with the intention of making a new permanent home there.

The importance of domicile is that for a non-UK domiciled individual:
- inheritance tax payable on UK situs assets only; and
- income and capital gains taxes are only payable on a "remittance" basis for non-UK source income and capital gains

Relevant foreign income means income which arises from a source outside the UK and includes:

- profits of an overseas property business
- dividends from overseas companies
- interest on foreign bank deposits/foreign securities
- overseas pensions

Profits of an overseas property business are taxed as non-savings income i.e. 10%, 22% and 40%.

Other forms of relevant foreign income income are taxed as savings income i.e. 10%, 20% and 40% (note: only 90% of pension taxed).

Dividends from overseas companies are taxed in the same manner as UK source dividends (i.e. include under the "dividends" column) at the 10% and 32.5% rates.

Note, that although the profit of an overseas property business is computed on the same principles as the profit of a UK property business (see Chapter 5) it is kept separate from any assessment on the UK property business.

Basis of assessment
The basis of assessment for relevant foreign income is the "arising" basis; income arises when received or when credited.

Non-UK domiciled
However, where the UK resident individual is non-UK domiciled (*or a British subject who is not ordinarily resident*) and thus taxed on the remittance basis *all* relevant foreign income is treated as *non-savings income* (even interest and dividends) and taxed accordingly i.e. taxed at the 10%, 22% and 40% rates (see Chapters 2 and 3).

Double Tax Relief
Double tax relief (DTR) may be available either unilaterally (i.e. under the UK's domestic tax laws) and/or under a relevant double tax agreement (i.e. a bilateral agreement between the UK and an overseas country under which each country agrees how each will tax certain types of income e.g. interest; dividends etc and taxpayers of both countries).

Any foreign income liable to UK tax is included "gross" (i.e. before foreign taxes are deducted).

In ascertaining the extent of any DTR credit for any foreign tax will be the lower of:

- the foreign tax paid on the foreign income and
- the UK tax on that foreign income

In calculating the UK tax on the foreign income the following method is adopted:

- calculate UK tax on both UK and the foreign income before DTR; then

- calculate the UK tax on all income except the foreign income;
- the difference between the two tax calculations represents the UK tax payable on the foreign income.

Where an individual receives more than one source of overseas income (e.g. foreign dividend income; foreign rental income) the order in which the overseas income is taxed may be taken to be that which is most favourable i.e. that which enables the greatest DTR to be obtained.

Usually this means identifying the highest taxed foreign source and removing this amount first followed by the removal of the next highest taxed foreign income etc.

Example 11.1

John Smith a UK resident individual received £25,000 salary taxable under ITEPA 2003 for the tax year 2005/06.

In addition during that tax year John also receives foreign rental income of £1,950 after foreign tax of £1,050 had been levied and interest on a foreign bank account of £8,000 after local foreign tax of £1,500 had been deducted.

Calculate John's income tax liability for 2005/06.

Answer

John is entitled to DTR on the two sources of foreign income.

First, it is necessary to calculate John's income tax liability on *all* (i.e. his UK and foreign source) income before being able to determine the amount of his DTR.

	Non-Savings	Savings	Dividends
Employee income	25,000		
Relevant foreign income:			
Rental income	3,000		
Bank interest		9,500	
Less:			
Personal allowance	(4,895)		
Taxable income	23,105	9,500	Nil

Taxable income	Rate of tax	Tax liability
2,090	10%	209
21,015	22%	4,623
23,105		
9,295	20%	1,859
32,400		
205	40%	82
32,605		6,773

Therefore income tax liability pre DTR = 6,773

This amount is reduced by any foreign tax credit i.e. foreign tax paid on overseas income.

The foreign rental income is subject to a foreign tax rate of 1,050/3,000 = 35%.

The foreign bank interest is subject to a foreign tax rate of 1,500/9,500 = 15.8%

To maximise DTR as the rental income is taxed at the higher rate of foreign tax this should be excluded first.

Thus, the income tax liability needs to be calculated but ignoring the rental income
i.e. Taxable income = (23,105 - 3,000 + 9,500) = 29,605

This gives an income tax liability of 6,072.

UK income tax thus levied on the foreign rental income = 6,773 − 6,072 = 701
Foreign tax levied on rental income = 1,050

Therefore DTR is the lower of the two figures i.e. 701.

This procedure is now repeated by excluding the foreign bank interest *in addition* to having excluded the rental income. This gives a revised Taxable income of £20,105 (i.e. 29,605 − 9,500). Income tax liability on 20,105 is 4,172.

The UK income tax thus levied on the foreign bank income = 6,072 − 4,172
$$= \quad 1,900$$
Foreign tax levied on bank income = 1,500

Therefore DTR is the lower of the two figures i.e. 1,500

Thus:

Income tax liability (pre DTR) =		6,773
Less:		
DTR on rental income	701	
DTR on bank income	1,500	
Total DTR		(2,201)
Net UK income tax liability		4,572

Note
In the case of the foreign bank interest source the UK income tax liability was less than the foreign tax paid on that income. As a consequence, any surplus foreign tax unutilised is simply lost.

SUMMARY

UK resident and domiciled individuals are liable to UK income tax on their world wide income (i.e. UK source income and relevant foreign income).

Non-domiciled individuals who are resident are liable to UK income tax on UK source income and remitted relevant foreign income.

Double tax relief is available to reduce any income tax liability on the relevant foreign income but such DTR cannot exceed the UK income tax liability on that particular source of relevant foreign income.

CHAPTER 12

Capital Gains Tax: General Principles

INTRODUCTION

This chapter introduces a new tax, capital gains tax.

It does not rely on the principles of income tax so far discussed.

The chapter will look at how an individual's capital gains tax and losses are calculated; the rates of tax of capital gains tax; and the relief that may enable a capital gains tax liability to be reduced or avoided.

Basic principles

Capital gains tax (CGT) is a tax on the profits which may be made from the sale of *capital* assets.

Only *individuals* are liable to capital gains tax. Companies are not liable to capital gains tax although they are liable to corporation tax on capital gains (see Chapter 16).

However, not all capital assets are liable to capital gains tax when sold (see below).

Technically speaking, a liability to capital gains tax arises when a chargeable person (e.g. an individual) makes a chargeable disposal (e.g. a sale) of a chargeable asset (e.g. a painting).

At its simplest a capital gain on the sale of a capital asset is computed as follows:

Sale proceeds	£350
Less:	
Cost of asset	<u>£150</u>
Capital gain	£200

As will be seen below the actual computation is a little more complicated.

For example, the "Cost of asset" may include elements of expenditure other than simply the original cost of the asset. In addition, in computing the capital gain there may also be an allowance for inflation (called indexation) and a further allowance called taper relief which depends upon how long the asset has been held prior to sale. Each of these areas is discussed below.

In any tax year capital gains from the sales of assets are aggregated and any capital losses are offset giving for any individual either a net capital gain or net capital loss (however, the manner in which losses are offset can be very important; see below).

As will be seen below an individual is entitled to an annual exemption for tax year 2005/06 of £8,500 (2004/05 of £8,200).

CAPITAL GAINS TAX

Chargeable assets
All assets are liable to CGT unless they are exempt.

Examples of capital (or more correctly chargeable assets) assets are:
- paintings
- jewelry
- listed and unlisted shares
- goodwill of a business
- plant and machinery
- land and buildings
- leases

Exempt capital assets include:
- national savings certificates and premium bonds
- motor vehicles suitable for private use
- most government securities
- decorations for valour, unless acquired through purchase
- life assurance policies when held by the original beneficial owner
- investments held within Individual Savings Accounts (ISAs)
- foreign currency for the individual's private use
- pension rights
- prizes and betting winnings
- tangible movable property (chattels) with a life of 50 years or less (tangible wasting assets)

Disposals on death or to a charity or public body are also normally exempt.

Disposal
A charge to CGT can arise whenever there is a disposal. The main types of disposal are:
- a sale *or*
- a gift

Other types of disposal include:
- the loss or destruction of an asset
- the creation of one asset out of another e.g. the grant of a lease out of a freehold
- the receipt of compensation (e.g. insurance proceeds; other than for personal injury or wrongs)

The timing of a disposal
This is normally the *date of an unconditional contract* for the disposal *not* the date of receipt of the proceeds.

A gift is made at the date it is made.

An asset lost is disposed of at the time of loss but, if compensation is received (e.g. from an insurance company) the date of disposal is normally the date of receipt of the compensation.

Allowable expenditure

This comprises four elements:

- *cost*
  (i.e. price paid or in some cases market value)

- *the incidental costs of acquisition and disposal*
  (e.g. fees for professional services; advertising costs)

- *enhancement costs so long as they are reflected in the nature of the asset at the date of disposal*
  (e.g. an extension to a property)

- *the costs of defending title to the asset*
  (e.g. legal costs in defending owner's title to the asset)

It is *not* possible to deduct expenditure which is:

- deductible from trading income as a trading expense; *or*
- interest on a loan taken out to acquire the asset; *or*
- recoverable from a third party.

Example 12.1

John Smith buys an asset in May 2002 for a gross cost of £15,000 which includes incidental costs of acquisition of £500. He sells the asset one year later for £17,500 which includes incidental costs of disposal of £250.

Calculate John's capital gain

Answer

Gross sale proceeds	17,500
Less:	
Incidental costs of disposal	(250)
Net sale proceeds	17,250
Less:	
Cost of asset	(15,000)
(includes incidental costs of acquisition)	
Capital gain	2,250

Indexation

An indexation allowance is an attempt to allow for inflation (i.e. the time value of money).

The indexation allowance is computed by multiplying the allowable expenditure of an asset by an Indexation factor. The resulting Indexation allowance is then deducted from any capital gain thus reducing the size of the capital gain.

The indexation factor is:

RPI for month of disposal (or April 1998 if earlier) - RPI for month of purchase
RPI for month of purchase

RPI refers to the Retail Price Index (a monthly figure calculated by the UK government).

The index factor is normally found as a decimal and rounded to 3 decimal places.

Indexation allowances cease on 5th April 1998. Thus, no indexation allowance will be given on assets purchased on nor after 6th April 1998 and on assets purchased before 6th April 1998 an indexation allowance will be available only up to and including 5th April 1998.

The reason for the cessation of any such allowance is that with effect from 6th April a new form of relief, taper relief, is available (see below).

An indexation allowance can only reduce any capital gain to nil; it cannot therefore turn a capital gain into a capital loss. Nor can an indexation allowance increase a capital loss.

Companies retain an entitlement to an indexation allowance beyond 5th April 1998 but are not entitled to taper relief; see Chapter 16.

No indexation allowance is available for the incidental *disposal* costs. Such costs are simply deducted from gross sale proceeds.

Example 12.2

John Smith sells an asset in April 1998 for £26,000 before selling costs of £400. John acquired the asset in May 1986 for £10,000.

Assume that the indexation allowance for the period May 1986 to April 1998 is £6,620.

Calculate John's capital gain.

Answer

Gross sale proceeds	26,000
Less:	
Incidental costs of disposal	(400)
Net sale proceeds	25,600
Less:	
Cost of asset	(10,000)
Unindexed capital gain	15,600
Less:	
Indexation allowance	(6,620)
Indexed capital gain	8,980

Example 12.3

John Smith sells an asset in April 1998 for £30,000 before selling costs of £1,000. John acquired the asset in March 1988 for £15,000.

In addition further capital expenditure was incurred enhancing the value of the asset as follows:

June 1995	£1,000
June 1998	£4,000

Assume that the Indexation allowance for the period March 1988 to April 1998 is £8,430 and for the period June 1995 to April 1998 is £85.

Calculate John's capital gain.

Answer

Gross sale proceeds		30,000
Less:		
Incidental costs of disposal		(1,000)
Net sale proceeds		29,000
Less:		
Cost of asset	15,000	
Enhancement expenditure	1,000	
Enhancement expenditure	4,000	
		(20,000)
Unindexed capital gain		9,000
Less:		
Indexation allowance	8,430	
Indexation allowance	85	
Total indexation allowance		(8,515)
Indexed capital gain		485

Notes

1. An indexation allowance is available only up to April 1998.
2. The enhancement expenditure of 4,000 was incurred after this date and therefore there is no indexation allowance for this expenditure.
3. The enhancement expenditure of 1,000 was incurred before April 1998 and therefore an indexation allowance for this expenditure is available from when it was incurred, i.e. June 1995, to April 1998 of 85.
4. An indexation allowance of 8,430 is also available in respect of the original cost of the asset for the period May 1988 to April 1998.
5. An indexation allowance applies separately to individuals items of cost (e.g. original purchase cost and enhancement expenditure).

As will be seen the indexation allowance simply reduces the amount of the unindexed capital gain.

Taper relief

Taper relief only applies to disposals made after 5th April 1998. A disposal made before this date does not attract taper relief. Taper relief is not available to companies. Companies simply get an indexation allowance up to the date of sale whether this date is before or after 5th April 1998.

Taper relief applies by reducing the indexed capital gain (i.e. after deducting any indexation allowance) by an appropriate percentage.

The percentage depends upon:
*   the number of *complete years* for which the asset was held; *and*
*   whether the asset qualifies as a *business* or *non-business* asset

Length of ownership of the asset is measured from the *later* of:
*   the date of acquisition; and
*   6th April 1998

For taper relief purposes *enhancement expenditure* (see *allowable expenditure* definition above) is deemed to have been incurred *not* when it is actually incurred but when the asset is first acquired (i.e. when the initial cost was incurred). This means that only one taper relief need be calculated.

Example 12.4

John Smith acquires an asset on 1st May 2003 and sells it on 31st July 2005.

Although the asset has actually been held for 2 years 3 months, for taper relief purposes the asset has been held for 2 *complete* years.

Example12.5

John Smith acquires an asset on 1st May 2003 and sells it on 31st March 2006.

Although the asset has actually been held for 2 years 11 months, for taper relief purposes the asset has been held for 2 *complete* years.

Example 12.6

John Smith acquires an asset on 1st May 1997 and sells it on 31st July 2003.

The asset has actually been held for 6 years 3 months.

Taper relief is, however, only available from 6th April 1998 (indexation being available before then).

The asset has therefore been held for taper relief purposes from 6th April 1998 to 31st July 2003 which is in complete years five years.

Business asset versus Non-business asset

As will be seen in the table below the amount of taper relief available not only depends upon how long an asset has been owned but also on whether it is a business or non-business asset.

Bonus year

In the case of a *Non-business* asset (i.e. not a business asset) after having identified the length of ownership in *complete years* an additional *bonus year* is added *if* the asset was owned on 16th March 1998 to give the total complete years of ownership.

Example 12.7

John Smith acquires a non-business asset on 1st May 1997 and sells it on 31st July 2005.

The asset has actually been held for 8 years 3 months.

Taper relief is, however, only available from 6th April 1998 (indexation being available before then).

The asset has therefore been held for taper relief purposes from 6th April 1998 to 31st July 2005 which is in complete years seven years.

However, as the non-business asset was owned on 16th March 1998 a bonus year is available. Therefore, for taper relief purposes the asset has been held for seven years plus one bonus year i.e. eight years.

Example 12.8

John Smith acquires a non-business asset on 1st May 2003 and sells it on 31st March 2006.

Although the asset has actually been held for 2 years 11 months for taper relief purposes the asset has been held for two *complete* years. As it is a non-business asset and was *not* owned on 16th March 1998 no bonus year arises.

The amount of taper relief available on both business and non-business assets is shown below:

CAPITAL GAINS TAX

Non Business Assets

Qualifying period of ownership in complete years (after 5.4.98)	% of chargeable gain *reduced*	% of chargeable gain *chargeable*
1	Nil	100%
2	Nil	100%
3	5%	95%
4	10%	90%
5	15%	85%
6	20%	80%
7	25%	75%
8	30%	70%
9	35%	65%
10 or more	40%	60%

Business Assets

Qualifying period of ownership in complete years (after 5.4.98)	% of chargeable gain *reduced*	% of chargeable gain *chargeable*
1	50%	50%
2 or more	75%	25%

Note

A *business asset* is:

- an asset used by individuals or partnership or trustees in a business carried on by them or by a qualifying company (see below); *or*
- shares in qualifying trading companies; *or*
- an asset held by an individual for the purpose of an employment with a person carrying on a trade

A *trading company* is a *qualifying company* where one of the following conditions applies:

- if shares *not* listed on a recognised stock exchange *or*
- where shares are listed individual holds 5% at least of voting rights *or*
- where shares are listed individual is an employee of company

A *non-trading company* is a *qualifying company* where individual is an employee of the company and holds no more than 10% of its voting rights etc.

A *non business asset* is any asset other than a business asset.

Example 12.9

John Smith sells a business asset on 10th May 2005 for £30,000 before selling costs of £700. John acquired the asset in May 1991 for £15,000.

Assume that the Indexation allowance for the period May 1991 to April 1998 is £4,320.

Calculate John's capital gain.

Answer

Gross sale proceeds	30,000
Less:	
Incidental costs of disposal	(700)
Net sale proceeds	29,300
Less:	
Cost of asset	(15,000)
Unindexed capital gain	14,300
Less:	
Indexation allowance	(4,320)
Indexed capital gain	9,980
Less:	
Taper relief of (75% x 9,980)	(7,485)
Chargeable gain	2,495

Notes
1. In calculating taper relief the asset is a business asset and was held for taper relief purposes from 6th April 1998 (later of 6th April 1998 and date of acquisition May 1991) to 10th May 2005 i.e. seven complete years.
2. Using the above table shows the taper relief percentage to be 75%.
3. Indexation allowance applied from May 1991 to 5th April 1998.

Example 12.10

John Smith sells a non-business asset on 15th May 2005 for £30,000 before selling costs of £700. John acquired the asset in May 1992 for £15,000.

Assume that the Indexation allowance for the period May 1992 to April 1998 is £4,320.

Calculate John's capital gain.

Answer

Gross sale proceeds	30,000
Less:	
Incidental costs of disposal	(700)
Net sale proceeds	29,300
Less:	
Cost of asset	(15,000)
Unindexed capital gain	14,300
Less:	
Indexation allowance	(4,320)
Indexed capital gain	9,980
Less:	
Taper relief of (30% x 9,980)	(2,994)
Chargeable gain	6,986

Note

The asset is a non-business asset and was held for taper relief purposes from 6th April 1998 (later of 6th April 1998 and date of acquisition May 1992) to 15th May 2005 i.e. seven complete years. The asset was also held on 16th March 1998, as it was acquired before then in May 1992, and therefore qualifies for a bonus year making eight years in total giving the taper relief percentage of 30% (see table above).

Business versus non-business

An asset may during its period of ownership partly qualify as a business asset and partly as a non-business asset.

In such cases the indexed gain on sale is split into that part of the gain attributable to the time period the asset qualified as a business asset and that time period it qualified as a non-business asset.

Taper relief is then calculated separately for each element of the split gain.

Note, however, that for each element of the gain the taper relief percentage is based on the *total* number of years of ownership of the asset not just the respective time periods the asset qualified as either business or non-business.

Example 12.11

John Smith sold a factory precipitating an indexed gain of £300,000.

John had owned the factory for 15 years. During this period John had used the factory in his trade for 10 years and he had let it out for the other 5 years to a third party for them to use in their trade.

Calculate John's capital gain.

Answer

John's business use amounted to 10 years.
John's non-business use amounted to 5 years.

Apportioning the indexed gain:
Business use gain =   10/15 x 300,000 = 200,000
Non-business use gain = 5/15 x 300,000   = 100,000

Business use chargeable gain after taper relief = 200,000 x 25% = 50,000
Non-business use chargeable gain after taper relief = 100,000 x 60% = 60,000
Total gain = 50,000 + 60,000 = 110,000

Notes

1. The split of the total indexed gain on sale is simply based on a straight forward time apportionment between business and non-business time period ownership.
2. The taper relief percentages for each gain are based on the total ownership period of the asset i.e. 15 years (i.e. not on the two time periods of 5 and 10 years).
3. For the business asset use gain the taper relief percentage is 75% (i.e. 25% chargeable); for the non-business use asset gain the taper relief percentage is 40% (i.e. 60% chargeable).

The annual exemption

Every individual is entitled to an annual exemption which is £8,500 for the fiscal year 2005/06 (£8,200 for 2004/05).

It represents the amount of gains which an individual can make in the tax year CGT free.

It is the last item to be deducted when calculating an individual's capital gains for a tax year.

It cannot be carried forward or backward if unused and it cannot be surrendered to any other individual (thus, for example, a husband cannot surrender any unused portion to his wife or vice versa).

It is not available to companies and special rules apply to trusts.

Pro- forma CGT computation

It is now possible to set out a pro-forma which should be followed when calculating an individual's chargeable gains/losses.

When computing an individual's CGT liability the following pro-forma should be used.

Gross disposal proceeds	X
Less	
Incidental disposal costs	(X)
	X
Less	
Allowable expenditure	(X)
Unindexed gain	UIG
Less	
Indexation allowance	(X)
Chargeable indexed gain	CIG
Less	
Taper relief	(X)
(i.e. % of CIG not taxable)	
Taxable amount	
(before annual exemption)	X
Less	
Annual exemption (2005/06)	(8,500)
Taxable amount	X

Notes

1. *Indexation factor* is applied to each element of *Allowable expenditure* separately other than *Incidental costs of disposal* which do not qualify for an Indexation allowance.

2. *Taper relief* simply reduces the *Chargeable indexed gain* according to the prescribed table % figure after indexation relief has been obtained but before deducting the Annual exemption.

Below are some examples adopting the pro-forma.

Example 12.12

John Smith bought a painting on 1st March 1994 for £7,000 incurring incidental costs of acquisition of £150.

John sold the painting for £23,000 on 30th April 2005 incurring incidental costs of disposal of £750.

Calculate John's capital gain.

Answer

Using the pro-forma above:

Disposal proceeds	23,000
Less Incidental disposal costs	(750)
	22,250
Less Allowable expenditure	(7,150)
Unindexed gain	15,100
Less Indexation allowance *	(1,008)
Chargeable indexed gain	14,092
Less Taper relief **	(4,228)
30% x 14,092	
Chargeable gain after TR	9,864
Less Annual exemption	(8,500)
Taxable amount	1,364

* Indexation allowance

Indexation factor $\quad = \quad \dfrac{162.6 - 142.5}{142.5} = 0.141$

Indexation allowance $\quad = \quad 0.141 \times 7,150 = 1,008$

** Taper relief (TR)

Painting is a Non-business asset, i.e. not used in a business.

Ownership from 6 April 1998 to 30 April 2005 = seven years 24 days i.e. in complete years = seven years (note that TR only applies from 6th April 1998 even though this asset was purchased prior to this date; however, for this prior period an indexation allowance applied).The painting was also held on 16 March 1998 and therefore a bonus year applies.

The painting was therefore held for TR purposes for seven years plus one bonus year = eight years.

TR percentage = 30%

Example 12.13

John Smith purchased a Non-business asset on 1st April 1997 for £10,000.

Enhancement expenditure of £3,000 was incurred on 1st July 1997.

The asset was sold on 30 April 2005 for £36,000.

Incidental costs of disposal were £1,000.

Calculate John's capital gain.

Answer

Using the pro-forma above:

Disposal proceeds	36,000	
Less Incidental disposal costs	(1,000)	
		35,000
Less Allowable expenditure:		
Original cost	10,000	
Enhancement exp.	3,000	
		(13,000)
Unindexed gain		22,000
Less Indexation allowance *		
(400+96)		(496)
Chargeable indexed gain		21,504
Less Taper relief **		
30% x £21,504		(6,451)
Chargeable gain after TR		15,053
Less Annual exemption		(8,500)
Capital gain subject to tax		6,553

* Indexation allowance

Original cost:

Indexation factor $= \dfrac{162.6 - 156.3}{156.3} = 0.04$

Indexation allowance $= 0.04 \times 10,000 = 400$

Enhancement expenditure:

Indexation factor $= \dfrac{162.6 - 157.5}{157.5} = 0.032$

Indexation allowance $= 0.032 \times 3,000 = 96$

** Taper relief

The asset is a Non-business asset.

Ownership for 6 April 1998 to 30 April 2005 = seven years 24 days i.e. in complete years = seven years (note that TR only applies from 6th April 1998 even though this asset was purchased prior to this date; however, for this prior period an indexation allowance applied).

The asset was also held on 16 March 1998 and therefore a bonus year applies. The asset therefore held for TR purposes for seven years plus one bonus year = eight years

TR percentage = 30%

Although enhancement expenditure was incurred in July 1996, for TR purposes, it is assumed to have been incurred when the asset was originally purchased i.e. April 1997. For indexation allowance, however, enhancement expenditure is indexed from July 1997.

Connected persons

An individual is connected with:

- his spouse
- his relatives (i.e. brothers, sisters, ancestors and lineal descendants)
- the relatives of his spouse
- the spouses of his and his spouse's relatives

The relevance of the connected person concept is that transactions between such persons are treated as if any gift or sale is, in fact, at market value of the asset at the appropriate date. The actual price paid, if any, is irrelevant.

In addition, any capital loss arising on a connected person transaction can only be offset against capital gains of the same or future tax years on disposals to the same person.

Inter-spouse transfers

Husband and wife are treated as two separate persons for CGT (and indeed for income tax purposes) and each are therefore entitled, inter alia, to their own annual exemption.

Losses of one spouse cannot be offset against the gains of the other.

Disposals between spouses (i.e. husband and wife) living together do not give rise to chargeable gains or allowable losses. At the date of the asset transfer the asset is assumed to have been transferred at its original cost plus an indexation allowance up to date of asset transfer. This will then give neither a loss nor gain to the transferring spouse.

The cost of the asset to the receiving spouse is the same i.e. original cost plus the indexation allowance.

On a subsequent sale of the asset the calculation would follow the normal rules. However, for taper relief purposes the asset is assumed to have been held from the date of original acquisition not just from the date of the transfer between the spouses.

Example 12.14

John Smith purchased a non-business asset in April 1997 for £13,000. He transferred it to his wife Mary on 16th July 2001. Mary then sold it on 1st June 2005 for £30,000. Indexation allowance for the period April 1997 to April 1998 is £520.

Show the CGT position for John and Mary.

Answer

When John transferred the asset to Mary no disposal for CGT purposes arises. Mary is assumed to have acquired the asset at no gain/no loss to John and thus will have acquired it for 13,000 + 520 = 13,520.

This is then the base cost of the asset for Mary. On sale by her:

Disposal proceeds	30,000
Less:	
Cost	(13,520)
Indexed gain	16,480
Less:	
TR (30%)	(4,944)
	11,536
Less:	
Annual exemption	(8,500)
Taxable amount	3,036

Notes
1. Indexation ceases on 5th April 1998.
2. For TR purposes Mary is assumed to have owned the asset from the original date of acquisition, i.e. April 1997, and thus also is deemed to own it on 16th March 1998 thus becoming entitled to the bonus year making eight complete years of ownership giving 30% TR.

Calculating the capital gains tax liability

A capital gain is taxed as though it is the highest part of an individual's income and is treated as Savings income (see Chapter 2).

In other words *income tax* is levied on non-savings, savings and then dividend income as normal (see Chapter 2) and then any capital gains are treated as on top of these categories and taxed appropriately.

As a capital gain is treated as savings income the capital gains tax rates are 10%, 20% or 40% (which also applies where top rate of income tax for the individual is the dividend rate of 32.5%).

Note: Personal allowances *cannot* be deducted from capital gains.

Date of payment of CGT

CGT is payable on the 31st January following the fiscal year in which the gain arose. There are no interim or payments on account as is the case for income tax (see Chapter 21).

Example 12.15

John Smith in the tax year 2005/06 has made capital gains of £14,500 before annual exemption. His other taxable income for the tax year is £32,500 all of which is Non-savings income.

Calculate John's CGT liability and state when it has to be paid.

Answer

Capital gains	14,500
Less:	
Annual exemption	(8,500)
Capital gain	6,000

Following the format used in Chapter 3:

Taxable income	Rate	Tax
	%	£
32,500 (taxable income)		
6,000 (gain)	40	2,400

As John's taxable income (i.e. 32,500) exceeds the 32,400 threshold all the capital gain is taxed at the 40% rate.

The CGT of 2,400 is payable on 31st January 2006.

Example 12.16

John Smith makes a capital gain after annual exemption of £4,600 in 2005/06. His taxable income (all non-savings) for the tax year 2005/06 is £28,000.

Calculate John's CGT liability.

Answer

Taxable income	Rate	Tax
	%	£
28,000 (taxable income)		
4,400 (gain)	20	880
32,400		
200 (gain: 4,600 – 4,400)	40	80

Therefore capital gains tax = 880 + 80 = 960

Note that a part (4,400) of John's capital gain is taxed at the 20% rate with the balance of the gain (200) then being taxed at the 40% rate.

Example 12.17

John Smith makes a capital gain after annual exemption of £4,600 in 2005/06. His taxable income (all dividends) for the tax year 2005/06 is £28,000.

Calculate John's CGT liability.

Answer

Taxable income	Rate	Tax
	%	£
28,000 (taxable income)		
4,400 (gain)	20	880
32,400		
200 (gain: 4,600 – 4,400)	40	80

Therefore capital gains tax = 880 + 80 = 960

Note

A part (4,400) of John's capital gain is taxed at the 20% rate with the balance of the gain (200) then being taxed at the 40% rate. The fact that John's taxable income is all dividend income taxable at 32.5% does not alter John's CGT liability (i.e. it is the same as in Example 12.16 above).

Using capital losses

On any sale of a capital asset a capital loss, as opposed to a capital gain, may arise. This would of course occur if the sale proceeds were less than original cost.

In such cases no indexation allowance would apply; an indexation allowance cannot increase a capital loss nor can it convert a taxable gain into a capital loss.

Example 12.18

John Smith bought an asset for a cost of £10,000 and sold it for sale proceeds of £8,000.

Answer

Capital gain = £8,000 - £10,000 = £2,000 capital loss.

No indexation allowance can be claimed.

Example 12.19
John Smith bought an asset for a cost of £15,000 on 1st January 1993. He sold it for sale proceeds of £15,500 on 31st August 2005.

Answer
Using the pro-forma:

Disposal proceeds	15,500
Less Incidental disposal costs	nil
	15,500
Less Allowable expenditure	(15,000)
Unindexed gain	500
Less Indexation allowance*	(500) **
Chargeable indexed gain	nil

* Indexation allowance =
    0.179 x 15,000 = 2,685

Note
** The indexation allowance of 2,685 has been restricted to 500 so as not to convert a capital gain of 500 into a capital loss but simply to produce no gain/loss.

Current year capital losses
Capital losses are offset against other capital gains of the same fiscal year.

Capital losses are offset against capital gains *after* indexation allowance but *before* taper relief.

It may be that in any tax year the total capital losses exceed the total capital gains; where this applies the excess capital losses can be carried forward to the succeeding tax years; but never carried back (except in year of death (see below)).

Carried forward capital losses
Surplus capital losses in any tax year may only be carried forward for offset against any net capital gains of future tax years.

Net capital gains for a tax year refers to capital gains less capital losses for that year. Thus, *current* year capital losses are offset against *current* year capital gains *before* any capital losses brought forward may be used.

Any capital losses brought forward can only be offset against the net capital gains for a tax year to the extent that at least an amount of net capital gains after offset of capital losses brought forward equal to the annual exemption remains in charge for that tax year.

Example 12.20

John Smith has the following gains and losses:

	2003/04	2004/05	2005/06
Gains	4,000	7,000	15,000
Losses	8,000	2,000	1,000

Gains are after indexation allowance and before taper relief.

Calculate John's capital gains/loss position for each of the above tax years. Ignore taper relief.

Answer

	2003/04	2004/05	2005/06
Gains	4,000	7,000	15,000
Losses	(8,000)	(2,000)	(1,000)
Current Net gains/losses	(4,000)	5,000	14,000
Less:			
Capital loss b/f	nil	nil*	(4,000)**
Net gains/losses	(4,000)	5,000	10,000

Notes

1. Capital loss brought forward from 2003/04 is 4,000. However, none of this may be used in 2004/05 as current year net gains for 2004/05 are only 5,000 which is less than the annual exemption for that year (i.e. 8,200). Thus, the 4,000 loss of 2003/04 is carried forward to 2005/06.
2. ** It is possible to use all 4,000 capital loss brought forward to 2005/06 as there is still left into charge net gains in excess of the 2005/06 annual exemption (i.e. 8,500)

Example 12.21

John Smith has capital losses brought forward from 2003/04 of £18,000 and made the following gains and losses:

	2004/05	2005/06
Gains	12,000	32,000
Losses	(7,000)	(12,000)

The gains are after indexation allowances but before taper relief.

Show how the capital losses can be used. Ignore taper relief.

Answer

	2004/05
Net gains in year (12,000 – 7,000)	5,000
Less: Losses b/f	nil
Net gains	5,000

	2005/06
Net gains in year (32,000 – 12,000)	20,000
Less: Losses b/f	(11,500)
	8,500
Less: Annual exemption	(8,500)
Taxable amount	nil

Losses available for carrying forward to 2006/07:
18,000 -11,500 = 6,500

2004/05   The net current year gains of 5,000 are already less than the annual exemption for that year. Therefore no part of the b/f loss of 18,000 can be used in this tax year.

2005/06   Of the b/f losses of 18,000 sufficient are used (i.e. 11,500) to reduce the net current year gains of 20,000 to the annually exempt amount for 2005/06 of 8,500.

Optimal usage of capital losses

Capital losses must be used in the most tax efficient manner. This means that in any tax year it is not acceptable simply to aggregate gains and deduct losses.

In order to minimise an individual's CGT liability the following rule should be followed:

Offset any capital loss against the capital gain on an asset which qualifies for the least amount of taper relief as measured in taper relief % terms irrespective as to whether the gain arises on an asset which is a business or non-business asset.

Therefore the order of offset will be:

> *first,* against a gain on which there is no taper relief
> *second,* against a gain with the smallest taper relief %
> *third,* against a gain with the next smallest taper relief % etc.

Gains and losses of business and non-business assets may be offset against each other in the most efficient manner i.e. for example, a loss on a business asset may be offset against a gain on a non-business asset and vice versa if appropriate.

Once the capital loss has been offset in the most tax efficient manner taper relief is applied to the net capital gain for each asset individually. The figures for each asset may then be aggregated before subtracting the annual exemption to give a single gain figure.

Example 12.22

John Smith sold three assets in 2005/06 as follows:

Asset	1 (a business asset)	acquired	1 October 1996	for	£50,000
		sold	1 March 2006	for	£270,000
	2 (a non-business asset)	acquired	1 July 1997	for	£100,000
		sold	1 February 2006	for	£220,000
	3 (a business asset)	acquired	1 August 1994	for	£170,000
		sold	1 March 2006	for	£50,000

Relevant amounts of indexation allowance are:

October 1996 – April 1998   £2,850

July 1997 – April 1998   £3,200

Show how John should use the capital loss most efficiently and calculate his net capital gain/loss for the tax year 2005/06.

Answer

	Asset 1	**Asset 2**	**Asset 3**
Sale proceeds	270,000	220,000	50,000
Less:			
Cost	50,000	100,000	170,000
Unindexed gain	220,000	120,000	(120,000)
Less:			
Indexation allowance	(2,850)	(3,200)	nil
Indexed gain	217,150	116,800	(120,000)
Less:			
Capital loss offset	(3,200)	(116,800)	
Net capital gains	213,950	nil	

Aggregate capital gains	213,950
Less:	
Taper relief (75%)	(160,463)
Net capital gain	53,488
Less:	
Annual exemption	(8,500)
Net capital gain	44,988

Notes

1. No indexation allowance is available on Asset 3 as a capital loss arises.
2. The offset of the Asset 3 capital loss is first against Asset 2 on which taper relief of 30% (i.e. eight years including bonus year) is available compared to the 75% taper relief available on Asset 1. The balance (i.e.120,000 – 116,800 = 3,200) of the capital loss may then be used against Asset 1.
3. After the offset of the capital loss, taper relief is applied to each asset individually (in this case Asset 1 only) with each of the net gains for each asset then being aggregated.
4. The annual exemption is then deducted from this aggregate figure.

Example 12.23

Using example 12.22 above assume that as at 6th April 2005 John also had a capital loss brought forward of £25,000.

How would this additional capital loss affect John's 2005/06 capital gains tax position?

Answer

	Asset 1	Asset 2	Asset 3
Sale proceeds	270,000	220,000	50,000
Less:			
Cost	<u>50,000</u>	<u>100,000</u>	<u>170,000</u>
Unindexed gain	220,000	120,000	(120,000)
Less:			
Indexation allowance	<u>(2,850)</u>	<u>(3,200)</u>	<u>nil</u>
Indexed gain	217,150	116,800	(120,000)
Less:			
Capital loss offset	(3,200)	<u>(116,800)</u>	
Less:			
Capital loss b/f	<u>(25,000)</u>		
Net capital gains	188,950	nil	

Therefore aggregate capital gains for 2005/06 = 188,950 less 75% taper relief (for Asset 1) giving a net gain of 47,238

From this figure of 47,238 the annual exemption of 8,500 may be deducted giving 38,738

Notes

1. No indexation allowance is available on Asset 3 as a capital loss arises.

2. The offset of the Asset 3 capital loss is first against Asset 2 on which taper relief of 30% (i.e. eight years including bonus year) is available compared to the 75% taper relief available on Asset 1. The balance (i.e. 120,000 – 116,800 = 3,200) of the capital loss may then be used against Asset 1.

3. After offsetting current year capital losses any capital losses brought forward may then be offset. This offset is against assets with the smallest taper relief percentages just as before. In this case the only capital gain available for offset is that on Asset 1.

4. Taper relief is then applied to each asset; the annual exemption is then deducted.

Year of death

In the year of death any capital losses arising in that year may be *carried back to the three tax years* preceding the tax year of death on a LIFO basis and offset against gains assessable in those years.

However, any losses in the year of death must be first offset against gains of that year to the fullest extent.

The losses carried back are relieved against the most recent tax year first but the losses so relieved must be such as to leave into charge in that tax year sufficient gains equal to the annual exemption for that tax year and similarly for earlier tax years.

Capital gains of companies

The capital gains tax computation of a company broadly follows that of an individual except that:

- there is no annual exemption
- there is no taper relief; the indexation allowance continues until the date of disposal (i.e. beyond 5th April 1998)
- many capital gains reliefs and exemptions are not relevant to companies

  e.g. main residence exemption; gifts relief (see later chapters)

With respect to sales of shares (see later chapter) there are also differences between individuals and companies:

- the FA 1985 pool for shares continues to the month of disposal i.e. does not cease at 5th April 1998
- matching of shares sold rules are different:
    - same day acquisitions
    - acquisitions in previous nine days
    - FA 1985 pool

Substantial shareholdings

Effective 1.4.02 chargeable gains made by a trading company on the disposal of the whole or any part of a substantial shareholding in another trading company are exempt.

A substantial shareholding is a shareholding of 10% or more which gives rise to a beneficial entitlement of at least 10% of profits available for distribution to shareholders *and* assets available for distribution on a winding up for a continuous period of 12 months during the two years preceding the disposal.

Similarly capital losses thereon are not allowable.

Chargeable gains roll over relief

Following the Finance Act 2002 chargeable gains roll-over relief is no longer available from 1st April 2002 for companies concerning the sale of intellectual property (e.g. goodwill; patents; etc). Gains and losses on such assets are taken into account under the new "intangible assets" provisions (see Chapter 13).

Chargeable gains roll-over relief continues to be available for other chargeable assets as previously.

SUMMARY

Only individuals are liable to capital gains tax. Companies are only liable to corporation tax.

Capital gains are treated as the highest part of an individual's taxable income and are treated as savings income. Thus, possible rates of capital gains tax are 10%, 20% and 40%.

Current year capital losses are offset against current year capital gains before any brought forward unused capital losses any be used.

Individuals are entitled to both an indexation allowance and taper relief in arriving at any capital gain. Indexation for individuals ceases on 5th April 1998; there-after taper relief applies.

Any capital gains tax liability is due for payment in one lump sum on the 31st January following the tax year in which the gains arose.

CHAPTER 13

Capital Gains Tax: Shares and Securities

INTRODUCTION

This chapter follows on from Chapter 12 and looks at the capital gains tax position on the sale of shares and securities for individuals and companies.

Securities

Government stocks and most commercial securities i.e. company debentures, loan stocks etc. are *exempt* from capital gains tax when they are held by individuals.

For companies, capital gains and losses on government and commercial securities would normally be treated as part of a non trading loan relationship gain or loss (see Chapter 16).

Shares

There is no equivalent exemption from CGT in respect of share sales by individuals. Sales of shares thus give rise to either capital gains and/or capital losses.

The main problem in working out the capital gain/loss which may arise on a share sale is identifying which shares of those acquired at various different times have in fact been sold.

Example 13.1

John Smith has purchased the following ordinary shares in ABC Ltd:
100 shares on 1st March 1996 for £4,000
50 shares on 3rd August 1998 for £1,400
350 shares on 6th October 2002 for £6,250

On 18th September 2005 John sold 380 shares.

The issue thus arises as to which of the shares which John had bought he has now sold.

Matching rules: for individuals

The tax legislation lays down the following so-called *matching rules* i.e. on any sale of shares of the *same class in the same company* the shares sold are to be matched as follows:
- with shares acquired *on the same day*, then
- with shares acquired *within 30 days after* the disposal on a FIFO basis, then
- with shares acquired *after 5th April 1998* on a LIFO basis, then
- with shares in the *1985 pool*

Same day

Any shares which have been acquired on the same day as any sales are assumed to have been sold first.

Following 30 days

This may seem strange. There are reasons for it but it is not necessary to understand them or be aware of them. Thus any shares which have been acquired within 30 days after the date of any sales are assumed to have been sold next.

Acquisitions after 5 April 1998

This date is used because at this date indexation allowances cease and taper relief begins (see Chapter 12). As taper relief applies after 5th April 1998, any purchases after this date are matched separately with any share sales.

1985 Pool

Contains shares acquired on or after 6 April 1982 but before 6 April 1998.

Any pool can only contain shares of the same class in the same company (e.g. ordinary shares in ABC Ltd; or ordinary shares in XYZ Ltd). Before any matching the value of the pool as at 5th April 1998 must be determined (i.e. the cost of any purchases prior to this date need to be indexed to this date).

The indexed value of the 1985 Pool as at 6th April 1998 will normally be given in any questions although occasionally it will be necessary to derive the pool value as at 5th April 1998 from the information given in the question.

Computational procedure

To work out the capital gain/loss on a share sale a number of separate calculations may be necessary.

Each of the calculations below is carried out *after* taking into account indexation allowances but *before* taper relief.

The basic approach is to work back in time matching shares sold with those purchased. Thus, those shares which are in effect deemed to have been sold first are those which were purchased later in time.

STEP 1

Match shares sold with shares acquired on same day.

Calculate capital gain/loss on this matching.

If number of shares sold exceed shares acquired on same day then continue to STEP 2 (if this is not the case no further computation is necessary).

STEP 2

Match shares sold not already matched under STEP 1 with shares acquired in next 30 days.

Calculate capital gain/loss on this matching.

If number of shares sold exceed shares matched under STEPS 1 and 2 then continue to STEP 3.

STEP 3

Match shares sold not already matched under STEPS 1 and 2 with shares acquired on or after 5th April 1998.

Calculate capital gain/loss on this matching.

If the number of shares sold exceed shares matched under STEPS 1, 2 and 3 then continue to STEP 4.

STEP 4

Match shares not already matched under STEPS 1, 2 and 3 with shares held in 1985 pool.

Calculate capital gain/loss on this matching.

STEP 5

Having matched all the shares sold under STEPS 1 to 4 a capital gain and/or capital loss will have arisen under each of STEPS 1 to 4. If there are no capital losses simply proceed to STEP 6. If there are any capital losses these must be first offset against the capital gains in the most optimal manner (i.e. use the rule laid down in Chapter 9).

STEP 6

Reduce the capital gains (after capital loss offset as under STEP 5 where necessary) by any taper relief.

STEP 7

Aggregate the net gains from STEP 6 to produce one single capital gain.

STEP 8

Deduct the annual exemption from the figure in STEP 7 to finally give the net chargeable gain arising on the share sale.

Example 13.2

On 1st March 2006, John Smith sold 5,000 shares in XYZ Ltd for £29,000 incurring £3,000 of incidental costs of disposal. John had purchased shares in XYZ Ltd which qualify as business assets for taper relief purposes as follows:

	Shares	Cost
16 September 2002	2,000	£5,000
3rd January 2005	1,500	£2,000
1st March 2006	400	£750
25th March 2006	300	£500

John had also purchased 7,500 shares between 6th April 1982 and 5th April 1998 for a total cost of £5,000. As at 5th April 1998 the indexed cost of these shares was £6,000.

Calculate John's capital gain/loss position for tax year 2005/06.

Answer

STEP 1 [same day]

Of the shares sold on 1st March 2006 400 are matched with the shares acquired on this date.

Sale proceeds [400/5,000 x £26,000]	2,080
Less:	
Cost	(750)
Gain	£1,330

STEP 2 [next 30 days]

Of the shares sold on 1st March 2006 300 are matched with shares purchased in the following 30 days after this date.

Sale proceeds [300/5,000 x £26,000]	1,560
Less:	
Cost	(500)
Gain	£1,060

STEP 3 [post 5th April 1998]

Of the shares sold on 1st March 2006 1,500 are matched with shares purchased on 3rd January 2005 and 2,000 are matched with shares purchased on 16th September 2002 (i.e. shares purchased on or after 5th April 1998).

In this example there are thus two matchings in this category. Shares sold are matched with shares in this category on a LIFO basis i.e. matched first with the 3rd January 2005 and then with 16th September 2002 purchases.

Sale proceeds [1,500/5,000 x £26,000]	7,800
Less:	
Cost	(2,000)
Gain	£5,800

Sale proceeds [2,000/5,000 x £26,000]	10,400
Less:	
Cost	(5,000)
Gain	£5,400

STEP 4 [1985 pool]

In STEPS 1 to 3 the total shares matched is 400 + 300 + 1,500 + 2,000 = 4,200.

Total shares sold are 5,000. Therefore, in Step 4, 800 shares remain to be matched. Thus, 800 shares need to be matched with share purchases prior to 6th April 1998.

Sale proceeds [800/5,000 x £26,000]	4,160

Less:					
Cost	[800/5,000 x £6,000]		(3,000)		
Gain			£1,160		

STEP 5

No capital losses arose on any of the share sale matchings. Therefore any taper relief may now be calculated individually.

	STEP 1	STEP 2	STEP 3		STEP 4
Gains	1,330	1,060	5,800	5,400	1,160
Less:					
Taper relief:					
50%			(2,900)		
75%				(4,050)	(870)
			2,900	1,350	290
Total gains		6,930			
Less:					
Annual exemption		(8,500)			
Net chargeable gain		£nil			

Notes

1. The annual exemption for 2005/06 of £8,500 could not be fully utilised as only net gains after loss offset and taper reliefs of £6,930 remained. Thus, only £6,930 of this exemption could be utilised; the balance of £8,500 minus £6,930 i.e. £1,570 is simply lost.
2. The order of offsets is important; first capital losses are offset (but in this case there are no capital losses) against any indexed capital gains; then taper relief is applied to the net gain on each asset; then the gains are aggregated and the annual exemption then deducted from the aggregated gains.
3. The only indexation allowance is that arising on the sale of the 1985 pool (Step 4). The cost of £6,000 includes any indexation allowance.

Normally in carrying out the above computation you would not show the words "STEP" as these have been included merely to illustrate the order in which the computation should be performed.

Example 13.3

John Smith sold 1,000 shares in John Smith Ltd, on 31st January 2006 for £20,000, which do not qualify for business asset taper relief. He bought 1,500 shares on 30th April 2004 for £18,000; 500 shares for £7,000 on 31st May 2004; and 200 shares for £3,600 on 10th February 2006.

Calculate John's chargeable gain.

Answer

Same day matching

No shares were bought on the sale date of 31st January 2006.

Following 30 days matching

200 shares were bought in this period on 10th February 2006. Thus 200 shares sold can be matched with the shares bought in this period.

Sale proceeds [(200/1,000) x £20,000]	4,000
Less:	
Cost	(3,600)
Gain	£400

Post 5th April 1998 matching

Shares in this period were bought on 30th April 2004 and 31st May 2004. Therefore shares sold can be matched with these purchases on a LIFO basis.

Sale 31st May 2004

Sale proceeds [(500/1,000) x £20,000]	10,000
Less:	
Cost	(7,000)
Gain	£3,000

Note: As 700 shares in total out of the 1,000 shares sold have now been matched only 300 shares out of those purchased on 30th April 2004 need to be matched:

Sale 30th April 2004

Sale proceeds [(300/1,000) x £20,000]	6,000
Less:	
Cost [300/1,500) x £18,000]	(3,600)
Gain	£2,400

There are no capital losses to offset (see STEP 5 above) and thus taper relief for each of the above gains can be calculated as appropriate (STEP 6). However, in no case have any of the shares purchased been held for at least three complete years. Therefore no taper relief applies to any of the gains.

John's total chargeable gains = £400 + £3,000 + £2,400 = £5,800

In then computing any CGT liability the annual exemption of £8,500 would be deducted there-from in fact giving rise to a nil chargeable gains amount for John in 2005/06.

Scrip and rights issues

Scrip issues

Scrip or bonus issues are a free issue of shares. The shareholder receiving the bonus shares does not pay anything for them.

For tax purposes the bonus shares are assumed to have been acquired at the same date as the original shares in respect of which they have been issued.

Rights issue

A rights issue is an issue of shares but unlike a bonus issue are shares which have to be paid for.

No indexation allowance is available in respect of any rights issue shares where the rights issue occurs after 5th April 1998.

On or before this date indexation applies to the cost of the rights issue shares from the date the rights issue shares are acquired which will typically be different from the date indexation applies in respect of the original cost of the shares.

For matching purposes the rights shares are deemed to have been acquired at the same time as the original shares and thus for taper relief purposes the rights shares are also assumed to have been acquired at the same time as the original shares not their actual date of acquisition.

Example 13.4

John Smith bought 1,500 ordinary shares in JS Ltd for £3,000 on 7th February 1996.

On 30th March 2001 a bonus issue of ordinary shares was made of 1 for 5.

Thus, John will have acquired an extra 1,500/5 i.e. 300 ordinary shares.

These extra 300 shares will be deemed to have been acquired on 7th February 1996 for no cost.

For taper relief purposes ownership of the total 1,800 shares at a cost of £3,000 will start from 6th April 1998 (i.e. the later of 7th February 1996 the date of acquisition of the original shares and 6th April 1998 the date from which taper relief starts).

For indexation allowance purposes the cost of the original shares will be indexed from 7th February 1996 to 5th April 1998 as normal. No indexation allowance is available for the bonus shares as simply there is no cost for these shares.

Example 13.5

John Smith bought 1,500 ordinary shares in JS Ltd for £3,000 on 7th February 2000.

On 30th June 2000 a bonus issue of ordinary shares was made of 1 for 5.

Thus, John will have acquired an extra 1,500/5 i.e. 300 ordinary shares.

These extra 300 shares will be deemed to have been acquired on 7th February 2000 for no cost.

For taper relief purposes ownership of the 1,800 shares at a cost of £3,000 will start from 7th February 2000 (i.e. the later of 7th February 2000 and 6th April 1998).

No indexation allowances as there are no shares held prior to 6th April 1998.

Example 13.6

John Smith bought 1,500 ordinary shares in JS Ltd for £3,000 on 7th February 1996.

On 30th March 1997 a rights issue of ordinary shares was made of 1 for 5 at a cost of £2.50/share.

Thus, John will have acquired an extra 1,500/5 i.e. 300 ordinary shares.

These extra 300 shares will be deemed to have been acquired on 30th March 1997 for £750 (300 x £2.50).

For taper relief purposes ownership of the 1,800 shares at a cost of £3,750 will start from 6th April 1998 (i.e. the later of 7th February 1996 and 6th April 1998).

However, for indexation allowance purposes the original cost of £3,000 is indexed from 7th February 1996 to 5th April 1998 as normal but the rights issue cost of £750 is indexed separately from 30th March 1997 to 5th April 1998.

Example 13.7

John Smith bought 1,500 ordinary shares in JS Ltd for £3,000 on 7th February 1996.

On 30th June 1998 a rights issue of ordinary shares was made of 1 for 5 at a cost of £2.50/share.

Thus, John will have acquired an extra 1,500/5 i.e. 300 ordinary shares.

These extra 300 shares will be deemed to have been acquired on 30th June 1998 for £750 (300 x £2.50).

For taper relief purposes ownership of the 1,800 shares at a total cost of £3,750 will start from 6th April 1998 (i.e. the later of 7th February 1996 and 6th April 1998).

However, for indexation allowance purposes the original cost of £3,000 is indexed from 7th February 1996 to 5th April 1998 but the rights issue cost of £750 which was incurred on 30th June 1998 does not qualify for an indexation allowance as it was incurred after 5th April 1998.

Effect of bonus and/or rights issues

The effect of each type of issue is of course to increase the number of shares held and in the case of a rights issue the total costs of the shares held.

Before matching shares sold with shares purchased, if either a bonus and/or a rights issue occurs prior to any sale of shares, it is first necessary to adjust the original shares purchased for the bonus/rights issue. Only after these adjustments are made can shares sold then be matched.

Example 13.8

John Smith sold 3,600 shares in John Smith Ltd for £20,400 in September 2005.

He bought 4,500 shares in January 2005 for £10,800 and a further 500 shares for £1,750 in May 2005. John Smith Ltd made a bonus issue of 1 for 5 in June 2005. The shares qualify for business asset taper relief.

Calculate John's chargeable gain pre annual exemption.

Answer
Same day matching
No matching is possible as no such shares were purchased.

Following 30 days matching
No matching is possible as no shares were purchased.

Post 5th April 1998 matching
Two sets of shares were purchased in this period i.e. on January 2005 and May 2005.
Before each of these purchases can be matched account of the bonus issue must be taken.
Taking the later purchase (i.e. LIFO) first:

May 2005
Shares	500 for £1,750
Bonus issue 1 for 5	100 for nil
Total	600 for £1,750

January 2005
Shares	4,500 for £10,800
Bonus issue 1 for 5	900 for nil

| Total | 5,400 for £10,800 |

May 2005 matching

Sale proceeds [(600/3,600) x £20,400]	3,400
Less:	
Cost	(1,750)
Gain	£1,650

January 2005 matching

Sale proceeds [(3,000/3,600) x £20,400]	17,000
Less:	
Cost [(3,000/5,400) x £10,800]	(6,000)
Gain	£11,000

No taper relief due as none of shares held for at least a year.

John's total chargeable gain = £1,650 + £11,000 = £12,650.

Example 13.9

John Smith sold 3,600 shares in John Smith Ltd for £20,400 in September 2005.

He bought 4,500 shares in January 2005 for £10,800 and a further 500 shares for £1,750 in May 2005. John Smith Ltd made a rights issue of 1 for 5 in June 2005 at a price of £2 per share. The shares qualify for business asset taper relief. This uses example 13.8 replacing the bonus issue with a rights issues.

Calculate John's chargeable gain, pre annual exemption.

Answer

Same day matching

No matching possible as no such shares was purchased.

Following 30 days matching

No matching possible as no shares purchased.

Post 5th April 1998 matching

Two sets of shares were purchased in this period i.e. on January 2005 and May 2005.

Before each of these purchases can be matched account of the rights issue must be taken.

Taking the later purchase (i.e. LIFO) first:

May 2005		
Shares	500 for £1,750	1,750
Rights issue 1 for 5	100 for £2 per share	200
Total	600 for	£1,950

January 2005		
Shares	4,500 for £10,800	10,800
Rights issue 1 for 5	900 for £2 per share	1,800
Total	5,400 for	£12,600

May 2005 matching

Sale proceeds [(600/3,600) x £20,400]	£3,400
Less:	
Cost	(1,950)
Gain	£1,450

January 2005 matching

Sale proceeds [(3,000/3,600) x £20,400]	17,000
Less:	
Cost [(3,000/5,400) x £12,600]	(7,000)
Gain	£10,000

No taper relief due as none of shares held for at least a year.

John's total chargeable gain = £1,450 + £10,000 = £11,450

Take-overs

A take-over occurs where one company acquires the shares of another company. In effect, the shareholder in, say, Company A swaps his/her shares for shares in Company B. Company B is the acquiring company and Company A is the target company or company being acquired.

Take-over bids can be:
- share for share, *or*
- cash for share, *or*
- a mixture of the two.

An entirely share for share bid (i.e. with no cash involved) is *not* a disposal for CGT purposes provided that as a result of the bid the acquiring company controls either:
- more than 25% of the ordinary share capital of the target company, or
- more than 50% of the voting power of the target company.

Share for share

The new shares received in the acquiring company will 'step into the shoes' of those originally held in the target company and will take their costs and dates of acquisition and give rise to no CGT disposal.

Cash for shares

If only cash is received (i.e. no shares are issued) there is a CGT disposal of the old holding in the normal manner with a resulting capital gain or loss.

Share plus cash for shares

Where there is a hybrid, i.e. the consideration is a mixture of cash and shares, the cost of the original shareholding must be split between the cash and value of the shares received and as cash has been received a CGT liability will arise.

The allocation of the cost of the original shareholding is done on a pro-rata basis according to the market values of the new shares immediately following the successful acquisition.

The consideration taken in new shares will "step into the shoes" of those shares originally held.

If the cash received on a take over is 'small' then there will be no immediate liability to CGT and the cash will be used to reduce the cost of the new shares etc. received. It will be 'small' where it does not exceed either 5% of the total value of the consideration received as a result of the take-over or £3,000.

Example 13.10

John Smith Ltd was acquired by XYZ Ltd in December 2004. XYZ Ltd offered the shareholders of John Smith Ltd one ordinary share and three preference shares for every one ordinary share held in John Smith Ltd.

John Smith owned 2,100 ordinary shares in John Smith Ltd purchased in March 1995 for £7,000.

The market values of the shares in XYZ Ltd on the day after the take-over were:
- £5 per share for the ordinary XYZ Ltd shares
- £3 per share for the preference shares in XYZ Ltd

The shares in John Smith Ltd and XYZ Ltd do not qualify as business assets for taper relief purposes.

In March 2006 John sells the whole of his ordinary shareholding in XYZ Ltd for £7.50 per share.

Indexation allowance for March 1995 to April 1998 is £987

Calculate John's capital gain on this sale.

Answer

The take-over was made only by way of an issue of shares. Therefore when John swapped his John Smith Ltd shares for shares in XYZ Ltd no CGT disposal arises.

The new shares are thus assumed to have simply replaced the original shares i.e. the new shares are assumed to have been acquired at the same time as the original shares and at their original cost.

First it is necessary to work out what consideration was received by John:
one ordinary XYZ Ltd share for every one John Smith Ltd ordinary share:
thus 2,100 XYZ Ltd ordinary shares were received
plus
three preference XYZ Ltd shares for every one John Smith Ltd ordinary share;
thus 6,300 XYZ Ltd preference shares were received

Second it is necessary to work out the value of this new shareholding:
2,100 ordinary shares at £5 market value each   =   10,500
6,300 preference shares at £3 market value each =   18,900
Total value   £29,400

Third it is necessary to allocate the original shareholding cost to the new shareholding:
Original cost of shares in John Smith Ltd was £7,000.

Allocate (10,500/29,400) x £7,000 to the new ordinary shares in XYZ Ltd i.e. £2,500

Allocate (18,900/29,400) x £7,000 to the new preference shares in XYZ Ltd i.e. £4,500

Fourth calculate capital gain on sale of XYZ Ltd ordinary shares

Sale proceeds 2,100 x £7.50	15,750	
Less:		
Cost	(2,500)	
Gain	£13,250	
Less:		
Indexation allowance	(987)	
Indexed capital gain	£12,263	
Less:		
Taper relief (30% x 12,263)	(3,679)	
Capital gain	£8,584	

Notes
1. The taper relief percentage of 30% is because the original shareholding (which the new shareholdings now replace) was acquired in March 1995 and John sold his new ordinary shares in March 2006. Ownership is therefore measured from 6th April 1998 to March 2006 i.e. seven years. However, a bonus year is also due as the old shares were owned on 16th

March 1998 (and as the new shares replaced the old shares they are also deemed to have been held on this date). Thus total number of years of ownership for taper relief purposes is 7 + 1 = 8 years which gives a 30% taper relief percentage. The shares are a non-business asset.

2. Indexation allowance is also available as the new XYZ Ltd shares are assumed to have been owned from March 1995 i.e. March 1995 to April 1998.

Detailed Rules for Companies

Where share disposals are made by companies rather than individuals although the above principles of computation apply the matching rules are slightly different.

Thus, shares sold are matched as follows:

- with acquisitions on the same day
- with acquisitions within the preceding nine days on a FIFO
- with shares in the 1985 pool

Companies are not entitled to taper relief (see Chapters 12 and 16). Instead an indexation allowance is permitted up to the date of a share sale even if this is on or after 6th April 1998.

Hence, there is no need to match shares according to whether they have been acquired on or before 5th April 1998 or thereafter as applied for individuals.

However, in the case of companies it may be necessary to derive the value of the FA 1985 pool at the date of any share disposals. In other words it may be necessary to work out the amount of any indexation allowances.

To do this it should be noted that the FA 1985 pool is comprised of:

- shares held by the company on 1st April 1985 and acquired on or after 1st April 1982; and
- shares acquired by the company on or after 1st April 1985

In deriving the pool the following approach must be taken:

first, index the cost of each share purchase between 1st April 1982 and 1st April 1985 to 1st April 1985; indexation factors used are rounded to three decimal places;

second, aggregate the total number of shares purchases between 1st April 1982 and 1st April 1985, their associated costs and their associated indexed costs;

third, continue to index the pool (however, for the post 1st April 1985 position no rounding to three decimal places occurs when working out any indexation factors) between successive operative events (i.e. subsequent purchases and sales).

Example 13.11

JS Ltd acquired 1,000 shares in ABC Ltd in July 1983 for £5,000. In August 1984 a further 2,000 shares in ABC Ltd were acquired for £7,000 and in October 1990 a further 1,500 shares in ABC Ltd were acquired for £4,000.

JS Ltd then sold 4,000 shares in ABC Ltd in May 2004 for £35,000.

JS Ltd prepares it s accounts to 31st March each year.

Indexation factors are as follows:

July 1983	85.30
August 1984	89.94
April 1985	94.78
October 1990	130.30
May 2004	186.50

What is JS Ltd's chargeable gain for its accounting period ended 31st March 2005?

Answer

No shares in ABC Ltd were purchased either on the same day of sale (i.e. May 2004) or in the 9 days prior to it.

Therefore any matching is with shares forming part of the FA 1985 pool. Before any matching can be done the value of the pool as at the date of the share sale must be worked out.

FA 1985 pool

	Shares numbers	Cost £	Indexed cost £
July 1985	1,000	5,000	5,000
August 1986	2,000	7,000	7,000
Indexation allowances to April 1985:			
[[94.78 – 85.30]/85.30]			
= 0.111 x £5,000			555
[[94.78 – 89.94]/89.94]			
= 0.054 x £7,000			378
As at 1.4.85 pool	3,000	12,000	12,933
Indexation allowance to October 1990			
[[130.30 – 94.78]/94.78]			
x £12,933			4,847
			17,780
October 1990 purchase	1,500	4,000	4,000
As at October 1990	4,500	16,000	21,780

Indexation allowance
to May 2004
[[186.50 – 130.30]/130.30]
x £21,780   9,387

As at May 2004   **4,500**   **£16,000**   **£31,167**

Out of the above 4,500 shares in ABC Ltd with a cost and indexed cost respectively of £16,000 and £31,167 JS Ltd sold 4,000 shares for £35,000.

Sale proceeds	£35,000
Less:	
Cost	
[£16,000/4,500] x 4,000	(14,222)
	£20,778
Less:	
Indexation allowance	
[[£31,167 – £16,000]/4,500]	
x 4,000	(13,482)
Chargeable gain	£7,296

Notes
1. Shares purchased prior to 1st April 1985 are each indexed to this date with the indexation factor restricted to three decimal places.
2. Once the pool as 1st April 1985 has been ascertained it is then indexed to each successive operative event (i.e. basically subsequent purchases) in turn until the pool value as at the date of any sale is known. Post 1st April 1985 indexation factors are not restricted to three decimal places.
3. The gain on sale can now be worked out using the pool values as at the date of sale.

Scrip and rights issues
The comments made in connection with bonus and rights issues for individuals earlier in this chapter apply equally to companies, subject to the fact that any indexation allowances do not stop as at 5th April 1998.

Example 13.12

JS Ltd carried out the following transactions:
May 1987 purchased 1,000 shares in XYZ Ltd for £2,000
July 2001 purchased 2,000 shares in XYZ Ltd for £6,000
March 2003 acquired rights issue shares for £3 each under a one for three issue.
May 2004 sold 1,500 shares in XYZ Ltd for £9,000.

Indexation factors are as follows:

May 1987   101.9
July 2001   173.3
March 2003   179.9
April 2004   185.7

Calculate JS Ltd's chargeable gain on the share sale.

Answer

No purchases were made either on the same day or the previous 9 days of the sale in April 2004. Any matching is therefore of shares in the FA 1985 pool.

FA 1985 pool

	Shares	Cost	Indexed cost
	nos	£	£
May 1987	1,000	2,000	2,000
Indexation allowance to July 2001 [[173.3 – 101.9]/101.9] x £2,000			1,401
	1,000	2,000	3,401
July 2001	2,000	6,000	6,000
	3,000	8,000	9,401
Indexation allowance to March 2003 [[179.9 – 173.3]/173.3] x £9,401			358
March 2003	3,000	8,000	9,759
Rights issue	1,000	3,000	3,000
As at March 2003	**4,000**	**11,000**	**12,759**

Out of the above 4,000 shares in XYZ Ltd with a cost and indexed cost respectively of £11,000 and £12,759 JS Ltd sold 1,500 shares for £9,000.

Sale proceeds	£9,000
Less:	
Cost	
[£11,000/4,000] x 1,500	(4,125)
	£4,875
Less:	
Indexation allowance	
[[£12,759 – £11,000]/4,000]	
x £1,500	(660)
Chargeable gain	£4,215

Notes

1. The procedure followed above is the same as that followed in the earlier Example 13.11.
2. The rights issue is another example of an operative event and thus prior purchases are indexed to the date of any rights issues.
3. No rounding to three decimal places when calculating the indexation factors.

SUMMARY

It is important when calculating a CGT liability on a sale of shares to first identify if the person selling the share is an individual or a company. This is of course necessary because the matching rules are different in each case.

The approach to take, however, is the same in either case which is:

- First, identify shares purchased in each of the categories (i.e. same day; next 30 days; etc)
- Second, adjust the shares purchased in each of these categories by any bonus and/or rights issues
- Third, match the shares sold with shares purchased in each of these categories until all shares sold have been matched
- Fourth, compute for each individual matching the associated capital gain or loss
- Fifth, offset any capital losses as appropriate
- Sixth, reduce the individual net capital gains by taper relief
- Seventh, aggregate the resulting capital gains and reduce this aggregate figure by the annual exemption to give the final chargeable gain.

CHAPTER 14

Deferral Methods: Business Asset Replacement

INTRODUCTION
This chapter follows on from Chapter 12 and introduces the concept of roll-over and hold-over reliefs.

Both these reliefs allow taxpayers to replace business assets (i.e. new business assets are bought to replace old business assets) used in their trade/business without incurring a liability to CGT on the sale of the "old" business assets at the date of sale. A number of conditions need to be satisfied.

Deferral: Roll-over
On the sale of a business asset where *all* the proceeds are reinvested in another business asset any gain on the sale of the first asset is not taxed immediately but is *deferred* until the replacement asset is itself sold without at that point any further reinvestment in further business assets.

This deferral is achieved by simply deducting the gain (*after* any indexation allowance) made on the sale of the old asset from the base cost of the replacement asset.

If all the sale proceeds from the sale of the old asset are not fully reinvested then only a partial roll-over arises (i.e. part of the gain is taxed immediately with part being deferred).

The terms roll-over and hold-over are often used differently by different writers. Roll-over is used in this text to mean that the gain on the sale of an asset is deducted from the base cost of the new asset. Hold-over relief is used to mean that the gain on the sale of an asset is not deducted from the base cost of the new asset but is literally treated as suspended or held over until it becomes chargeable at a later date (see below).

Conditions for roll-over relief to apply
The general conditions for complete roll-over relief are:
- both 'old' and 'new' assets must be used wholly for trade purposes, *and*
- assets must both be within the *qualifying classes of assets* but need not
- belong to the same class, *and*
- the 'new' asset must be acquired within *one year before to three years after*
- the disposal of the 'old' asset, *and*
- all the sale proceeds from the sale of the old asset must be reinvested

The words 'old' and 'new' relate to the asset's position in relation to the particular business. In other words the asset may be bought as a second hand asset from someone else but is still categorised as new for the business which is buying it.

CAPITAL GAINS TAX

Qualifying assets

The qualifying assets for deferral include:

- land and buildings occupied and used for trading purposes
- fixed (i.e. immovable) plant and machinery
- goodwill (not for companies)
- ships, airplanes and hovercraft
- satellites, space stations and spacecraft

Example 14.1

John Smith sold land and buildings, which had been used in a trade carried on by him, for £140,000 in March 2001 which he had bought for £100,000 in July 1993. In September 2001 he bought a replacement asset, land and buildings, for £200,000.

In June 2005 he sold the replacement asset for £220,000 without any further reinvestment.

Calculate John Smith's CGT position (pre annual exemption).

Answer
Original asset

Sale proceeds	140,000
Less:	
Cost	(100,000)
Unindexed gain	40,000
Less	
Indexation allowance*	(15,600)
Indexed gain	24,400

$$* \frac{162.6 - 140.7}{140.7} \times 100,000 = 0.156 \times 100,000$$

(remember, indexation only up to 5th April 1998 and any indexation factor is normally always rounded down to only three decimal places)

Replacement asset

The indexed gain of £24,400 can now be rolled-over against the cost of the replacement asset i.e. deducted from it:

Cost of replacement asset	200,000
Less:	
Rolled-over gain	(24,400)
New base cost	175,600

Sale of new asset		
Sale proceeds	220,000	
Less		
New base cost	(175,600)	
Chargeable Gain	44,400	
Less:		
Taper relief (75%)	(33,300)	
Capital gain	11,100	

Thus no capital gain is taxed in tax year 2000/01 but a capital gain is taxed in tax year 2005/06.

Notes

1. Any claim for rollover relief means that any taper relief which may have been available when the old asset is sold is in fact lost i.e. no taper relief available; thus no taper relief available in above for period 6th April 1998 to March 2001.

2. Any eventual taper relief (business) due is based only upon the period of ownership of the replacement (i.e. new) asset when it is sold, i.e. September 2001 to June 2005 (i.e. four years; 75%).

Only partial reinvestment

Where the disposal proceeds of the old asset are *not* fully reinvested the surplus cash retained reduces the gain allowed to be rolled over (and in fact if the surplus cash proceeds are greater than the gain there will be no rollover at all). In effect a partial roll-over occurs whilst at the same time a CGT liability arises.

Example 14.2

John Smith sold a business asset for proceeds of £130,000 making an indexed gain of £45,000 in tax year 2004/05. He reinvested £105,000 in a replacement business asset in tax year 2005/06.

Show John's CGT position (pre annual exemption).

Answer

Gain on sale of old asset which is capable of roll-over is 45,000.

However, some (130,000 - 105,000) i.e. 25,000 of the sale proceeds from the sale of the old asset has not been reinvested in any new asset.

Therefore the gain eligible for roll-over = 45,000 - 25,000 = 20,000.

Thus, 20,000 will reduce the cost of the replacement asset to 85,000 (i.e. 105,000 - 20,000).

The balancing amount of 25,000 (i.e. 45,000 - 20,000) which was not reinvested will be taxed on John immediately i.e. in tax year 2005/06. This part of the gain will, however, be eligible for taper relief and the percentage will depend upon how long the old asset had been owned (say, one year i.e. 50% taper relief applies).

Note that if the sale proceeds reinvested had been, say, 85,000 (i.e. 45,000 not reinvested) then the whole indexed gain of 45,000 would have been immediately chargeable with no part being eligible for roll-over.

Non-business use

Where the asset being replaced has not been used entirely for business purposes during its period of ownership the roll-over relief is scaled down.

This can be achieved by assuming the asset is in fact two assets one of which is that which was used entirely for business purposes and one asset which was not.

Two separate CGT calculations are then performed normally assuming that the costs and proceeds are pro rated in the same manner. Alternatively a single computation may be carried out reducing pro rata according to the amount of business and non-business use.

Example 14.3

John Smith purchased a factory in July 1991 for a cost of £500,000. 15% of it was let out as John did not need it for his trade. In May 2005 the factory was sold for £800,000 and a replacement factory was bought for £900,000. The indexation allowance for the period July 1991 to 5th April 1998 is £107,500.

Calculate John Smith's CGT position (pre annual exemption).

Answer
Original asset

Sale proceeds	800,000
Less	
Cost	(500,000)
Gain	300,000
Less:	
Indexation allowance	(107,500)
Indexed gain	192,500
Taxable element of gain = 15% x 192,500 =	28,875
Less taper relief (30%)	(8,663)
(April 1998 to May 2005 = seven years	
plus bonus year = eight years in total)	

Taxable gain   20,212

Thus, 85% of 192,500 is eligible for roll-over = 163,625

Base cost of new asset 900,000 – 163,625 = 736,375

Note

The above taper relief percentage of 30% is based upon the non-business asset table as this part of the business asset was not in fact used for business purposes and thus qualifies as a non-business asset.

Deferral: Hold-over

Rollover relief is modified where the new asset purchased is a "depreciating asset". A depreciating asset for this purpose is an asset with an expected life of 50 years or less at the time of acquisition (or will become so in the next 10 years).

Unlike rollover relief, the held over gain on sale of the old asset does not reduce the cost of the new asset. This gain is simply "held over" until the earliest of one of the following three occurrences and then at that time is charged to CGT:

- the sale of the 'new' depreciating asset, *or*
- the cessation of its use in the business, *or*
- the 10th anniversary of acquisition of the depreciating asset.

Leases of 60 years or less and plant and machinery are examples of depreciating assets.

Taper relief on the held over gain is given when the gain is assessed (i.e. on the earliest of one of the above three events) but is still based only on the period of ownership of the asset that produced the original held over gain.

Example 14.4

John Smith bought a factory in June 1990 for £250,000. He then sold it for £600,000 in January 2003. In August 2003 he bought some fixed plant and machinery for £750,000 selling it in March 2006 for £1,250,000. The indexation allowance for the period June 1990 to 5th April 1998 is £70,750.

Show John Smith's CGT position.

Answer

The reinvestment of the proceeds from the sale of the factory was into a depreciating asset (i.e. plant and machinery). Only *hold-over* relief is thus available.

Indexed gain on sale of factory = 600,000 – [250,000 + 70,750] = 279,250

This gain is held over until the earliest of the events mentioned above which in this case is the sale of the replacement plant and machinery in March 2006.

This gain of 279,250 is now taxable in tax year 2005/06 (not 2002/03 when it was in fact sold):

Gain (after indexation allowance)	279,250
Less	
Taper relief (75%)	(209,438)
(4 years ownership; business asset)	
Taxable gain	69,812

Note

Taper relief is based on actual period of ownership i.e. later of June 1990 and 6th April 1998 to January 2003 (*not* to March 2006)

In addition, gain on sale of plant and machinery is taxable in tax year 2005/06:

Sale proceeds	1,250,000
Less	
Cost	(750,000)
Gain	500,000
Less	
Taper relief (75%)	(375,000)
(2 years ownership; business asset)	
Taxable gain	125,000

Partial reinvestment

As for roll-over relief, full hold-over relief on the gain on the disposal of the old asset(s) is only available if the whole of the disposal proceeds are reinvested in 'new' asset(s). If part of the proceeds is not reinvested, there will be an immediate assessment on that part and only the remainder of the gain can be held-over. For individuals (companies not being entitled to taper relief) taper relief will be deducted from the gain immediately assessed as normal.

Example 14.5

If in Example 14.4 above the replacement fixed plant and machinery had cost £500,000 (instead of £750,000) then, of the indexed gain of £279,250 arising on the sale of the factory, only £179,250 could be held-over to 2005/06 i.e. [279,250 − (600,000 − 500,000)]. The balance of the gain, £100,000 (i.e. 279,250 − 179,250) would be immediately taxable in 2002/03 albeit less 75% taper relief.

Hold-over converted into roll-over relief

If a gain is initially held over (i.e. reinvestment was into a depreciating asset) and, before this gain crystallises (i.e. before one of the above three events occurs) a non-depreciating asset is acquired, it is possible to then change the original hold-over to a roll-over claim. The original gain is then offset against the base cost of the cost of the newly acquired non-depreciating asset as normal.

Example 14.6

John Smith sold a freehold office block, which he used in his trade, in September 2000 for £2,000,000. It had cost £500,000 in November 1995. In October 2000 he bought some plant and machinery for £2,250,000. In May 2004 John bought a replacement freehold factory for £2,500,000. The indexation allowance for the period November 1995 to 5th April 1998 is £42,500.

Calculate John's CGT position.

Answer
Old asset

Sale proceeds	2,000,000
Less:	
Cost	(500,000)
Gain	1,500,000
Less:	
Indexation allowance	(42,500)
Indexed gain	1,457,500

This gain can only be *held-over* as the replacement asset (i.e. the plant and machinery) is a depreciating asset.

However, prior to the earliest of the three events occurring (see above), at which time this held over gain would have become chargeable subject to taper relief, a non-depreciating asset (i.e. factory) is purchased. As a consequence, this originally held over gain may now in fact be rolled-over against the base cost of the new non-depreciating asset. Thus:

Base cost of new asset = 2,500,000 - 1,457,500 = 1,042,500

Transfer of a business to a company

Subject to satisfying certain conditions so-called incorporation relief may be available when a person transfers his sole trader-ship business to a company.

Incorporation relief permits the transfer to take place without any capital gains tax liability arising on the deemed sale of the chargeable business assets which would otherwise occur. The capital gains which would otherwise arise are rolled-over against the cost of the shares issued to the sole trader in exchange for the acquisition of the sole trader's business.

However, for complete roll-over relief to apply all the consideration for the trade transfer must be in shares of the acquiring company. If a part of the consideration is in cash a partial roll-over may apply and a CGT liability will immediately arise on the cash element received. In this latter case the amount of gain eligible for roll-over relief is given by:

Capital gain x	Value of shares received
	Total consideration received

Example 14.7

John Smith a sole trader who set up his business in 1995 has decided to transfer his entire business to a limited company JS Ltd on 31st December 2005 in exchange for an issue of ordinary shares. The assets and liabilities as at 31st December 2005 are as follows:

	Cost	Market Value
	£	£
Assets		
Cash	4,000	4,000
Freehold property	15,000	30,000
Furniture/fittings	10,000	2,000
Trading stock	3,000	1,200
Goodwill	nil	3,000
Debtors	nil	1,000
TOTAL	**32,000**	**41,200**
Liabilities		
Trade creditors	nil	1,200
Net assets	**32,000**	**40,000**

Assume the indexation allowance is £2,000 for the freehold property.

What is John Smith's CGT position for tax year 2005/06 and what difference would it make if John received his consideration as shares worth £30,000 and cash of £10,000 (i.e. a total consideration of £40,000 the sole trader's net worth)?

Answer

Chargeable gains on the transfer of chargeable assets are as follows:

Freehold property:	30,000 – (15,000 + 2,000)	=	13,000
Goodwill:	3,000 – (nil)	=	3,000
Total gain			16,000

(note that the only other chargeable asset for CGT purposes are the fixtures and fittings which are sold at less than cost thus giving rise to an appropriate balancing allowance/charge obtained for capital allowance purposes, but no capital gain/loss).

Gain eligible for roll-over relief = 16,000 as all consideration in the form of shares.

Base cost of new shares = 40,000 – 16,000 = £24,000

Had the consideration been shares plus cash then of the £16,000 of gain above only:

[30,000/40,000] x 16,000 = £12,000 of gain can be rolled over against the cost of the shares of £30,000.

The balancing gain of £4,000 (i.e. 16,000 – 12,000) is taxable immediately albeit subject to taper relief of 75% (i.e. seven years business assets).

SUMMARY

The CGT liability which arises on a sale of business assets may be rolled-over where the new business asset purchased is a non-depreciating asset. If the purchased asset is a depreciating asset (e.g. plant and machinery) then hold-over relief applies.

Under either scenario the reliefs are only available where the various conditions are satisfied.

Where roll-over relief applies the gain rolled-over is the gain after indexation but before taper relief.

The failure to reinvest all of the sale proceeds precipitates an immediately taxable gain on some part of the overall gain.

CHAPTER 15

Gifts of Business Assets by Individuals

INTRODUCTION

Chapter 14 examined the various business reliefs when a qualifying business asset is replaced by another such asset. This chapter examines the relief which is available where certain assets are either gifted or sold for less than their true market value.

General

Gifts of assets are deemed to be made at their market value at the date of the gift. In other words, even though no sale proceeds are received, for CGT purposes a disposal is deemed to have been made and thus a gain/loss will also be deemed to have arisen.

However, a capital gain deemed to have been made on a gift can be deferred by way of gift relief provided:

- the donor (the person making the gift) and donee (the person receiving the gift) jointly elect within five years from 31st January following the end of the fiscal year in which the disposal is made, *and*
- the donee is resident or ordinarily resident in the UK, *and*
- the asset is a qualifying asset.

Qualifying assets

These are:

- business assets and
- transfers of assets subject to an immediate charge to inheritance tax (the tax which is levied on death and on lifetime gifts)

Only gifts of business assets are relevant for present purposes.

Transfers of business assets are transfers of:

- business assets used by the donor in his or her business *or* used by his or her personal trading company
- shares or securities held in the donor's personal trading company
- shares or securities in an unquoted trading company

A *personal company* is one in which the donor controls at least 5% of the voting rights and can be either quoted or unquoted.

An unquoted company includes those dealt in on AIM or on OFEX.

Note that unlike the position for roll-over and hold-over relief discussed in Chapter 11 for replacement of business assets, in the case of gift relief there is no restriction on the type of assets which qualify other than that they must be used in the business.

Thus it can be seen that gift relief would not apply to for example a gift by say a mother to her daughter of a piece of family jewellery or painting as neither asset are used in any business.

Effect of gift relief

There are two effects of the donor and donee claiming gift relief:

- the donor will be treated as making neither gain nor loss on the gift; *and*
- the donee will be treated as taking the asset at its market value - the deemed disposal proceeds - but this market value will be reduced by the amount of the gain deferred on the part of the donor.

In the following examples the annual exemption (£8,500 for 2005/06) is ignored for ease of understanding. It will be recalled (see Chapter 12) that it is in fact the last deduction made.

Example 15.1

John Smith gave a business asset to his son Jim in May 1999 when its market value was £30,000. John originally bought the asset in January 1996 for £22,000. John and Jim are agreed that gift relief should be claimed. Assume the indexation allowance available to John is £1,816.

What is the CGT position of both John and Jim?

Answer

John

Deemed sale proceeds	30,000
Less:	
Cost	(22,000)
Unindexed gain	8,000
Less:	
Indexation allowance	(1,816)
Indexed gain	6,184
Less:	
Gift relief	(6,184)
Chargeable gain	nil

Jim

Market value of asset acquired	30,000
Less:	
Gift relief	(6,184)
Base cost of asset	23,816

Taper relief

One adverse consequence of claiming gift relief is that taper relief is not available on the making of the gift. Thus in the above example taper relief was not available to John on making the gift.

On a subsequent disposal by the donee at arm's length (i.e. where the asset is actually sold for its market value) taper relief is then available to reduce any gain but depends only upon the ownership period of the asset by the donee (i.e. from the date the donee received the gift) and, of course, whether the asset qualifies as a business or non-business asset since the receipt of the gift.

Example 15.2

Using the figures in example 15.1 assume Jim subsequently sells the asset in December 2005 for £35,000 also assuming that during Jim's ownership the asset continued to qualify as a business asset.

Calculate Jim's capital gain.

Answer

Sale proceeds	35,000
Less:	
Cost	(23,816)
Gain	11,184
Less:	
Taper relief (75%)	(8,388)
Capital gain	2,796

Jim held the asset from May 1999 until sale in December 2005 i.e. six complete years giving 75% taper relief. The ownership period of John is totally ignored.

Had the asset once received by Jim ceased to qualify as a business asset during his ownership then the taper relief would have been 20% (i.e. six years of ownership).

Not pure gift

Gift relief also applies where the "gift" is in fact a sale albeit at less than its true market value.

However, in such cases only a part of the gain can be subject to gift relief with some part of the gain becoming immediately chargeable.

The part of the gain which is chargeable immediately is the excess of the cash received by the donor over the donor's original cost, ignoring indexation allowance. The balance of the gain can then be deferred i.e. subject to gift relief.

Example 15.3

John Smith purchased shares in an unquoted trading company for £50,000 in December 1989. He then sold them to his son Jim for £80,000 in February 2006 when their market value was £175,000. John and Jim intend to claim gift relief on the transaction.

What is the CGT position for John and Jim?

Answer

John

Deemed sale proceeds	175,000
Less:	
Cost	(50,000)
Unindexed gain	125,000
Less:	
Indexation allowance	
(162.6 – 118.8/118.8) x 50,000	(18,450)
Indexed gain	106,550
Less:	
Gift relief	76,550
Chargeable gain (pre Taper relief)	30,000
Less:	
Taper relief (7 years; 75%)	(22,500)
Chargeable gain	7,500

Jim

Market value of shares acquired	175,000
Less:	
Gift relief	(76,550)
Base cost of shares	98,450

Notes

1. If John had simply gifted the shares to Jim gift relief of 106,550 would have been available.
2. However, as Jim paid John 80,000 then John is immediately chargeable on 30,000 (i.e. 80,000 – 50,000). Only 76,550 (i.e. 106,550 – 30,000) is thus available for gift relief.

Assets not used wholly for business purposes

Business assets other than shares

It may be that during an individual's ownership of an asset it qualifies as a business asset for part of the time and as a non-business asset for the rest of the time.

This may occur because the asset was itself used only partly for business purposes throughout its period of ownership or alternatively the asset was used wholly for business purposes but only for a part of its period of ownership.

For individual trading assets (e.g. land and buildings; plant and machinery; goodwill) the overall gain is simply pro-rated accordingly.

Example 15.4

John Smith owns a factory which he purchased in May 1999 for £100,000. In July 2002 John gave the asset to Jim when its market value was £300,000. 80% of the factory has been used in John's business with the remaining 20% being let out to a third party (i.e. this part is not used in John's business).

Show John and Jim's CGT position.

Answer

Of John's gain of 200,000 (i.e. 300,000 - 100,000) 20% of it (i.e. 40,000) is chargeable immediately subject to non-business asset taper relief.

The balancing 80% (i.e. 160,000) is eligible for gift relief.

Jim will therefore receive the asset at its market value of 300,000 less gift relief of 160,000 giving a base cost of 140,000.

Shares

In the case of a gift of shares the above rule is applied differently.

Where a gift of shares in a personal trading company is made and not all of the company's assets are business assets then some part of the gain on the sale of the shares is not eligible for gift relief.

Only the gain on the shares attributable to any underlying *chargeable* **business** *assets* as opposed to *chargeable assets* of the company qualifies for gift relief calculated as follows:

Gain on share gift	x	Market value of chargeable *business* assets
		Market value of company's chargeable assets

An example of chargeable assets of a company which are not chargeable *business* assets would be investments held by the company. Thus, the company may have used its surplus cash to invest in other company shares. These are investments and thus not business assets (i.e. they are not used in the company's business).

Example 15.5

John Smith gave his shares in his personal trading company to his son Jim in June 2005 when their market value was £125,000. John had originally purchased the shares for £40,000 in September 2002.

At the date of the gift the company's net assets were as follows:

Freehold building	55,000
Goodwill	40,000
Investments	20,000
Net current assets (none chargeable to CGT)	10,000
Total net assets	125,000

What is the CGT position of John and Jim?

Answer

John

Deemed disposal proceeds	125,000
Less:	
Cost	(40,000)
	85,000
Gift relief:	
(95,000/115,000) x 85,000	(70,217)
Chargeable gain (pre Taper relief)	14,783

Jim

Market value of assets acquired	125,000
Less:	
Gift relief	(70,217)
Base cost of shares	54,783

Notes

1. The only chargeable *business* assets were the freehold building and goodwill i.e. 55,000 + 40,000 = 95,000. However, total chargeable assets were 55,000 + 40,000 + 20,000 = 115,000.
2. John's chargeable gain for 2005/06 is 14,783 pre taper relief.

SUMMARY

It needs to be noted that gift relief:

- only applies to certain (i.e. business) assets, not all assets
- applies not just to gifts but also to sales at below market value
- taper relief is lost by the donor where gift relief is claimed
- taper relief of donee based upon ownership only of donee
- gift relief is *after* any indexation allowance but *before* taper relief
- gift relief needs the consent of both donor and donee

CHAPTER 16

Corporation Tax: General Principles

INTRODUCTION

This chapter looks at the basic rules in relation to the taxation of companies. Companies are not liable to income tax. Companies are liable to corporation tax on their profits.

Liability to corporation tax

A company's liability to corporation tax depends upon its fiscal residence. A company which is resident in the UK is liable to corporation tax on its worldwide profits.

The basic rule: place of incorporation

If a company is incorporated in the UK then it will be treated as UK resident.

Place of central management and control

If it is not incorporated in the UK, it may still be UK resident if it is controlled and managed in the UK. Basically, the control and management of a company is exercised where its board of directors meet and take strategic decisions in relation to the company.

The meaning of "profits chargeable to corporation tax"

A company is liable to *corporation tax* on its *profits chargeable to corporation tax (PCTCT)* arising in an *accounting period*.

PCTCT includes:

* income *and*
* chargeable gains

Note: companies are liable to corporation tax on chargeable gains not capital gains tax.

The meaning of "profits"

Although companies, as indicated above, are liable to corporation tax on *PCTCT* for an accounting period the *rate* of corporation tax which applies to the PCTCT is determined by the amount of the company's PROFIT which is defined as:

PROFIT = PCTCT + FII

FII means *franked investment income* which is dividend income from other UK companies (FII equals net dividends plus tax credit). Dividend income from other UK companies is **not** itself subject to corporation tax but is used to determine the applicable rate of corporation tax. Dividends from other group companies (see Chapter 18) are ignored; they do *not* form part of FII.

CORPORATION TAX

Accounting period

A period of account is any period for which a company may prepare its accounts. This may be for twelve months, less than or more than twelve months.

An accounting period however, as stated above, cannot be longer than twelve months.

An accounting period *starts*:
- when a company starts to trade; *or*
- otherwise becomes liable to corporation tax; *or*
- immediately after the previous accounting period ends

An accounting period *ends* on the earliest of the following:
- twelve months after its start
- end of the company's period of account
- company's ceasing to be resident in the UK
- company's ceasing to be liable to corporation tax
- commencement of the company's winding up

Rates of corporation tax and financial years

Rates of corporation tax are determined not for income tax years/years of assessment but for *financial years* (FY). The financial year 2005 refers to the period 1st April 2005 to 31st March 2006.

The rates for financial year 2005 (or FY 2005 (1.4.05 to 31.3.06)) are:

Profits up to £10,000	0% (starting rate)
Profits between £50,000 and £300,000	19% (small companies rate)
Profits above £1.5 million	30% (main rate)

Note 1

For Profits between £10,000 and £50,000 there is not a single rate of corporation tax; corporation tax on Profits between these limits is computed as follows (between these limits marginal relief is available):

$$0.19 \times PCTCT - [(M - P) \times PCTCT/P \times MRF]$$

M = Upper limit = £50,000   P = Profit   MRF (Marginal relief fraction) = 19/400

Note 2

For Profits between £300,000 and £1.5 million there is not a single rate of corporation tax; corporation tax on Profits between these limits is computed as follows (between these limits marginal relief is available):

$$0.30 \times PCTCT - [(M - P) \times PCTCT/P \times MRF]$$

M = Upper limit = £1.5 million   P = Profit   MRF = 11/400

Example 16.1

JS Ltd has PCTCT of £2 million for its accounting period 1st April 2005 to 31st March 2006. It has FII of £250,000 for the same period.

Calculate the corporation tax liability of JS Ltd for the accounting period 1.4.05 to 31.3.06

Answer

STEP 1

Determine the *rate* of corporation tax which applies for this accounting period to PCTCT.

PROFIT = PCTCT + FII = £2 million + £250,000 = £2,250,000

As will be seen from above this gives a rate of 30% (i.e. PROFIT exceeds £1.5 million)

STEP 2

Apply the rate determined under STEP 1 to the PCTCT for the accounting period.

Corporation tax = 30% x PCTCT = 30% x £2million = £600,000

Example 16.2

JS Ltd has PCTCT of £30,000 and FII of £25,000 for its accounting period 1st April 2005 to 31st March 2006.

Calculate the corporation tax liability of JS Ltd for the accounting period 1.4.05 to 31.3.06

Answer

Profit = £30,000 + £25,000 = £55,000

Therefore rate of corporation tax = 19%

Corporation tax = 19% x PCTCT = 19% x £30,000 = £57,000

Example 16.3

JS Ltd has PCTCT of £20,000 and FII of £15,000 for the accounting period 1st April 2005 to 31st March 2006.

Calculate JS Ltd's corporation tax liability for this accounting period.

Answer

Profit = £20,000 + £15,000 = £35,000

The Profit falls between the £10,000 and £50,000 limits where the actual rate of corporation tax varies.

In such cases to calculate the corporation tax requires use of the formula set out above:

Corporation tax = 0.19 x PCTCT − [(M − P) x PCTCT/P x MRF]

Corporation tax = 19% x 20,000 − [(50,000 − 35,000) x 20,000/35,000 x19/400]
$$= 3,800 − 407 \quad = 3,393$$

Corporation tax liability $\quad = £3,393$

Example 16.4

JS Ltd has PCTCT of £400,000 and FII of £20,000 for the accounting period 1st April 2005 to 31st March 2006.

Calculate JS Ltd's corporation tax liability for this accounting period.

Answer

Profit = £400,000 + £20,000 = £420,000

The Profit falls between the £300,000 and £1.5 million limits where the actual rate of corporation tax varies.

In such cases to calculate the corporation tax requires use of the formula set out above:

Corporation tax = 0.30 x PCTCT − [(M − P) x PCTCT/P x MRF]

Corporation tax = 30% x 400,000 − [(1.5 million − 400,000) x 400,000/420,000 x 11/400]
$$= 120,000 − 28,206 = £91,794$$

Example 16.5

JS Ltd has PCTCT of £1,600,000 for the accounting period of 1st April 2005 to 31st March 2006. It receives net dividends of £90,000.

Calculate JS Ltd's corporate tax liability for 1.4.05 to 31.3.06.

Answer

Profit = 1,600,000 + FII = 1,600,000 + [90,000 + (1/9 x 90,000)] = 1,700,000

As Profit exceeds £1.5 million the rate of corporation tax is 30%.

Corporation tax = 0.30 x £1,700,000 = £510,000

Accounting period straddles Financial Years (i.e. accounting period does not end on 31 March)

In each of the Examples above the accounting period matched a financial year (the 2005 financial year) exactly i.e. 1st April 2005 to 31st March 2006.

However, if an accounting period straddles two financial years it is necessary to apportion on a time basis into the two financial years the company's Profit and PCTCT.

Two separate computations are then carried out and then aggregated to get the company's overall corporation tax liability.

It is also necessary to apportion the "limits" for the Profit figures for each financial year to determine the rates of corporation tax.

Example 16.6

JS Ltd has PCTCT of £1.2 million and FII of £400,000 for its accounting period 1st September 2004 to 31st August 2005.

Calculate the company's corporation tax liability.

Answer
STEP 1
Compute Profit.

Profit = 1.2 million + 400,000 = 1.6 million.

STEP 2
Apportion on a time basis both Profit and PCTCT into the two financial years FY 2004 and FY 2005 covered by the accounting period.

	Profit	**PCTCT**
1.9.04 to 31.3.05	7/12 x 1.6million = 933,333	
1.4.05 to 30.8.05	5/12 x 1.6million = 666,667	
1.9.04 to 31.3.05		7/12 x 1.2 million = 700,000
1.4.05 to 30.8.05		5/12 x 1.2 million = 500,000

STEP 3
Apportion the "limits" used to determine the rate of corporation tax for each financial year. The limits are:

FY 2004

Profits up to £10,000 x 7/12 i.e. 5,833	0%
Profits (£50,000 - £300,000) x 7/12 i.e. between 29,167 and 175,000	19%
Profits above £1.5 million x 7/12 i.e. 875,000	30%

FY 2005

Profits up to £10,000 x 5/12 i.e. 4,167	0%
Profits (£50,000 - £300,000) x5/12 i.e. between 20,833 and 125,000	19%
Profits above £1.5 million x 5/12 i.e. 625,000	30%

CORPORATION TAX

STEP 4

Compare Profit figures from STEP 2 with limits from STEP 3 to obtain relevant rates of corporation tax for each Financial Year to apply to PCTCT for that financial year.

For FY 2004 rate is 30% (as 933,333 exceeds 875,000)
For FY 2005 rate is 30% (as 666,667 exceeds 625,000)

STEP 5
Compute corporation tax for each FY applied to the PCTCT for each FY.

FY 2004   FY 2005
30% x 700,000 = 210,000   30% x 500,000 = 150,000

STEP 6
Aggregate figures from STEP 5 to get corporation tax liability for the whole 12 month accounting period i.e. 1st September 2004 to 31st August 2005.

CT = 210,000 + 150,000 = 360,000

Accounting period

The period of account (i.e. the period for which a company prepares its accounts) for a company can be:

- 12 months long
- less than 12 months long
- longer than 12 months.

However, a period of account is not necessarily the same as an accounting period.

As noted above, however, corporation tax is levied on PCTCT for an *accounting period.*

Short accounting period

Where the company's period of account is less than 12 months long this period of account is also the company's accounting period.

Corporation tax is computed as above except the limits in determining the rate of corporation tax are adjusted accordingly:

Example 16.7

JS Ltd prepares its accounts for the nine month period 1st April 2005 to 31st December 2005.

In this case the Limits used to determine the rate of corporation tax will be:
£10,000 x 9/12 = £7,500
£50,000 x 9/12 = £37,500
£300,000 x 9/12 = £225,000
£1.5 million x 9/12 = £1,125,000

Thus, if Profit for the accounting period 1st April to 31st December 2005 is £200,000 then as this falls between £37,500 and £225,000 the rate of corporation tax is 19%.

Example 16.8

JS Ltd prepares its accounts for the 6 month period 1st April 2005 to 31st September 2005.

In this case the Limits used to determine the rate of corporation tax will be:

£10,000 x 6/12 = £5,000

£50,000 x 6/12 = £25,000

£300,000 x 6/12 = £150,000

£1.5 million x 6/12 = £750,000

Thus, if Profit for the accounting period 1st April to 31st September 2005 is £200,000 then as this falls between £150,000 and £750,000 the rate of corporation tax will depend upon the marginal relief calculation.

CT = 0.30 x PCTCT – [(M – P) x PCTCT/P x MRF]

= 0.30 x 200,000 – [(750,000 – 200,000) x 200,000/200,000 x 11/400]

= 60,000 – 15,125

= 44,875

Notes

1. Profit and PCTCT in this example are the same as there is no FII.
2. As the accounting period is less than 12 months the limits have been adjusted and thus "M" itself is also reduced. In this case "M" is reduced from £1.5 million to £750,000.

Long period of account

Where the company's period of account is more than 12 months (referred to as a long period of account) this complete period cannot be an accounting period because the accounting period of a company for corporation tax purposes must be no longer than 12 months.

In such cases the period of account must be split into two separate accounting periods, one of 12 months; and one for the balance of the time. Two calculations are then necessary producing two separate corporate tax liabilities for each accounting period which are *not* then aggregated.

Example 16.9

JS Ltd prepared its accounts for the 15 months 1ˢᵗ January 2005 to 31ˢᵗ March 2006.

To compute JS Ltd's corporation tax liability the above period of account must be split into two separate accounting periods:

1ˢᵗ January 2005 to 31ˢᵗ December 2005 (i.e. 12 months long) and

1ˢᵗ January 2006 to 31ˢᵗ March 2006 (i.e. the balance).

Two totally separate calculations are then carried out for each of these two accounting periods.

Two corporation tax liabilities result which remain separate i.e. they are not aggregated.

Where the company's period of account exceeds 12 months, before any calculations can be carried out it becomes necessary to split the individual items of income (e.g. rental income; interest income; etc) comprising the company's Profit and the company's FII for the whole period of account between the two accounting periods created. This split is carried out using the following rules:

- trading income *before* capital allowances is time apportioned
- capital allowances need to be calculated separately for each accounting period
- property business profit is time apportioned
- other income is allocated to accounting period to which it relates (i.e. accruals basis)
- chargeable gains/losses allocated to accounting period in which realised
- charges on income allocated to accounting period in which paid
- dividends allocated to accounting period in which received

Example 16.10

JS Ltd has the following results for the 16 months to 31 December 2006:

Trading profit   320,000 (pre capital allowances)
Property business profit   160,000

Bank interest received and accrued to 31 December 2006	8,000
Capital gain made on 30 August 2006	89,000
UK dividend received 1 September 2006	36,000

Tax written down value of plant and machinery as at 1ˢᵗ September 2005 was £100,000.

No purchases or sales were made during the period of account.

Calculate the PCTCT and Profit for the two accounting periods and the corporation tax liability for each accounting period.

Answer
The period of account 1st September 2005 to 31st December 2006 is divided into an accounting period of 1st September 2005 to 31st August 2006 and an accounting period of 1st September 2006 to 31st December 2006.

	1.9.05 to 31.08.06	1.9.06 to 31.12.06
Trading profit		
320,000x 12/16	240,000	
320,000x 4/16		80,000
Capital allowances (see below)	(25,000)	(6,250)
Property business profit		
160,000x 12/16	120,000	
160,000x 4/16		40,000
Interest income		
8,000x 12/16	6,000	
8,000x 4/16		2,000
C. Gain	89,000	
PCTCT	**430,000**	**115,750**
FII		40,000
PROFIT	**430,000**	**155,750**

Capital allowances
1.9.05 to 31.8.06
TWDV as at 1.9.05   100,000
WDA (25%)   (25,000)
1.9.06 to 31.12.06
TWDV as at 1.9.06   75,000
WDA (25% x 4/12)   (6,250)

1.9.05 to 31.8.06
Corporation tax liability = 0.3 x 430,000 – 11/400 x [(1,500,000 – 430,000)]
= 99,575

1.9.06 to 31.12.06
Corporation tax liability =
0.3 x 115,750 – 11/400 x [(500,000 – 155,750) x 115,750/155,750]
= 27,690

Notes

1. These are two separate tax liabilities for two different accounting periods and they are thus not added together; they are also paid at different times; see Chapter 21.
2. Profit limits needed to be adjusted for accounting period 1.9.06 to 31.12.06 by multiplying limits by 4/12.
3. Thus the 'M' in the formula has had to be adjusted for the accounting period 1.9.06 to 31.12.06 to 4/12 of the £1.5 million i.e. £500,000.

Associated companies

When determining the rate of corporation tax to apply to the PCTCT of a particular company for a particular accounting period not only is the length of the accounting period and whether the accounting period straddles different financial years relevant it is also necessary to take into account the number of companies which are associated with this company.

The number of associated companies affects the limits for the various rates of corporation tax.

More specifically, for a particular company these limits are divided by the number of associated companies the company has for the relevant accounting period plus 1 (e.g. if a company has four associated companies the corporation tax limits are divided by 4 + 1 i.e. 5).

Definition

One company is associated with another company if one company controls the other company or where both companies are controlled by a third person (the term person means a company or an individual).

Broadly, control occurs where more than 50% of a company's ordinary share capital is owned directly or indirectly by another company.

The following companies are taken into account in determining the number of associated companies:

- UK and non-UK resident companies; and
- companies even if only controlled for part of an accounting period (which occurs when a company joins or leaves a group)

Dormant companies are *ignored* (a dormant company is one which undertakes no activities of any description) in the accounting period.

Example 16.11

```
                    A Ltd
          60%                 40%
        B Ltd                C Ltd
         60%
        D Ltd
```

To work out the corporation tax liability of any of the above companies (e.g. A) requires that the number of associated companies be determined (e.g. the number of associated companies of A).

Take A Ltd
A Ltd controls B Ltd (as it owns directly more than 50% of B Ltd's shares)
Therefore A and B are associated.

What about B Ltd and D Ltd?
B Ltd controls D Ltd
Therefore B and D are associated

What about A Ltd and D Ltd?
A Ltd controls B Ltd; and B Ltd controls D Ltd; therefore A Ltd controls D Ltd through B Ltd.
Therefore A and D are associated.

A Ltd does *not* control C Ltd (as it owns less than 50%)
Therefore A and C are *not* associated.

Thus, two companies are associated with A, namely B and D. Therefore the profit limits for determining the rate of corporation tax need to be divided by three (not two i.e. number of associated companies plus one); the three associated companies being A, B and C.

Notes
1. In ascertaining if companies are associated it is never acceptable to multiply share ownership percentages to see if the 50% threshold is exceeded.
2. Thus, to work out in the above Example if A Ltd and D Ltd are associated multiplying 60% by 60% (i.e. A's interest in B and B's interest in D to get A's effective interest in D) and getting 36% indicating that A owns less than 50% of D would *not* be correct.

Example 16.12

Mr John Smith

	62%		80%	
	P Ltd		T Ltd	
83%	67%	80%		
Q Ltd	S Ltd	M Ltd		

To work out the corporation tax liability of any of the above companies requires that the number of associated companies be determined.

P Ltd and T Ltd are controlled by the same third person, John Smith, even though John Smith is an individual. Therefore as P and T are controlled by the same person they are associated.

P controls Q and therefore P and Q are associated.
P controls S and therefore P and S are associated.
P controls M and therefore P and M are associated.
Therefore, there are 5 associated companies P, Q, S, M and T.

Example 16.13
JS Ltd prepared its accounts for the nine month period to 31st December 2005. During this accounting period JS Ltd was associated with two other companies (i.e. there are 3 associated companies in total). What are the relevant limits used to work out the rate of corporation tax to apply to JS Ltd's PCTCT.

Answer
The relevant limits need to be multiplied by 9/12 because of the nine month period *and* then be divided by 3 to represent the three associated companies, i.e.

£10,000 x 9/12 x 1/3 =	£2,500
£50,000 x 9/12 x 1/3 =	£12,500
£300,000 x 9/12 x 1/3=	£75,000
£1.5m x 9/12 x 1/3 =	£375,000

JS Ltd's Profits would then be compared to these new limits to determine the relevant rate of corporation tax to apply to its PCTCT.

Profit: make up and Pro-Forma
Corporation tax is levied on the PCTCT of an accounting period as stated above.

PCTCT is equal to the aggregate of the income and chargeable gains made by a company in the accounting period. This would include, for example, any property business profit, trading/business profit and bank interest etc.

In computing the corporation tax liability for an accounting period the following pro-forma should be followed:

Property business profit	x
Trading profit	x
Net interest income	x
Income from foreign securities	x
Income from foreign possessions	x
Chargeable Gains	x
Total profits	X
Less: Charges on income (gross)	(x)
Profits chargeable to	
corporation tax - PCTCT	X
Plus:	
FII	x
"Profit"	X

("Profit" = PCTCT + FII)

Taking each of these items in turn:

Property business profit

Property business profit is determined in a very similar manner as applies to individuals (see Chapter 5); thus, the accruals basis applies (e.g. dates of receipt of rent irrelevant). It is, however, assessed for an accounting period (not a year of assessment as for individuals).

Property business profit comprises:

- rents
- premiums received on grant of a short lease (i.e. a lease of 50 years or shorter)

In computing the amount of property business profit the normal rules relating to the calculation of trading profits also apply here (see Chapters 5 and 6):

e.g. expenses must have been wholly and exclusively incurred for the business;

capital expenditure disallowed;

general provision for bad debts disallowed etc.

Property business profits from more than one property are aggregated producing a single assessable property business profit figure.

One important point to note here, is that where a company pays interest on a loan to purchase or improve rented property such interest is *not* allowed as an expense in computing the property business profit (as is the case for individuals; see Chapter 5). The interest is in fact deductible against any interest income of the company under the so-called loan relationship rules. This may give rise to net interest income or loss (see below).

Premiums received for grant of short lease

For this purpose a short lease is one of 50 years or less.

A premium is simply a lump sum payment by tenant to landlord in consideration of the grant of lease.

A premium is in effect treated as if it was additional rent in the accounting period in which the lease is granted. However, only part of the premium is actually chargeable to tax:

Amount of premium chargeable =

Premium – [2% x Premium x (duration of lease in complete years – 1)]

Example 16.14

J S Ltd received a premium of £10,000 on 1st June 2005 when it let out a property under a 10 year lease which it owned. A monthly rent of £500 payable on 1st of each month is also chargeable.

Calculate J S Ltd's property business profit to be included as part of its profit for the accounting period 1st April 2005 to 31st March 2006.

Answer

Both the rent (on an accruals basis) and a proportion of the premium (in accounting period of granting of lease) are taxable.

Taxable element of premium = 10,000 – [2% x 10,000 x (10 – 1)] = 8,200

Rents accrued from 1.6.05 to 31.3.06 = £500 x 10 = 5,000

Therefore:

Property business profit = £8,200 + £5,000 = £13,200

Grant of a sub-lease

Where a tenant grants a sub-lease to a sub-tenant any premium charged to the subtenant is assessed on the grantor tenant as above.

However, if that tenant had paid a premium on receiving its own lease then a measure of relief from assessment on the sub-lease premium is available. The relief is:

Duration of sublease   x Taxable premium for headlease
Duration of headlease

Example 16.15

A Ltd grants a lease to B Ltd for 40 years on 1.3.1994 with a premium of £16,000 paid by B to A.

B Ltd grants a sub-lease to C Ltd on 1.6.2005 for 10 years with C paying B a premium of £30,000.

A, B and C each prepare their accounts to 31st March each year.

How is B Ltd taxed?

Answer

Taxable element of Premium received by B on sub-lease =

30,000 – [2% x 30,000 x (10 – 1)]	=	24,600

Less:

Allowance for premium paid by B to A =

[16,000 – [2% x 16,000 x (40 – 1)]] x 10/4	=	<u>880</u>

Premium taxable on B for accounting period 1.4.05 to 31.3.06 =   23,720

Just as the premium is assessed on the recipient company so a deduction is available to the payor company. The amount allowable as an expense to the payor company is equal to the amount assessable on the landlord (per above) divided by the number of years of the lease. This amount is then deductible each year for the life of the lease.

Example 16.16

J S Ltd received a premium of £10,000 on 1st June 2005 when it let out a property under a 10 year lease to ABC Ltd. A monthly rent of £500 payable on 1st of each month is also chargeable. ABC Ltd uses the property concerned in its own trade. Each company prepares its accounts to 31st March each year.

Show the deduction available to ABC Ltd.

Answer

J S Ltd

Both the rent (on an accruals basis) and a proportion of the premium (in accounting period of granting of lease) are taxable.

Taxable element of premium = 10,000 – [2% x 10,000 x (10 – 1)] = 8,200

Rents accrued from 1.6.05 to 31.3.06 = £500 x 10 = 5,000

Therefore property business profit assessment on J S Ltd for accounting period is:

= £8,200 + £5,000 = £13,200

ABC Ltd

For ABC Ltd it can claim a trading expense for the rent of £5,000 (i.e. 10 months) for its accounting period ended 31st March 2006 and £6,000 annually thereafter.

For the accounting period ended 31st March 2006 it will also be able to claim trading expense treatment of:

Amount of premium assessed on J S Ltd = £8,200 x 10/12 = £683

Duration of lease   10

For each accounting period thereafter a deduction of £820 will be available with a balancing deduction of [£820 x 2/12] in the final accounting period in which the lease terminates.

Note

The annual expense of £820 is reduced to £683 for year ended 31st March 2006 because the lease is taken out only on 1st June 2005 and therefore only 10 month of accrual applies.

Property business losses

A property business loss for an accounting period may be set off against non-property business income and chargeable gains of the accounting period of the loss before charges on income, and then may be carried forward and offset against future income and chargeable gains of future accounting periods before charges on income.

Alternatively, a part or whole of the loss may be surrendered as group relief (see Chapter 18).

Trading profits

Companies are taxed on their trading profit for the accounting period on the normal accruals basis and the normal rules regarding deductibility of expenses apply (see Chapter 6).

Unlike the case for sole traders:

- there are no commencement or cessation rules and no overlap profits
- there is no disallowance for any private proportion of any expenses (i.e. the full amount of the expense is deductible; this is because in the case of companies any private part of an expense (e.g. private fuel costs of a company car) is taxed as income on the part of the relevant employee; see Chapter 10)
- there is no restriction for the private element of any capital asset in respect of which capital allowances may be claimed (see Chapter 7).

Capital allowances

Capital allowances are given for accounting periods by reference to acquisitions and disposals in that accounting period.

First year allowances and writing down allowances are in principle calculated as for sole traders (see Chapter 7) using the same rates (note the new 50% FYA applicable to small businesses on expenditure incurred between 1st April 2004 and 31st March 2005 inclusive).

Period of account exceeds twelve months

As an accounting period cannot for corporation tax purposes exceed 12 months writing down allowances can never exceed 25% of the relevant tax written down values/costs (compare this with that of the sole trader where a 15 month period of account may produce writing down allowances of:

25% x 15/12; see Chapter 6 and 7).

Where the period of account is in excess of 12 months two separate capital allowance computations are necessary for each of the two accounting periods which are created (see Example 16.10 above).

Period of account less than twelve months

Where the period of account is *less* than 12 months writing down allowances are reduced as appropriate.

As stated above no reduction in writing down allowances occurs where private use of any assets occurs.

Capital allowances are deductible from trading income.

Interest income

Non-trading loan relationships

Interest income and interest expenses are dealt with under the loan relationship provisions.

Interest income related to a non-trading relationship primarily consists of interest income from bank and building society deposits and on loans to other companies. *Interest expenses* consist of the interest payable on a borrowing incurred to buy property for renting out (i.e. for a property business).

In essence, such interest income/expense items are not received/paid as part of the company's trade (see below).

Such income and expenses are taxed on an accruals basis and are simply aggregated to produce the net interest income/expense figure.

Note that unlike individuals UK companies receive bank and building society interest *gross* i.e. without tax at source having been first deducted (compare that for individuals; see Chapter 3).

Interest received from other UK companies is also received *gross*.

Excess of interest expense over interest income
Where the aggregate interest expense exceeds the aggregate interest income the loss arising may be relieved by:
- set against total profits of same accounting period (*after* trading loss b/f but *before* trading loss of same or future periods and *before* charges on income)
- surrendered as group relief
- carried back and set against surpluses on non-trading relationships for previous 12 months
- carried forward and set against future non trading profits

Trading loan relationships
Trading loan relationships refer to the position where the interest payable or receivable is paid/received as part of the company's trade. In such cases interest payable is allowed as a trading expense (e.g. incidental costs of loan finance) and interest receivable is treated as trading income (normally any interest income will not be treated as trading income but income as part of a non-trading relationship; see above).

Chargeable gains
Companies:
- do *not* pay capital gains tax but corporation tax on chargeable gains for an accounting period
- are *not* entitled to taper relief
- are *not* entitled to an annual exemption

Indexation allowance, however, applies to the date of disposal of the asset even if after 5th April 1998.

With respect to share sales the matching rules are similar, but not identical, to those applying to individuals.

The matching rules for companies are as follows:
- same day purchases
- previous nine days purchases
- FA 1985 pool purchases

On the sale of certain business assets roll-over/hold-over relief may be claimed as also applies to sole traders (see Chapter 14).

Charges on income

The only example of a charge on income for corporation tax purposes is a payment(s) to a charity under the Gift Aid scheme (patent royalty payments and qualifying interest payments which are charges for individuals are not so for companies; see Chapter 3 and below).

Such payments are made gross (i.e. no tax at source is deducted from the payment; where an individual makes a Gift aid payment tax at 22% is deemed to have been deducted).

Charges on income are deductible from total profits from all sources.

Only charges which are actually paid in an accounting period are deductible.

Prior to 1.4.02 patent royalties were also treated as charges on income. However, from this date such payments are to be treated as trading expenses and are thus now deductible on an accruals (not payments) basis in computing trading profit.

A charitable donation incurred for trade purposes and not within the Gift Aid scheme is deductible in computing trading profit (generally speaking this is unlikely).

Franked investment income (FII)

FII refers to dividends from other UK resident companies plus the attaching tax credit of 1/9th of the net dividend (it excludes dividends from 51% group companies which are outside the scope of corporation tax and are thus ignored).

FII is not taxable but is used in determining the rate of corporation tax to apply to PCTCT by being added to PCTCT to get the Profit figure (see above).

Remember

$$\text{Profits} = \text{PCTCT} + \text{FII}$$

Turning to an example which pulls all the above together:

Example 16.17

JS Ltd has the following results for the accounting period 1st April 2005 to 31st March 2006.

Property business profit	20,000
Trading profit	1,200,000
Net interest income	7,000
Chargeable gains	175,000
Dividends received from other UK companies (net)	108,000
Gift Aid payment	15,000

Bank interest is the amount received in the accounting period. No interest was owed to the company at 1st April 2005 but an amount of £2,700 is owed to the company as at 31st March 2006.

Answer

Adopting the pro-forma above:

Property business profit	20,000
Trading profit	1,200,000
Net interest income	9,700
Chargeable Gains	175,000
Total profits	1,404,700
Less: Charges on income (gross)	(15,000)
Profits chargeable to corporation tax - PCTCT	1,389,700
FII	120,000
"Profit"	1,509,700

Corporation tax 30% x £1,389,700 = £416,910

Notes

1. Net interest income is taxed on an accruals basis. Therefore the amount of interest owed to the company as at 31st March 2006 (i.e. £2,700) needs to be included with the amount accrued and received during the accounting period (i.e. £7,000).
2. Gift Aid payments are made gross (i.e. without deduction of income tax at source) and are treated as a charge on income payment.
3. Dividends received of 108,000 are received net. Therefore a tax credit equal to 1/9th (1/9th of 108,000) needs to added to get the gross dividend or FII of 120,000.
4. Although PCTCT is below £1.5 million, Profit exceeds £1.5 million and therefore the rate of corporation tax applicable is 30% (which is applied to PCTCT i.e. Corporation tax = 30% x £1,389,700 = £416,910).

Very small companies

New legislation has been introduced which is effective from 1st April 2004 which alters the way in which corporation tax is levied on very small companies.

A very small company is a company where the underlying rate (see below) of corporation tax is less than 19%.

The new legislation only applies where the underlying corporate tax rate is less than 19% *and* the company has made a dividend payment to one or more *non-corporate* shareholders (i.e. individual shareholders).

Where the legislation applies the corporation tax liability of the company is the sum of the underlying rate of corporation tax as applied to the amount of the PCTCT which is not paid out as dividends to individuals plus the rate of 19% applied to the amount of dividends paid.

Thus, if none of a company's PCTCT is paid out as dividends this new legislation cannot apply and even if dividends are paid out the company's underlying rate of corporation tax must be less than 19% for it to apply.

The underlying corporate tax rate is determined by dividing the corporation tax liability calculated as normal by the company's PCTCT.

Dividends are treated as relating to the accounting period in which they are paid.

Example 16.18

JS Ltd for the accounting period 1st April 2005 to 31st March 2006 has PCTCT of £45,000 of which £35,000 was paid out as dividends to individuals and an amount of £2,500 was paid to corporate shareholders.

Calculate JS Ltd's corporation tax liability for the accounting period.

Answer

On a PCTCT of £45,000 the corporation tax liability is calculated as normal (see above):

$$CT = 0.19 \times 45,000 - [(50,000 - 45,000)] \times 45,000/45,000 \times 19/400$$
$$= £8,550 - £238 = £8,312$$

Underlying tax rate = 8,312/45,000 = 18.47% (i.e. less than 19%)

JS Ltd is thus a very small company.

$$CT = 0.19 \times 35,000 + 0.1847 \times (45,000 - 35,000)$$
$$= 6,650 + 1,847 = £8,497$$

$$CT = £8,497$$

Notes
1. JS Ltd is a very small company as its rate of corporation tax calculated in the normal way is less than 19%.
2. The effect of the new legislation is to tax the dividends (but only those to individuals; i.e. 35,000) at the full 19% rate and to tax the amount of PCTCT left after such dividends (i.e. 45,000 – 35,000) at the underlying rate of corporation tax (i.e. 18.47%).
3. The rate of underlying corporation tax is simply the corporation tax calculated as normal divided by the PCTCT (i.e. 8,312/45,000).

It may be that dividends paid by a company to its individual shareholders are of an amount which exceeds the level of PCTCT for the accounting period under consideration (e.g. part of the dividends are paid out of pre-existing retained earnings of the company).

In such cases the excess (i.e. Dividends less PCTCT) is simply treated as a dividend of the following accounting period together with any dividends which may also be paid in that next accounting period. Note, however, that there are no carry back provisions.

Example 16.19

JS Ltd for the accounting period 1st April 2005 to 31st March 2006 has PCTCT of £45,000 of which £50,000 was paid out as dividends to individuals on 30th September 2005 and an amount of £2,500 was paid to corporate shareholders.

JS Ltd for the accounting period 1st April 2006 to 31st March 2007 has PCTCT of £35,000 of which £5,000 was paid out as dividends to individuals on 30th September 2006.

Calculate JS Ltd's corporation tax liability for the accounting periods ended 31st March 2006 and 2007.

Answer
For the accounting period ended 31st March 2006:
On a PCTCT of £45,000 the corporation tax liability is calculated as normal:

$CT = 0.19 \times 45,000 - [(50,000 - 45,000)] \times 45,000/45,000 \times 19/400 = £8,550 - £238$
$= £8,312$

Underlying tax rate = 8,312/45,000 = 18.47% (i.e. less than 19%)
JS Ltd is thus a very small company.

$CT = 0.19 \times 45,000 + 0.1847 \times (45,000 - 45,000^*) = 8,550$
(Dividends actually 50,000 not 45,000 but the result is nil).

$CT = £8,550$

For the accounting period ended 31st March 2007:
On a PCTCT of £35,000 the corporation tax liability is calculated as normal:

$CT = 0.19 \times 35,000 - [(50,000 - 35,000)] \times 35,000/35,000 \times 19/400$
$= £6,650 - £713 = £5,937$

Underlying tax rate = 5,937/35,000 = 16.96% (i.e. less than 19%)

JS Ltd is thus a very small company.

$CT = 0.19 \times 10,000 + 0.1696 \times [35,000 - (5,000 + 5,000)] = 1,900 + 4,240$

$CT = £6,140$

Notes

1. For the accounting period ended 31st March 2006 as the whole of the PCTCT was paid out as dividends there is in fact no need to compute an underlying tax rate as the PCTCT to which it applies is 45,000 – 50,000 i.e. nil.

2. The excess dividends paid (i.e. 50,000 – 45,000 = 5,000) in the accounting period ended 31st March 2006 are carried forward to the next accounting period i.e. 31st March 2007.

3. Thus, in the accounting period ended 31st March 2007 dividends of 10,000 are deemed to have been paid which represents the 5,000 brought forward from the prior accounting period and the 5,000 paid on 30th September 2006 in the accounting period.

SUMMARY

Corporation tax is levied on a company's PCTCT for an accounting period which cannot be longer than 12 months. The rate of corporation tax is determined by the company's Profit for the accounting period.

Profit equals PCTCT plus FII.

Where an accounting period exceeds 12 months it must be split into two accounting periods of 12 months and the balance of the period with income etc apportioned as appropriate.

The number of associated companies will affect the rate of corporation tax levied as will the length of the accounting period.

Dividends from UK resident companies are never subject to corporation tax and their gross amount is referred to as FII.

CHAPTER 17

Company Trading Losses

INTRODUCTION

This chapter will examine how a trading loss may be used by the company which incurs it.

The following chapter will look at how a company's trading loss may be used by other companies which are said to be in the same *group* as the loss making company.

Types of loss

A company may for an accounting period make various types of loss. These losses are:

- trading loss
- property business loss
- net interest loss (under the loan relationship rules)
- capital loss

The manner in which a property business loss and a net interest loss may be relieved is considered in Chapter 16.

Capital loss

A capital loss may be offset against any chargeable gains of the same accounting period and any unrelieved amount of loss may then be carried forward for offset against future chargeable gains.

Capital losses may not be carried back to earlier accounting periods.

Unlike the position for individuals (see Chapter 12) there is no restriction on the use of brought forward capital losses; they are all available for use.

Trading losses

Trading losses of an accounting period can be used in two ways:

offset against income and chargeable gains of the accounting period (*before* charges on income) of the loss under section 393(A)(1)(a) with any surplus unrelieved loss then being eligible for carry back for offset against the income and chargeable gains of the previous 12 month period (*before* charges on income) under section 393(A)(1)(b);

and

carried forward and offset against future *trading profits* of future accounting periods under section 393(1)

A trading loss is computed exactly the same as a trading profit for any accounting period.

Where section 393(A) above is used it is not possible to carry back any trading loss for 12 months until the loss has first been offset against income and gains of the accounting period of the loss (this is different from the position for sole traders under the equivalent section 380; see Chapter 8) i.e. section 393(A)(1)(a) must be used before section 393(A)(1)(b) can be used.

There is, however, no requirement to carry back any unrelieved loss. After the loss has been offset against the income and chargeable gains of the accounting period of loss any unrelieved loss may then simply be carried forward under section 393(1). However, in practice optimal use of the loss will invariably require that a carry back of the loss occurs.

As is the case with the usage of losses, once a section to use has been chosen (e.g. section 393(A)(1)(a)) the loss must then be relieved to the maximum amount possible. It is not possible, for example, under section393 (A)(1)(b) to carry back to the previous 12 months only some proportion of the unrelieved loss; the maximum possible relievable loss must be carried back.

Example 17.1

JS Ltd has the following results:

	Year ended		
	31.12.03	**31.12.04**	**31.12.05**
Trading profit	(350,000)	250,000	115,000
Chargeable gains	50,000	40,000	30,000
Net interest income	25,000	15,000	40,000

Show how section 393(1) is used.

Answer

	Year ended		
	31.12.03	**31.12.04**	**31.12.05**
Trading profit	nil	(250,000)	115,000
Less:			
Section 393(1)	nil	(250,000)	(100,000)
Chargeable gains	50,000	40,000	30,000
Net interest income	25,000	15,000	40,000
PCTCT	75,000	55,000	85,000

Note

Under section 393(1) the trading loss of the accounting period ended 31.12.03 is simply carried forward and offset to the maximum extent possible against future trading profits of future accounting periods.

Example 17.2

JS Ltd has the following results:

	Year ended 31.12.03	3 months to 31.3.04	Year ended 31.3.05
Trading profit	(350,000)	250,000	115,000
Chargeable gains	50,000	40,000	30,000
Net interest income	25,000	15,000	40,000

Show how section 393(1) is used.

Answer

	Year ended 31.12.03	3 months to 31.3.04	Year ended 31.3.05
Trading profit	Nil	250,000	115,000
Less:			
Section 393(1)	nil	(250,000)	(100,000)
Chargeable gains	50,000	40,000	30,000
Net interest income	25,000	15,000	40,000
PCTCT	75,000	55,000	85,000

Note

The change of accounting date from a December to a March year end does not affect the use of section 393(1).

Section 393(1) and section 393(A)

The use of section 393(1) is straight forward as illustrated above. The important point to note is where in the corporation tax pro-forma to insert the section 393(1) line.

In the case of section 393(A) where to insert the section 393(A) line is also important but unlike section 393(1) above, a change of accounting date does affect the manner in which section 393(A) is used (see Example 17.4 below).

Loss strategy

Trading losses (or indeed any type of loss) must be used in the most tax efficient manner. Generally speaking, this will mean using the loss as soon as possible.

Thus, for companies section 393(A)(1)(a) should be used first; then section 393(A)(1)(b); and then section 393(1).

As for sole traders (see Chapter 8) where in an accounting period a trading loss arises then the assessment for trading profit will be "nil".

Example 17.3

JS Ltd has the following results:

| | Year ended | | |
	31.12.03	31.12.04	31.12.05
Trading profit	350,000	(750,000)	115,000
Chargeable gains	50,000	40,000	30,000
Net interest income	25,000	15,000	40,000
Charges on income	12,000	3,000	15,000

Show how section 393(A) is used.

Answer

The loss strategy set out above requires that the trading loss for the accounting period ended 31.12.04 should be used first against its own income and gains; then against those of the previous 12 months (i.e. accounting period ended 31.12.03) and finally if any surplus loss still remains it should be carried forward to accounting period ended 31.12.05.

| | Year ended | | |
	31.12.03	31.12.04	31.12.05
Trading profit	350,000	nil	115,000
Less:			
Section 393(1)	nil	nil	(115,000)
Chargeable gains	50,000	40,000	30,000
Net interest income	25,000	15,000	40,000
Total profit	425,000	55,000	70,000
Less:			
Section 393(A)(1)(a)		(55,000)	
Section 393(A)(1)(b)	(425,000)		
Less:			
Charges on income	(12,000)	(3,000)	(15,000)
PCTCT	Nil	Nil	55,000

Notes

1. Trading loss of 750,000 for accounting period ended 31.12.04 was first used against "total profit" of 55,000. The surplus was then carried back and offset against "total profit" of 425,000 with the balance then be carried forward for offset against the trading profit of 115,000.

2. Of the trading loss of 750,000 some 595,000 was used leaving for future carry forward under section 393(1) 155,000.

3. The charges on income for the accounting periods ended 31.12.03 and 31.12.04 are unrelieved. They cannot be carried back or forward for relief. However, they can be group relieved (see Chapter 18).

Accounting periods of different lengths

It may be that a company's accounting year end may change. This would then mean that the length of the accounting period will vary.

For example, a company may make its accounts up to 31st December each year. Following the preparation of the accounts to say 31st December 2003 the company may then decide to change to a 31st March year end. A set of accounts will then be prepared to 31st March 2004 and 31st each year thereafter. The accounting period to 31st March 2004 will thus be only three months long.

In such a case care is needed in offsetting any trading losses.

Example 17.4

JS Ltd has the following results:

	Year ended 31.12.03	3 months to 31.3.04	Year ended 31.3.05
Trading profit	50,000	150,000	(750,000)
Chargeable gains	50,000	40,000	30,000
Net interest income	25,000	15,000	40,000
Charges on income	12,000	3,000	15,000

Show how section 393(A) is used.

Answer

The loss strategy set out above requires that the trading loss for the accounting period ended 31.3.05 should be used first against its own income and gains; then against those of the previous 12 months. In this case, however, the previous 12 months is the period 1.4.03 to 31.3.04.

This period includes nine months of the accounting period ended 31.12.03 (i.e. 1.4.03 to 31.12.03) and the 3 months from 1.1.04 to 31.3.04.

Finally if any surplus loss still remains it should be carried forward to accounting period ended 31.03.06.

	Year ended 31.12.03	3 months to 31.3.04	Year ended 31.12.05
Trading profit	50,000	150,000	nil
Less:			
Section 393(1)	nil	nil	nil

Chargeable gains	50,000	40,000	30,000
Net interest income	25,000	15,000	40,000
Total profit	125,000	205,000	70,000
Less:			
Section 393(A)(1)(a)			(70,000)
Section 393(A)(1)(b)	(93,750)	(205,000)	
Less:			
Charges on income	(12,000)	(3,000)	(15,000)
PCTCT	19,250	nil	nil

Notes

1. Trading loss of 750,000 was first used against "total profit" of 70,000 leaving 680,000. This surplus was then carried back and offset against "total profit" of 205,000. However, the 680,000 can under section 393(A)(1)(b) be carried back 12 months. 205,000 of it has been carried back only three months.

2. The balance (i.e. 680,000 less 205,000) can still be carried back a further nine months covering the period 1.4.03 to 31.12.03. The profits available for offset thus are for this nine months i.e. 9/12 x 125,000 = 93,750.

3. Of the trading loss of 750,000 some 368,750 has been used leaving for future carry forward under section 393(1) 381,250.

4. The charges on income for the accounting periods ended 31.3.04 and 31.3.05 are unrelieved. They cannot be carried back or forward for relief. However, they can be group relieved (see Chapter 18).

Terminal losses

Where a company ceases to trade terminal losses may arise.

A terminal loss is a trading loss for the last 12 months of trading.

Unlike other trading losses a terminal loss may be carried back (under section 393(A)) to the three previous years and offset against income and gains (before charges on income).

Example 17.5

JS Ltd has the following results:

	Year ended 31.12.03	Year ended 31.12.04	3 months to 31.3.05
Trading profit	50,000	50,000	(300,000)
Chargeable gains	50,000	40,000	30,000
Net interest income	25,000	15,000	40,000
Charges on income	12,000	3,000	15,000

JS Ltd ceased to trade on 31st March 2005.

Show how the loss may be used.

Answer

	Year ended 31.12.03	Year ended 31.12.04	3 months to 31.3.05
Trading profit	50,000	50,000	nil
Less:			
Section 393(1)	nil	nil	nil
Chargeable gains	50,000	40,000	30,000
Net interest income	25,000	15,000	40,000
Total profit	125,000	105,000	70,000
Less:			
Section 393(A)(1)(a)			(70,000)
Section 393(A)(1)(b)	(125,000)	(105,000)	
Less:			
Charges on income	(12,000)	(3,000)	(15,000)
PCTCT	Nil	Nil	Nil

Notes

1. Under section 393(A)(1)(a) 70,000 of the trading loss for the three months ended 31.3.05 has been offset. In addition, under section 393(A)(1)(b) a further 105,000 of the trading loss has been used.

   Thus, only 125,000 of the trading loss remains unrelieved.

2. The terminal loss is for the last 12 months (i.e. 1.4.04 to 31.3.05) and is the aggregate of the trading losses for the periods 1.4.04 to 31.12.04 and 1.1.05 to 31.3.05 after the trading losses for these periods have been relieved.

3. For the period 1.4.04 to 31.12.04 a trading profit not a trading loss arose. For the purpose of calculating the terminal loss this is ignored (see Chapter 8). Hence the terminal loss is simply the 300,000 trading loss which arose in the period 1.1.05 to 31.3.05 less losses already relieved of 175,000 giving a terminal loss of 125,000.

4. The 125,000 can now be carried back three years prior to the period of loss.

SUMMARY

Trading losses are relievable by carrying forward against future trading profits. Alternatively, more immediate relief may be available by offsetting such losses against income and gains of the accounting period of the loss and possibly by carry back for 12 months for offset against the income and gains of this 12 month period.

Where a company ceases to trade a terminal trading loss may arise which can be carried back for three years rather than the one year which normally applies.

CHAPTER 18

Groups of companies

INTRODUCTION

Chapters 16 and 17 examined the corporation tax position of a single company.

This chapter will look at the position where there is more than one company and together the companies form what is called a *group* for corporation tax purposes. As will be seen there are a number of advantages for group companies.

Where a group exists four key issues arise:

- the limits for UK corporation tax purposes (see Chapter 16) used to determine the rate of corporation tax applicable to the PCTCT of a company are adjusted where the company concerned is a member of a group of companies
- the trading losses of one group company can be transferred and used by other companies in the same group (referred to as group relief)
- the chargeable assets of one group company can be transferred to another company in the same group without precipitating an immediate chargeable gain/loss
- chargeable gains roll-over and hold-over reliefs are available amongst group companies

Definition of group

There is not one single definition of a group for corporation tax purposes. The definition depends upon whether the objective is to ascertain whether group relief is available or whether tax free intra-group asset transfers is possible.

Group relief

The term group relief is the term which refers to the ability of one company in a group (referred to as the *surrendering* company) to give or surrender a trading loss to another company in the same group (referred to as the *claimant* company).

In addition to group relieving trading losses, a company can also surrender unrelieved charges on income and unrelieved property business losses of an accounting period to another group company.

For group relief (see below) purposes two companies are members of the same group if one of the companies is a 75% subsidiary of the other *or* both companies are 75% subsidiaries of a third company.

A company is a *75% subsidiary* of another company if:

- 75% or more of its ordinary share capital is owned directly or indirectly by the other company; *and*
- the other company is entitled to at least 75% or more of its profits available for distribution to ordinary shareholders; *and*
- the other company is entitled to at least 75% of the assets in the event of a winding up of the company

---

Example 18.1

A Ltd

75%

B Ltd

75%

C Ltd

B Ltd is a direct 75% subsidiary of A Ltd. Therefore A Ltd and B Ltd *are* in the same group.

C Ltd is a direct 75% subsidiary of B Ltd. Therefore B Ltd and C Ltd *are* in the same group.

What about A and C?

Is C a 75% direct or indirect subsidiary of A? A's indirect shareholding interest in C is 75% x 75% = 56.25%. Therefore C is not either a direct or indirect 75% subsidiary of A and therefore A and C are *not* in the same group.

Thus there are in effect two separate groups for group relief i.e. A and B; and B and C. Thus, A and B can surrender losses to each other and so can B and C. However, C cannot surrender its loss to B which in turn then surrenders it to A.

A, B and C are, however, all associated (see Chapter 16) i.e. there are three associated companies.

Note

For *group* purposes it is necessary to multiply percentage share ownerships to ascertain whether one company is an indirect subsidiary of another (e.g. A and C above). However, to work out if companies are *associated*, shareholding percentages are never multiplied; in this case the issue is whether one company controls another company (see Chapter 16).

Example 18.2

A Ltd

75%　　75%

B Ltd　　　　　　　C Ltd

A and B are in the same group.
A and C are in the same group.

In addition, as B and C are both 75% subsidiaries of the same third company (i.e. A) then B and C are also in the same group (see group definition above).

Therefore A, B and C are all in the same group.

A, B and C are also all associated companies.

Example 18.3

A Ltd

75% 60% 75%

B Ltd　　　　　C Ltd　　　　　D Ltd

A and B are in the same group.
A and D are in the same group.
B and D are in the same group as both are 75% subsidiaries of A.

Therefore A, B and D are in the same group.

A and C are *not* in the same group (C is *not* a 75% subsidiary of A).
B and C are *not* in the same group (as both are not 75% subsidiaries of the same company).
C and D are *not* in the same group (as both are not 75% subsidiaries of the same company).
C is simply not part of any group as it is not a 75% subsidiary of any company.

Notes
1. A, B, C and D *are* all associated for associated companies purposes (because A controls B, C and D i.e. owns more than 50% of each of the companies' shares). Thus, C may not be in a group due to the lack of at least a 75% shareholding but it is still controlled by A and therefore is associated. In working out the corporate tax liabilities of each company therefore the profit limits would need to be divided by four (as there are four associated companies in total).

> 2. "A" may choose to surrender its trading loss to "B" in the same group rather than use the loss itself because, for example, A may have no other profits against which it can offset the trading loss or, alternatively, more corporation tax might be saved by B rather than A using the trading loss.

Group relief may be used without the company with the trading loss first using the loss itself (e.g. under section 393(A)). The option chosen will depend upon where the greatest tax saving can be made.

Current trading loss surrender only

The trading loss (or surplus charges on income or property business loss) to be surrendered must be that of a current accounting period (e.g. trading losses carried forward or carried back cannot *then* be surrendered).

The surrendering company can surrender its trading loss for an accounting period either in whole or in part and does not first need to try and use the trading loss itself (note, however, that in the case of surplus charges and property business losses the surrendering company must have first tried to itself obtain relief for these two items before they can be surrendered).

The trading loss surrendered may be surrendered simply to one other group company or may be split amongst any number of group companies. As will be seen below there is an approach to loss surrender which ensures maximum relief for the group as a whole.

Use by claimant company of trading loss

The claimant company can offset the trading loss against its own PCTCT (i.e. after charges on income).

This therefore means that before the claimant company can use the trading loss claimed from another group company it must have:

> offset any of its own trading loss carry forward against trading profits (section 393(1)); any current year trading loss against profit before charges on income (section 393(A)(1)(a); but not section 393(A)(1)(b)); and deducted any charges on income of the current accounting period.

Group relief is, however, utilised before deductions of any reliefs from a *subsequent* accounting period (e.g. trading loss carried back; section 393(A)(1)(b)).

A claimant company cannot claim an amount of trading loss from a surrendering company which exceeds its own PCTCT against which the trading loss is to be offset. In other words the claimant company can group relief the *lower* of its own PCTCT and the loss available for group relieving.

Example 18.4

A Ltd has a 100% wholly owned subsidiary B Ltd. Both companies prepare their accounts to 31st March each year.

For the year ended 31st March 2006 A Ltd has a trading loss of £250,000 and no other profits.

B Ltd has a trading profit of £90,000; interest income of £25,000; property business income of £45,000; and chargeable gains of £60,000; and makes a Gift Aid payment of £30,000. B Ltd also has a trading loss carried forward from an earlier accounting period of £25,000 and FII of £15,000.

Show how A Ltd might use its trading loss under the group relief provisions.

Answer

Adopting the pro-forma from Chapter 16 for B Ltd (the claimant company) for the accounting period 1.4.05 to 31.3.06:

Property business profit		45,000
Trading profit	90,000	
Less: Trading loss b/f	(25,000)	
		65,000
Interest income		25,000
Chargeable Gains		60,000
Total profits		195,000
Less: Charges on income (gross)		(30,000)
Profits chargeable to corporation tax –		
PCTCT		165,000
Less:		
Group relief		(165,000)
Revised PCTCT		Nil

Notes

1. Note where the additional lines have been entered in the original corporate tax pro-forma i.e. insert the trading loss brought forward under the trading profit; and insert group relief once PCTCT (pre group relief) has been ascertained.

2. Only 165,000 of A Ltd's trading loss of 250,000 could be surrendered by A Ltd to B Ltd as B Ltd only had PCTCT of 165,000.

3. The balance of the trading loss of (250,000 - 165,000) i.e. 85,000 can either be carried forward by A Ltd for offset against future trading profits (but cannot then be surrendered as group relief) or offset against its current year and prior year's profits (before charges on income).

Corresponding accounting periods

As indicated above a trading loss of an accounting period can be offset against the PCTCT of another group company. However, for the whole of the trading loss to be potentially available for surrender and offset against the other group company's PCTCT for an accounting period both companies accounting periods must coincide exactly (said to be coterminous accounting periods).

In Example 14.4 this occurred as both companies accounting periods ended on 31st March each year.

Where the companies involved in the group relief claim do not have coterminous accounting periods (i.e. their respective accounting periods end on different dates) then any trading loss surrendered may only be used by the claimant company against its PCTCT for the *corresponding accounting period* i.e. that part of the accounting period of the claimant company which falls in the accounting period of the surrendering company's accounting period.

In fact, both the trading losses surrendered and the corresponding PCTCT are time apportioned.

Example 18.5

JS Ltd makes a trading loss of £24,000 for its year ended 30th June 2005.

AB Ltd has PCTCT of £36,000 and £20,000 for its years ended 30 September 2004 and 2005 respectively.

How can the group relief provisions be used assuming both companies are in the same group?

Answer

JS Ltd and AB Ltd do not have coterminous accounting periods. Some apportionment is therefore necessary.

JS Ltd			1.7.04	(24,000)	30.6.05	
AB Ltd	*1.10.03*	36,000	*30.9.04*	20,000		*30.9.05*

AB Ltd year ended 30th September 2004

Only the period 1.7.04 to 30.9.04 falls within JS Ltd's accounting period ended 30th June 2005.

Therefore AB Ltd can potentially claim JS Ltd trading loss attributable to 1.7.04 to 30.9.04

i.e. 3/12 x (24,000) = (6,000) for offset against its PCTCT for this corresponding period

---

i.e. AB Ltd's PCTCT for this period is 3/12 x £36,000 = 9,000

As AB Ltd's PCTCT for this corresponding period exceeds the available trading loss of JS Ltd the whole £6,000 loss may be claimed by AB Ltd.

AB Ltd year ended 30th September 2005
AB Ltd can also potentially claim JS Ltd's trading loss attributable to 1.10.04 to 30.6.05
i.e. 9/12 x (24,000) = (18,000)
AB Ltd's PCTCT for this period is 9/12 x £20,000 = 15,000.

In this case AB Ltd's PCTCT is smaller than the trading loss of JS Ltd available for relief.

Thus for its accounting period ended 30.9.05 AB Ltd can only claim the lower of the trading loss potentially available i.e. £18,000 and its PCTCT for the corresponding period i.e. £15,000. Thus the loss claimed is restricted to £15,000.

In total therefore of JS Ltd's trading loss for the accounting period ended 30.6.05 of £24,000 some £6,000 + £15,000 = £21,000 can be group relieved as shown above.

The balance of the trading loss of £3,000 which cannot be group relieved is available for use by JS Ltd against its current and prior year's profits and/or later trading profits under sections 393(A) and 393(1) respectively.

Optimum use of group relief
Where a group comprises more than two companies and one company incurs a trading loss then the question arises as to how that loss should be group relieved. In other words, against which of the other companies' PCTCT in the group should the loss be surrendered.

The answer is that the loss should be surrendered initially to the group company whose marginal rate of corporation tax is the highest.

More precisely, a sufficient amount of the loss should be surrendered to the company subject to the highest marginal rate of corporation tax such that after the relief for the loss its (i.e. the claimant's) PCTCT is subject to a marginal rate of corporation tax which is smaller than that of other group companies.

Any trading loss still not group relieved should then be claimed by the company in the group subject to the next highest marginal rate of corporation tax etc.

CORPORATION TAX

Marginal rates of corporation tax

The marginal rate of corporation tax is the rate of corporation tax applicable to the highest part of a company's Profit. It means that for each extra £ of Profit the rate of corporation tax is the marginal rate.

Chapter 16 highlighted the nominal rates of corporation tax, namely, 0%, 19% and 30%. These are the rates which should be used to calculate a company's corporation tax liability.

However, for group relief determinations only *marginal* rates of corporation tax are to be used.

These rates for Financial year 2005 (and 2004) are as follows:

Profit	$\leq$	£10,000	0%
Profit	>	£10,000 and <£50,000	23.75%
Profit	$\geq$	£50,000 and $\leq$ £300,000	19%
Profit	>	£300,000 and < £ 1.5 million	32.75%
Profit	$\geq$	£1.5 million	30%

For interest only set out below is how these marginal rates are computed:

	Marginal small companies			*Marginal starting rate companies*		
	Limits	*Rate*	*Tax*	*Limits*	*Rate*	*Tax*
U	1,500,000 ×	30% =	450,000	50,000 ×	19% =	9,500
L	300,000 ×	19% =	57,000	10,000 ×	0% =	0
	1,200,000		393,000	40,000		9,500

Marginal rate on profits between limits:
393,000/1,200,000 = 32.75%   9,500/40,000 = 23.75%

Note: The calculation of the marginal rates of tax is not affected by the number of associated companies.

For examination purposes never use marginal rates of corporation tax to compute a company's corporation tax liability. Always use the method set down in Chapter 16. Marginal rates are only ever used in determining the optimum allocation of group relief and for no other purpose.

Group relief procedure

In allocating a trading loss available for group relief to other group companies requires the following steps:

first, identify the company whose marginal rate of corporation tax is 32.75% (i.e. the highest)

second, surrender to such company only so much of the trading loss that reduces the company's Profit to exactly £300,000 (because, below this figure the rate of marginal corporation tax is only 19%)

third, identify the company whose marginal rate of corporation tax is 30% (i.e. the next highest)

fourth, surrender to such company only so much of the trading loss that reduces the company's Profit to exactly £300,000 (because, below this figure the rate of marginal corporation tax is only 19%)

fifth, identify the company whose marginal rate of corporation tax is 23.75% (i.e. the next highest)

sixth, surrender to such company only so much of the trading loss that reduces the company's Profit to exactly £10,000 (because, below this figure the rate of marginal corporation tax is 0%)

seventh, identify the company whose marginal rate of corporation tax is 19% (i.e. the next highest)

eighth, surrender to such company only so much of the trading loss that reduces the company's Profit to exactly £10,000 (because, below this figure the rate of marginal corporation tax is 0%)

It needs to be noted, however, that where a group exists there will inevitably be two or more associated companies. It will be recalled from Chapter 16 that the number of associated companies affects the limits for determining the rates of corporation tax which apply. Thus, the above limits of £10,000 etc will need to be adjusted first before the marginal rates of corporation tax will be known for each group company.

Nevertheless the rates of marginal tax remain the same irrespective of the adjustments to the limits by however many associated companies there may be.

Example 18.6

For the accounting period ended 31st March 2006 the following group companies had PCTCT as shown below:

J Ltd	(£90,000)
K Ltd	£20,000
L Ltd	£85,000
M ltd	£96,000
N Ltd	£325,000

In addition, K, L, M, and N each received FII of £5,000 for the accounting period ended 31st March 2006 whereas J received FII of £1,500 for this period. Show how the group relief provisions would work.

Answer

The five companies are associated companies.

Therefore the first calculation is to revise the limits for corporation tax purposes by dividing each of them by 5 (see Chapter 16):

£10,000	limit becomes	£2,000
£50,000	limit becomes	£10,000
£300,000	limit becomes	£60,000
£1.5 million	limit becomes	£300,000

Marginal rates of corporation tax are therefore:

0%	Profit up to	£2,000		
23.75%	Profit between	£2,000	and	£10,000
19%	Profit between	£10,000	and	£60,000
32.75%	Profit between	£60,000	and	£300,000
30%	Profit above	£300,000		

	J	K	L	M	N
PCTCT	nil	20,000	85,000	96,000	325,000
FII	1,500	5,000	5,000	5,000	5,000
PROFIT	1,500	25,000	90,000	101,000	330,000
Marginal rates of corporation tax	0%	19%	32.75%	32.75%	30%
Trading loss surrendered	nil	nil	(30,000)	(41,000)	(19,000)
Revised Profit	1,500	25,000	60,000	60,000	311,000
Revised PCTCT (i.e. PCTCT – Loss)	nil	20,000	55,000	55,000	306,000

Corporation tax liability

0%	nil				
19%			3,800	10,450	10,450
30%					91,800

Notes

1. Trading loss is *first* surrendered to any company subject to a marginal rate of corporation tax of 32.75% (i.e. the highest marginal rate). Thus, a part (i.e. 30,000) of the 90,000 trading loss has been surrendered to company L and a part (i.e. 41,000) to company M.

2. The amount of loss surrendered to each company is just enough to bring the marginal rate for each company down to 19%. Thus, sufficient loss has been surrendered to reduce Profit of each company to 60,000 (remember there are five associated companies). As each company is subject to a marginal rate of 32.75% it does not matter to which company L or M a group loss is first surrendered.

3. After surrendering trading losses of 30,000 to L and 41,000 to M this leaves 90,000 – (30,000 + 41,000) = 19,000.

4. Trading loss is *second* surrendered to company subject to next highest marginal rate of corporation tax i.e. N which is subject to a 30% marginal rate. The whole of the 19,000 is then surrendered to N as N's Profit still is higher than the 300,000 Profit limit and thus even after this group relief is still liable at the 30% marginal rate of tax.

Example 18.7

A, B and C are three UK resident companies that form a 75% group for loss relief purposes. All companies prepare accounts to 31st March annually.

The results for the year ended 31st March 2006 for each company are as follows:

	A	B	C
Trading profit	200,000	(250,000)	80,000
Property business profit	5,000	15,000	20,000
Interest income	20,000	nil	10,000
Chargeable gains	20,000	3,000	2,000
Gift aid paid	(5,000)	(2,000)	(15,000)

Company A has an unrelieved trading loss b/f at 1st April 2005 of £60,000.

Show how the losses may be used.

Answer

	A	B	C
Trading profit	200,000	nil	80,000
Less:			
Section 393(1) relief	(60,000)	nil	nil
Property business profit	5,000	15,000	20,000
Interest income	20,000	nil	10,000
Chargeable gain	20,000	3,000	2,000
Less:			
Section 393(A)(1)(a)	nil	nil	nil
Less: Charges on income	(5,000)	2,000)	(15,000)
PCTCT	180,000	16,000	97,000
Profit	180,000	16,000	97,000
Group relief			
Unrelieved charges on income			

Notes

1. Until the marginal rates of tax are known for each company it is not possible to decide how to use B's trading loss of 250,000.

2. The first stage involves inserting all figures into the pro-forma but ignoring any losses at this stage. Also do *not* add up the columns to get the PCTCT and PROFIT figures.

3. A's carry forward trading loss can only be used by A against its own trading profits. This figure of 60,000 can thus be inserted (on the section 393(1) line) as there is no choice as to how it may be used.

4. At this stage nothing should be inserted in the section 393(A)(1)(a) line as it cannot be known at this stage whether it would make sense for B to use some of its 250,000 trading loss itself rather than surrendering it.

5. The PCTCT and PROFIT figures can now be worked out by adding the columns.

6. Remember there are three associated companies and therefore the limits for corporation tax become 3,333; 16,667; 100,000 and 500,000.

7. PCTCT equals Profit in this case as there is no FII. The respective rates of marginal tax for A, B and C are 32.75%, 23.75% and 19% (note that the Profit limits have been divided by three as there are three associated companies).

8. Thus, of B's loss of £250,000 some £80,000 should be surrendered to A reducing A's Profit to £100,000 which is then taxed at 19%.

9. Of the balance of the loss of £170,000 some £12,667 should be used by B (marginal rate 23.75%) under section 393(A)(1)(a) against its own income and gains to reduce its Profit to £3,333 which is then taxed at 0%.

10. Of the balance of £157,333 some £93,667 should be group relieved to C (marginal rate 19%) reducing C's Profit to £3,333 which is then taxed at 0%.

11. Both B and C are now taxed at 0%. However, A is still subject to 19% tax on its post group relief Profit of 100,000. Therefore it makes sense for B to surrender all its remaining unused loss of £157,333 less £93,667 i.e. £63,666 to A reducing A's Profit even further to £100,000 less £63,666 i.e. £36,334.

12. The final result is therefore a PCTCT of £3,333 for B; a PCTCT of £3,333 for C; and a PCTCT of £36,334 for A. Remember PROFIT and PCTCT are the same in this example as there is no FII.

As was illustrated in the above example in some cases it may be appropriate for the company incurring the trading loss to use some of it itself under section 393(A)(1)(a) rather than surrendering it to other group companies.

Thus, B in the above example used some £12,667 (see Note 9) of its own trading loss after it had surrendered £80,000 to A (see Note 8) as its own marginal rate of corporation tax was 23.75% and thus higher than C's which was only 19%.

Chargeable gains group

For chargeable gains relief to apply a group is defined differently to that which applies for group relief.

For this purpose a chargeable gains group is one with a principal (or top) company plus its 75% subsidiaries plus the subsidiaries' 75% subsidiaries and so on subject to the principal company itself also possessing at least a 51% interest in each company.

Example 18.8

Using the structure of Example 18.1:

A Ltd

75%

B Ltd

75%

C Ltd

A is the principal or top company.

B is a direct 75% subsidiary of A. Therefore A and B *are* in the same group.

C is a direct 75% subsidiary of B. Therefore B and C and indeed A *are* all in the same group if in addition A possesses a greater than 50% shareholding in C. In fact A's shareholding in C is 75% x 75% = 56.25%.

A, B and C therefore form a chargeable gains group even though they do not form a group for group relief purposes (see Example 18.1).

A, B and C are also associated (see Chapter 16) i.e. there are three associated companies.

It should therefore be noted that a group for group relief purposes may be a different group than one for chargeable gains purposes as shown in the above example.

However, the groups may also be the same (see below).

Example 18.9

Using the structure of Example 18.2:

A Ltd

75%   75%

B Ltd   C Ltd

A is the principal or top company.

B and C are 75% subsidiaries of A and therefore A, B and C are in a chargeable gains group and are also in the same group for group relief purposes.

A, B and C are also associated companies.

Example 18.10

A Ltd

75%   75%

B Ltd   C Ltd

60%   75%

D Ltd   E Ltd

A is the principal company.

B and C are 75% subsidiaries of A and therefore A, B and C form a chargeable gains group.

D is not a 75% subsidiary of B. Therefore D is not a part of a chargeable gains group.

E is a 75% subsidiary of C. In addition A indirectly holds 75% x 75% = 56.25% of E. Therefore, E is also a part of the A, B and C chargeable gains group.

For group relief purposes the group comprises A, B and C, and C and E.

Relevance of chargeable gains group
The existence of a chargeable gains group allows two forms of relief to apply:
- assets may be transferred inter-group without gains or losses arising
- roll-over relief may apply as if all the group companies were a single company

Intra group chargeable gains relief
Chargeable gains relief refers to the ability of a chargeable gains group of companies to transfer chargeable assets amongst themselves at no gain and no loss thus avoiding a corporate tax liability on the transfers. The asset is thus deemed to have been transferred at original cost plus indexation allowance to the date of the inter-group transfer.

As and when the chargeable asset is eventually sold outside the group a gain or loss will arise at that time and then be subject to corporation tax.

The advantage of this facility is that it enables the capital gains of one group company to be offset against the capital losses of another group company. This is achieved by the transfer of the asset from the one company to the other prior to sale to a third party so that the same company makes the gain and the loss.

As to which company should make the transfer i.e. the company about to make the loss or the company about to make the gain) will depend upon the marginal rates of corporation tax each company is paying (as above for group relief).

Note, however, that any capital losses carried forward within a company must remain within that company. Thus if one company is about to sell an asset at a gain then the asset on which the gain arises must be transferred to the company with the capital loss carried forward if these losses are to be used.

Example 18.11

JS Ltd acquired a chargeable asset in January 1992 for £100,000. It transferred it to ABC Ltd a chargeable gains group company in January 2002 when its market value was £175,000. ABC Ltd subsequently sold the asset outside the group in May 2005 for £300,000. Both companies prepare their accounts to 31st March each year.

The indexation allowances for Jan 1992 to Jan 2002 and Jan 2002 to May 2005 are £31,400 and £11,169 respectively.

Show the position for both companies.

Answer

Transfer on January 2002

JS Ltd is deemed to have transferred the asset to ABC Ltd at no gain and no loss i.e. at its original cost to JS Ltd plus indexation to Jan 2002:
Asset transferred at £100,000 + £31,400 = £131,400

Thus base cost of asset to ABC Ltd =	£131,400

Sale on May 2005

Sale proceeds	300,000
Less:	
Cost	(131,400)
	168,600
Less:	
Indexation	(11,169)
(Jan 2002 to May 2005)	
Indexed gain	157,431

> **Note**
>
> The market value of the asset at the date of the inter-group transfer (i.e. £175,000) is irrelevant.

Notional intra group transfers

It has been assumed above that in order for one chargeable gains group company to offset for example its own gains against the capital losses of another group company requires that an actual transfer of an asset from one company to another occurs.

However, effective 1st April 2003 instead of an actual transfer of the relevant asset from one company to the other the two relevant companies can simply elect that such a transfer has been deemed to have occurred. The capital losses and capital gains can then be offset as set out above.

This election therefore does not affect any of the above discussion but merely enables in practice companies to avoid all the legal hassles associated with having to effect actual transfers of legal title of the assets.

Intra group chargeable gains roll-over relief

On the sale of certain business assets (i.e. land and buildings and fixed plant and machinery) *and* subject to satisfying certain conditions (i.e. reinvestment of the sale proceeds from the sale of the old asset in another new business asset must occur within one year before and three years after the sale of the old asset) a company may claim roll-over relief on the gain on the sale of the old asset (see Chapter 14 for equivalent relief for sole traders).

Roll-over relief applies by allowing the company to reduce the base cost of the new asset by the indexed gain on the sale of the old asset.

However, where a chargeable gains group exists it is also possible for the indexed gain on the sale of a business asset by one company to be rolled-over against the acquisition cost of a business asset by another group company subject to satisfying the above conditions.

> **Example 18.12**
>
> JS Ltd sells a factory in January 2005 for £250,000 which had cost it £75,000 in March 1992. In March 2005 ABC Ltd a chargeable gains group company purchased another factory for £350,000.
>
> Assume the indexation allowance for March 1992 to Jan 2005 is £29,475
>
> What is the position for each of the two companies?

Answer

JS Ltd

Sale proceeds	250,000
Less:	
Cost	(75,000)
	175,000
Less:	
Indexation allowance	(29,475)
Indexed gain	145,525

ABC Ltd

The base cost of the asset acquired by ABC Ltd is £350,000 - £145,525 = £204,475.

Where the equivalent amount of the sale proceeds received by one company on the sale of a business asset are not reinvested by another chargeable gains group company only a partial roll-over of the gain occurs and a balancing chargeable gain immediately occurs.

Example 18.13

If in Example 18.12 above ABC Ltd had bought a business asset for £225,000 then the position for each company would be as follows:

JS Ltd

Indexed gain (as above)	145,525
Less:	
Excess of sale proceeds over reinvestment (250,000 – 225,000)	(25,000)
Gain eligible for roll-over	120,525
Gain immediately chargeable on JS Ltd	25,000

(this gain will be subject to corporation tax in the accounting period in which the sale by JS Ltd occurred).

ABC Ltd

The base cost of the asset acquired by ABC Ltd is
£350,000 - £120,525 = £229,475

Intangible assets

For companies (not for individuals; see Chapter 14) intangible assets (e.g. goodwill) acquired on or after 1st April 2002 are no longer part of the capital gains regime.

Thus, the above roll-over rules for companies do not apply to such assets.

Intangible assets are, effective 1st April 2002, treated as part of a company's trading profit and the roll-over relief operates within the computation of trading profit.

For companies therefore the above rules only apply to the purchase and sale of:

- land and buildings
- fixed plant and machinery

SUMMARY

Groups of companies may be entitled to various forms of relief:

- group relief
- chargeable gains/loss relief
- chargeable gains business asset roll-over relief

The definition as to what constitutes a group differs according to the relief under consideration.

Whenever a group of any description exists a number of associated companies will occur. Thus, the limits used to determine the rate of corporation tax will need to be adjusted accordingly.

CHAPTER 19

Overseas Tax for Companies

INTRODUCTION

This chapter will look at the tax position where a UK resident company receives income from overseas i.e. outside the UK. The main category of overseas income examined is foreign source dividend income.

In addition, other aspects of the UK tax system which impact on overseas income will also be briefly examined.

Determination of UK residence

A UK resident company is liable to corporation tax on its worldwide profits whether those profits are remitted to the UK or not. There are two tests to determine whether a company is UK resident. Thus, a company is resident in the UK if:

- it is incorporated in the UK; *or*
- its central management and control is exercised from within the UK (a company's central management and control may said to reside where its board of directors meet and take strategic decisions concerning the company's affairs).

Foreign profits

The foreign profits of a UK resident company will include items equivalent to those which may arise from within the UK such as trading profits, investment income and capital gains.

However, it is highly likely that such overseas income will have been subject to some form of overseas taxes. When computing the quantum of foreign income to include in the corporation tax computation all such income must be included gross i.e. the foreign income must be included before any foreign taxes.

Double taxation

As may be observed, foreign income may thus be subject to tax twice i.e. once in the foreign country in which it arises and again in the UK. This issue is referred to as double taxation.

Double taxation in the UK may be relieved in one of two ways:

- under the UK's domestic law under the so-called unilateral tax provisions; *or*
- under the relevant double taxation agreement

Whilst there may be subtle differences between the two forms of relief the basic approach under each is that the form of double tax relief should be by way of a tax credit. In simple terms, for every £1 of foreign tax paid the UK corporation tax liability thereon should be reduced by £1.

Tax credit relief

Whilst the principle of the credit relief mechanism is as stated above the rules are a little more complicated.

In particular:

- double tax relief is computed on a source by source basis
- the tax credit available is in fact the lower of the foreign tax paid on the income and the UK corporation tax thereon
- double tax relief is available for underlying tax in certain cases

Taking each in turn:

Source by source basis

All sources of foreign income (e.g. foreign rents; trading profits; dividends; etc.) are not simply aggregated when working out the UK corporation tax liability.

In calculating the extent of any foreign tax credits which may be available for offset against the UK corporation tax charge each source of foreign income must be considered separately. Thus, the UK corporation tax charge on each source is computed and any foreign tax paid on that particular foreign source is then offset against that UK corporation tax liability.

This approach is repeated for each foreign source.

Lower of UK and foreign tax

Following on from the above, the foreign tax which may be offset against the UK corporation tax liability on that particular source must be the lower of the two amounts. In other words the foreign tax credit will always be the lower of the foreign tax actually paid on that source of income and the UK corporation tax liability thereon.

In some cases there will be a net UK corporation tax liability and in others no net UK corporation tax charge will arise (because the foreign tax will have been greater). Where the foreign tax exceeds the UK corporation tax on that income relief for the excess is possible by way of carry back and/or carry forward.

This excess is referred to as surplus foreign tax credits.

Underlying tax relief

Underlying tax refers to the foreign tax which a foreign company has paid on its own profits (broadly the overseas country's equivalent of UK corporation tax).

Underlying tax relief only applies where a UK resident company receives foreign dividend income from a foreign company in which it possesses at least 10% of the voting power.

A less than 10% holding means that no double tax relief will be available for any underlying tax which may have been paid; only dividend withholding tax will be creditable.

The amount of underlying tax which may be available for double tax relief is determined by the following formula:

$$\frac{\text{Gross dividend}}{\text{Profits available for distribution}} \quad x \quad \text{Foreign tax paid on profits}$$

- *Foreign tax paid* is the actual foreign tax paid on profits *not* the amount which may be shown in the accounts (e.g. by way of a provision)
- *Gross dividend* is the net dividend received in UK + any dividend withholding tax
- *Profits available for distribution* is the amount shown in the financial statements as the profit after tax or net profit

The reference above to *dividend withholding tax* is a reference to foreign tax which is often levied when dividends are paid to an overseas recipient (e.g. a UK resident company). Thus, when a foreign company pays such a dividend then before the dividend arrives in the UK an amount of foreign tax is deducted from it; this amount deducted is referred to as a dividend withholding tax and is usually in the 5% to 20% range.

The UK corporation tax which is attributable to any foreign source dividend income is calculated using the *average rate* of corporation tax on PCTCT i.e.

$$\frac{\text{Corporation tax liability on PCTCT}}{\text{PCTCT}}$$

This average rate will thus vary between 10% and 30% depending on the tax status of the company.

Corporation tax pro-forma

The pro-forma corporation tax computation of a company incorporating overseas profits and double tax relief is as follows:

	£ UK	£ OVERSEAS	£ TOTAL
UK profit (e.g. trading profit)	XX		
Overseas profits (inclusive of overseas taxes)		XX	
Less: Charges on income	(X)		
PCTCT	X	XX	3X
FII			F
PROFIT			3X + F
Tax liability on PCTCT of 3X			T1+T2
Average rate applied to X and XX	(T1)	(T2)	
Less: double tax relief		(Y)	(Y)
Net UK corporation tax payable	T1	(T2-Y)	(T1+T2-Y)

Notes
1. Any overseas income is always included gross (i.e. before deduction for foreign taxes)
2. Charges on income are deducted from UK source income first
3. Any trading losses eligible for relief (e.g. under section 393(1)) should be offset against UK source profits first
4. The *average* corporate tax rate [(T1 + T2)/3X] is applied to each UK and overseas source income to obtain the UK corporate tax charge thereon (i.e. T1 and T2).

Foreign income

Foreign income includes foreign rental income and foreign dividends (and under certain circumstances foreign trading income).

Income from foreign investments (e.g. interest on foreign securities) is taxed as part of the loan relationship rules.

Foreign dividend income is *not* FII (FII only refers to UK source dividends; other than group dividends).

As indicated above any charges on income and/or trading losses available for relief are to be offset:
- *first*, against UK source income
- *second*, against the foreign source income taxed overseas at the lowest tax rate;

- *third*, against the foreign source income taxed at the next lowest tax rate; etc

This approach will maximize the amount of double tax relief (see Example 19.5 below).

Example 19.1

JS Ltd a UK resident company has UK trading profits of £1.75 million for the accounting period ended 31st March 2006.

The company receives a dividend from its wholly owned overseas subsidiary, ABC Ltd.

ABC Ltd paid foreign tax of £62,500 on its pre-tax profits of £250,000 and a net dividend of £45,000 was received in the UK after a 10% dividend withholding tax was levied.

Calculate JS Ltd's corporate tax liability for the accounting period ended 31st March 2006.

Answer

First step is to compute the foreign income chargeable to UK corporation tax. This comprises the gross overseas dividend computed as follows:

Net dividend received	45,000
Plus	
Dividend withholding tax (10%)	5,000
Gross dividend	50,000
Plus	
Underlying tax:	
[62,500 x 50,000]	16,667
187,500	
Foreign dividend income	66,667

Therefore UK corporation tax liability:

	UK	OVERSEAS	TOTAL
UK trading profit	1,750,000		
Foreign income (dividends)		66,667	
PCTCT	1,750,000	66,667	1,816,667
PROFIT			1,816,667

Based on PROFIT of 1,816,667 rate of corporation tax is 30%.

UK corporation tax (30%)	525,000	20,000

Less:

Double tax relief i.e. *lower* of:

Foreign tax (5,000 + 16,667) = 21,667

UK tax on foreign income = 20,000   (20,000)

NET UK Corporation Tax   <u>525,000</u>   <u>Nil</u>   <u>525,000</u>

Notes
1. JS Ltd and ABC Ltd are associated companies (see Chapter 16) and therefore in working out the rate of corporation tax the relevant limits must be divided by two. Profit equals 1,816,667 which exceeds the limit of 750,000 (i.e. £1.5 million divided by 2) and thus 30% applies to PCTCT. This is in fact also the average rate of corporation tax which is then applied to each UK and Overseas source separately giving 525,000 and 20,000 (before double tax relief).
2. Underlying tax relief is available because JS Ltd owned more than 10% (in fact 100%) of ABC Ltd.
3. ABC Ltd's *Profit available for distribution* = 250,000 – 62,500 = 187,500
4. In this case some 21,667 - 20,000 = 1,667 of overseas tax paid. This excess can be carried forward or carried back (three years).

Example 19.2
JS Ltd has received a dividend of £428,400 after local withholding tax of 10% in the year ended 31 March 2006 from a foreign company XYZ Ltd in which it has a 40% shareholding.

The details of the foreign company from which the dividend was received are as follows.

	£	£
Profit before tax		1,500,000
Tax charge		
Current provision	270,000	
Deferred tax	25,000	
Under provision – previous year	15,000	
		(310,000)
Profit after tax		1,190,000

The eventual actual foreign corporation tax paid in respect of the period by XYZ Ltd was £500,000.

JS Ltd has UK trading profits of £4,000,000 but no other sources of UK income or gains.

Calculate the corporation tax liability of JS Ltd for the year ended 31 March 2006.

Answer

First step is to compute the foreign income chargeable to UK corporation tax. This comprises the gross overseas dividend.

Net dividend received	428,400
Plus	
Dividend withholding tax (10%)	47,600
Gross dividend	476,000
Plus	
Underlying tax:	
[500,000 x 476,000]	200,000
1,190,000	
Foreign income	676,000

Therefore UK corporation tax liability:

	UK	OVERSEAS	TOTAL
Trading profit	4,000,000		
Foreign income		676,000	
PCTCT	4,000,000	676,000	4,676,000
PROFIT			4,676,000

Based on PROFIT of £4,676,000 rate of corporation tax is 30%.

UK corporation tax (30%)	1,200,000	202,800	1,402,800

Less:
Double tax relief i.e. *lower* of:

Foreign tax (47,600 + 200,000) = 247,600			
UK tax on foreign income = 202,800		(202,800)	(202,800)
NET UK Corporation Tax	1,200,000	Nil	1,200,000

Notes
1. Foreign tax paid by XYZ Ltd on its profits of £500,000 is not the figure provided in the foreign accounts. However, it is tax actually paid which is important in calculating underlying tax relief i.e. it is not possible to get double tax relief for foreign tax which is not actually paid.
2. The excess foreign tax paid is (247,600 – 202,800) which can be carried forward or carried back.

Example 19.3

JS Ltd, a UK resident company, has a 30% interest in a UK resident company. It also owns 7% in a foreign resident company.

For the year ended 31st March 2006 JS Ltd's results are as follows:

	£
Trading profit	110,000
Dividends received from the UK resident company	72,000
Dividends received from non-resident company	60,000
Gift Aid payments	105,000

The foreign dividend received of £60,000 was after a 20% foreign dividend withholding tax had been levied. Tax paid by the foreign company on its profits was £125,000.

JS Ltd had an unrelieved trading loss brought forward at 1st April 2005 of £65,000.

Calculate the corporation tax liability of JS Ltd for the year ended 31st March 2006.

Answer

As JS Ltd does not own at least 10% in the foreign company JS Ltd is not able to obtain double tax relief for any underlying tax.

Double tax relief is therefore only available for any dividend withholding tax.

Thus:

Foreign income = £60,000 + £15,000 = £75,000.

Therefore UK corporation tax liability:

	UK	OVERSEAS	TOTAL
Trading profit	110,000		
Less: Section 393(1) relief	(65,000)		
Revised Trading profit	45,000		
Foreign income		75,000	
Less: Gift aid	(45,000)	(60,000)	
PCTCT	Nil	15,000	15,000
FII			80,000
PROFIT			95,000
UK corporation tax (19%*)	Nil	2,850	2,850
Less:			
Double tax relief i.e. *lower* of:			
Foreign tax (15,000) = 15,000			
UK tax on foreign income = 2,850		(2,850)	(2,850)
NET UK Corporation Tax	Nil	Nil	Nil

* Based on PROFIT of £95,000 rate of corporation tax is 19%.

Notes
1. The Gift aid payment is relieved first against UK source income to the maximum possible and the balance of the unrelieved payment (i.e. 60,000) is then relieved against the overseas source income. This maximises the extent of any double tax relief by leaving into charge to UK corporation tax the maximum amount of foreign source income.
2. No underlying double tax relief is available as JS Ltd owns less than 10% of the overseas company. Only double tax relief for the dividend withholding tax (of £15,000) is available.
3. The offsetting of part of the Gift Aid payment against the foreign source income has meant that a surplus foreign tax credit arises of (15,000 – 2,850).

Example 19.4
JS Ltd receives foreign rental income of £30,000 after foreign tax at the rate of 20% has been applied.

In addition JS Ltd receives a net dividend from an overseas company of £75,000 after a dividend withholding tax of 25% had been applied. JS Ltd's shareholding in the overseas company is 5%.

JS Ltd's trading profit is £300,000.

All figures are in respect of the accounting period ended 31st March 2006.

Calculate JS Ltd's corporation tax liability for the accounting period ended 31st March 2006.

Answer
JS Ltd's shareholding in the overseas company is below 10% and therefore only a tax credit for the dividend withholding tax will be available.

Gross dividend =   75,000 + 25,000 = 100,000
Gross rental income = 30,000 + 7,500 = 37,500
UK corporation tax:

	UK	Overseas	Overseas	TOTAL
UK trading profit	300,000			
Foreign income:				
Dividends		100,000		
Rents			37,500	
PCTCT	300,000	100,000	37,500	437,500
PROFIT				437,500

UK corporation tax (23.32% *)	69,960	23,320	8,745
Less:			
Double tax relief re dividends *lower* of:			
(1) Foreign tax = 25,000			
(2) UK tax on foreign income = 23,320			
		(23,320)	
Double tax re rents *lower* of:			
(1) foreign tax = 7,500			
(2) UK tax on foreign income = 8,745			(7,500)
NET UK Corporation Tax	69,960	Nil	1,245

* Based on PROFIT of £437,500 rate of corporation tax is between 19% and 30%:

UK corporation tax =

$$0.30 \times 437,500 - 11/400 \times [1,500,000 - 437,500] \times 437,500/437,500$$
$$= 131,250 - 29,219$$
$$= 102,031$$

Average rate of corporation tax = 102,031/437,500 = 23.32%

Notes
1. The overseas foreign tax paid on the overseas dividend income is greater than the UK corporate tax thereon and thus no net UK corporate tax is due; this contrasts with the UK tax position on the overseas rental income.
2. Each foreign source of income (i.e. the foreign dividends and foreign rent) must be kept separate when working out the amount of double tax relief for each source. Different sources of foreign source income must not be aggregated for this purpose.
3. Rounding errors account for the different corporation tax figures of 102,031 and 102,025.

Example 19.5
JS Ltd receives foreign rental income of £30,000 after foreign tax at the rate of 20% has been applied.

In addition JS Ltd receives a net dividend from an overseas company of £75,000 after a dividend withholding tax of 25% had been applied. JS Ltd's shareholding in the overseas company is 5%.

JS Ltd trading profit profit is £70,000. All figures are in respect of the accounting period ended 31st March 2006.

JS Ltd has a trading loss brought forward of £30,000 and pays a Gift aid payment of £50,000.

Calculate JS Ltd's corporation tax liability for the accounting period ended 31st March 2006.

Answer
JS Ltd's shareholding in the overseas company is below 10% and therefore only a tax credit for the dividend withholding tax will be available to it.

Gross dividend   = 75,000 + 25,000 = 100,000 (overseas tax rate 25,000/100,000 = 25%)

Gross rental income = 30,000 + 7,500 = 37,500 (overseas tax rate 7,500/37,500 = 20%)

UK corporation tax:

	UK	Overseas	Overseas	TOTAL
Trading profit	70,000			
Less: Section 393(1) relief	(30,000)			
Revised Trading profit	40,000			
Foreign income:				
Dividends		100,000		
Rents			37,500	
Less: Charge on income	(40,000)		(10,000)	
PCTCT	Nil	100,000	27,500	127,500
PROFIT				127,500
UK corporation tax (19%*)	Nil	19,000	5,225	24,225
Less:				
Double tax relief re dividends *lower* of:				
(1) Foreign tax	= 25,000			
(2) UK tax on foreign income	= 19,000			
		(19,000)		(19,000)
Double tax re rents *lower* of:				
1) Foreign tax	= 7,500			
2) UK tax on foreign income	= 5,225			
			(5,225)	(5,225)
NET UK Corporation Tax	Nil	Nil	Nil	Nil

* Based on PROFIT of £127,500 rate of corporation tax is 19% (no associated companies).

Therefore, average rate of corporation tax = 19%

Notes

1. The overseas foreign tax paid on both the overseas dividend and rental income is greater than the UK corporate tax thereon and thus no net UK corporate tax is due.
2. The Gift aid payment should be offset against UK source income first and then against the foreign source income which has been subject to the lowest foreign tax rate which in this case is the rental income.

Overseas branch

A UK resident company may set up a foreign subsidiary and receive foreign dividend income on its shareholding. Such dividends are taxed as set out above (ie grossed-up as appropriate).

Alternatively, the UK company may simply set up an overseas branch operation.

Whereas an overseas subsidiary is a separate entity, an overseas branch remains a part of the UK company. As a consequence, the trading profit of the overseas branch is simply treated as a part of the UK company's trade. Any foreign tax which may be paid on the foreign trading profit will be eligible for double tax credit relief.

Whereas any trading loss of the branch will immediately (i.e. automatically) be relievable against the UK source trading profit any trading loss of the foreign subsidiary cannot be so relieved. The foreign subsidiary's trading loss is locked into the subsidiary and can be used as prescribed under the tax laws of its country of residence (remember a non-UK resident company is not able to be part of a group relief claim; see Chapter 18).

Transfer Pricing

Companies under common control may set inter-company prices and charges at such that overall taxes are minimised. This is particularly likely to be the case where the inter-group transactions are between UK and non-UK resident companies.

It would clearly make sense from a tax perspective to ensure that most profit arises to companies which are resident in low tax as opposed to high tax countries.

However, legislation exists which precludes the above from occurring. In other words the legislation provides that where companies are under common control then any inter-group transactions must be carried out at arm's length. This means that the prices and charges levied must be in line with those that would be levied if the transaction had been with a third party.

In practice, precisely what is an arm's length price or charge may be somewhat difficult to determine.

In view of the difficulties which may arise provision is made in the legislation for companies to enter into what are called Advance Pricing Arrangements ("APA") with the relevant tax authority. Basically, following discussions the arm's length prices and charges will be agreed between taxpayer and tax authority. This, for the company, has the advantage of certainty. The APAs are normally for a fixed period (e.g. three or five years) following which both sides review the position.

In view of the fact that companies like individuals must self-assess (see Chapter 21) it is important that the corporation tax estimated for an accounting period reflect arm's length arrangements if interest and/or penalties are to be avoided.

Controlled foreign companies
(Note: The following section on CFCs is not part of the Paper 2.3 syllabus).

The CFC provisions are anti-avoidance provisions. They are designed to prevent UK resident companies accumulating overseas profits in overseas subsidiaries where such profits are taxed at low or even nil rates of tax.

Definition of CFC
A CFC is one which:
- is resident outside the UK *and*
- is controlled by UK resident persons *and*
- is subject to a low level of taxation in its country of residence

"Control" refers to owning more than 50% of the ordinary share capital.

"Low level of tax" refers to a comparison of the tax the CFC pays in its territory of residence with the UK tax it would have paid if it was UK resident. Where the overseas tax is less than 75% of the UK equivalent tax the CFC is then regarded as subject to a low level of tax.

Example 19.6
XYZ Ltd is resident in the Bahamas and its share capital owned as follows:

UK resident company	40%
UK resident individual	12%
USA resident company	48%

Is XYZ Ltd "controlled" by UK residents?

Answer
As more than 50% of XYZ Ltd's shares are owned by UK residents it *is* controlled from the UK for CFC purposes.

Note that, in applying this test, both individual and company shareholdings are included.

Example 19.7
XYZ Ltd is resident in Ruritania and pays tax in its territory of residence at rate of 25%.

Its local taxable profit is 300.

If XYZ Ltd were UK resident it would pay corporation tax at the 30% rate.

Is XYZ Ltd subject to a low level of tax?

Answer
Overseas tax paid = 25% x 300 = 75

UK equivalent tax = 30% x 300 = 90

As 75 is more than 75% x 90% (i.e. 67.50) XYZ Ltd is *not* subject to a low level of tax.

UK equivalent tax computation
Strictly speaking the computation of the UK equivalent tax involves first of all recomputing the profit of the overseas company on UK tax principles rather than using the local tax principles *before* comparing the taxes paid in the overseas territory and the UK.

Example 19.8
Using the figures from Example 19.7 above:

Assume however that the local taxable profit of 300 when recomputed on UK tax principles gives a figure of 400.

Answer
As above overseas tax paid = 75.

UK equivalent UK tax now based on profit of 400 not 300.

UK tax = 30% x 400 = 120.

Now overseas tax 75 is less than 75% of UK tax of 120 i.e. 80.

XYZ Ltd *is* therefore subject to a low level of tax.

In addition, the comparison of taxes must also take into account any tax paid by the overseas company outside of its territory of residence in respect of which double tax relief will be available.

Example 19.9

XYZ Ltd resident in Ruritania pays tax in its territory of residence at rate of 25%

Its local taxable profit is 300. Assume however that the local taxable profit of 300 when recomputed on UK tax principles gives a figure of 400.

If XYZ Ltd were UK resident it would pay corporation tax at the 30% rate.

XYZ Ltd has a branch in a third country where tax paid on its profit was 50.

Is XYZ Ltd subject to a lower level of tax?

Answer

UK equivalent tax = 30% x 400 = 120 less double tax relief for foreign tax of 50 (i.e. tax suffered in third country) = 70.

Tax paid in overseas country of residence =

$$(25\% \times 300) - 50 = 25.$$

As tax paid in overseas country (i.e.25) is less than 75% of UK equivalent tax of 70 (i.e. 52.50) XYZ Ltd *is* subject to a lower level of tax.

Designer rate regimes

To circumnavigate these CFC provisions a number of overseas territories permitted local companies to choose the amounts of local tax to pay in order to avoid being classified as a CFC. These territories were referred to as "designer rate regimes" by the UK tax authority. Now even if a company pays local tax in excess of 75% of the UK equivalent tax under such provisions the company will still be regarded as being subject to a low level of tax.

Appropriation of profit of CFC

The consequence of CFC classification is that any UK resident *company* owning at least 25% of the shares of the CFC will be subject to an apportionment of the CFC's chargeable profits as recomputed on UK tax principles equal to their shareholding percentage.

UK corporation tax will then be levied thereon at the rate of 30%.

Any tax paid by the CFC in its territory of residence (or elsewhere) may also be apportioned to the UK company shareholder and treated as creditable against the UK tax charged.

Example 19.10

A Ltd a company resident in Cyprus is owned as to 75% by B Ltd a UK resident company. Its other shareholders are not UK resident.

It pays tax at 4% in Cyprus.

Its profits chargeable to tax in Cyprus are 500.

On UK tax principles the profit becomes 700.

What are the CFC consequences?

Answer

A Ltd is a CFC as the three conditions are satisfied.

B Ltd is therefore subject to an apportionment of:

$$75\% \times 700 = 525$$

B Ltd is therefore required to include in its profits 525 which will then be subject to UK corporation tax at 30% i.e. 30% x 525 = 157.50.

However, A Ltd paid local tax in Cyprus of 4% x 500 = 20.

B Ltd will therefore be able to reduce the UK tax charge of 157.50 by the creditable overseas tax of 20 x 75% = 15 (i.e. 15 is B Ltd's share of the local overseas tax paid).

Therefore B Ltd net UK tax liability = 157.50 – 15 = 142.50.

Exceptions

As the CFC provisions are not designed to penalize legitimate overseas companies a number of so-called "let-outs" apply.

Some of these let-outs if satisfied will mean that no apportionment will occur. However, satisfaction of the other let-outs may ameliorate the impact of the CFC provisions.

The let-outs, any one only need be satisfied if an apportionment is to be avoided:

- where the company is *engaged in exempt activities* (broadly, trading activities with third parties)
- where the company is *publicly quoted* in its territory of residence and at least 35% of voting power held by public
- where company's *chargeable profits* (i.e. ignoring chargeable gains) are £50,000 or less for a twelve month accounting period
- where the company does not exist wholly or mainly to reduce UK tax by diverting profits from the UK and reduction is minimal or incidental (referred to as the *motive let out*)

- where company is resident and carrying on business in a country listed in the so-called *Excluded Countries* regulations.

The let-out where satisfaction ameliorates the CFC provisions requires that:

- the company pursues an acceptable distribution policy

  (i.e. dividends paid for an accounting period of the CFC to the UK must equal at least 90% of the CFC's chargeable profits as computed on UK tax principles) and the dividends must be paid within 18 months after the end of the relevant CFC accounting period.

Reporting requirements

For accounting periods after 30th June 1999 UK companies must "self assess" their corporation tax liabilities in respect of CFCs.

If the company pays its tax in instalments any tax relating to CFCs must be included.

Full details of all CFCs must be disclosed on the Supplementary Pages CY 600B of the corporation tax return CT 600 (e.g. name of CFC; territory of residence; etc.).

If one of the let-outs does not apply for a particular CFC then in addition its chargeable profits, creditable tax and UK tax due must also be reported.

Where, however, one of the let-outs referred to above applies a note is made on the Return and information re chargeable profits, etc is not then provided.

Clearance procedure

Any UK company with an interest in an actual or possible CFC may apply for advance clearance in respect of any aspect of the CFC legislation.

SUMMARY

Double tax relief is available to a UK resident company which receives foreign taxed income. The form of the relief is by way of a tax credit.

The amount of any double tax relief is the lower of the UK corporation tax charged on the foreign income and the foreign tax paid thereon. Each source of foreign income must be considered separately.

Underlying tax is available for credit if the UK resident company owns at least 10% of the voting power of the overseas company; it only applies to foreign dividend income.

Dividend withholding foreign tax is always in principle creditable irrespective of the size of the shareholding.

Any UK reliefs (e.g. charges on income) must be offset against UK before foreign source income.

Provisions exist to ensure that transactions between related companies must be of an arm's length nature (i.e. the transfer pricing provisions).

Provisions also exist under which the profits of an overseas company may be still subject to UK corporation tax (i.e. the CFC provisions).

CHAPTER 20

National Insurance Contributions (NIC)

INTRODUCTION

NICs are payments made to the UK Government. They are payments which are made in addition to any income tax which may be due.

They are paid by employees, employers and the self employed. The amount of NICs which are payable depend upon which Class of NIC applies.

A significant increase in NICs became effective from 6th April 2003. The rates below refer to those applying for tax year 2005/06.

Classes of contributions

There are four classes of NIC; namely, Classes 1, 2, 3 and 4. In addition there is also a Class 1A.

Class 1

Employee

NICs under this class are paid by both employees *and* employers.

An employee pays what are referred to as Class 1 *Primary* NICs on *gross earnings* at the rate of 11%.

The 11% rate applies on gross earnings above a threshold of £4,895 per annum (£94 per week) up to a maximum of £32,760 per annum (£630 per week). In addition, employees must also pay 1% on gross earnings above £32,760 per annum (£630 per week) without further limit.

Gross earnings are any remuneration from an employer paid in money (but note also included are certain readily convertible assets, e.g. wine, gold bars). No deductions for contributions to an employer's approved pension scheme or charitable donations under the payroll giving scheme or any expenses borne by the employee are allowed in arriving at gross earnings.

Excluded from gross earnings are mileage allowances payments to an employee who uses his own car on business (see Chapter 10) and where such payments are within the allowed limits for business mileage (any payments in excess of the allowed limits are subject to both primary and secondary Class 1). Certain other benefits which may be paid to an employee (e.g. relocation expenses within the tax free limit; car parking near the place of work; reimbursement of business expenses) are also excluded as are tips received directly from a customer.

The employee must be 16 years or older to be liable to NICs.

GENERAL TAX ADMINISTRATION

No Class 1 contributions are payable by an employee who reaches pensionable age but an employer is still liable for secondary contributions (see below).

Employer

An employer pays what are referred to as Class 1 *Secondary* NICs on the employee's *gross earnings* at the rate of 12.8% above the threshold of £94 per week with no upper limit.

Example 20.1

John Smith is an employee and for the tax year 2005/06 earns £200 per week.

His own (primary) Class 1 NICs = 11% x (£200 – £94) = £11.66 per week

His employer (secondary) NICs = 12.8% x (£200 – £94) = £13.57 per week

Example 20.2

John Smith is an employee and for the tax year 2005/06 earns £900 per week.

His own (primary) Class 1 NICs =

11% x (£630* – £94) + 1% x (£900 – £630) = £58.96 + £2.70 = £61.66 per week

*capped at £630 per week for employee

His employer (secondary) NICs =

12.8% x (£900 – £94) = £103.17 per week

Class 1A

Class 1A NICs are only paid by employers (i.e. not employees) and are payable at the rate of 12.8% on the value of any benefits provided for the private use of employees (e.g. company cars; car fuel; etc; see Chapter 10).

However, no Class 1A is payable with respect to benefits provided to lower paid employees (see Chapter 10).

Example 20.3

John Smith is a higher paid employee and in addition to his salary for the tax year 2005/06 receives a company car which has a taxable benefit of £3,750 and private fuel paid for by his employer which has a taxable benefit of £1,500.

No employee NICs are payable by John on the benefits (John will of course pay the normal Class 1 NICs on his salary).

However, his employer is required to pay Class 1A NICs of

12.8% x (£3,750 + £1,500) = £544

Class 2

Class 2 NICs are only paid by the self employed at a flat rate of £2.10 per week.

However, where *annual accounting profits* (not the tax adjusted profits) falling in the 2005/06 tax year i.e. from 6th April 2005 to 5th April 2006 (thus apportionment may be necessary where the sole trader's accounts are drawn up to a date other than 5th April which will almost certainly be the case) are below £4,345 no Class 2 NICs are payable.

The sole trader must be 16 years or older to be liable to NICs. No NICs are payable on reaching pensionable age.

Class 4

Class 4 NICs are only paid by the self employed at the rate of 8% on *taxable profits* assessed to income tax for the tax year above £4,895 up to a maximum of £32,760.

In addition, a further 1% is levied on *taxable profits* above £32,760 assessed for the tax year.

Class 4 are payable in addition to Class 2.

Taxable profits are arrived at for NIC purposes after allowing for a deduction for any trading losses. However, any personal pension contributions are not deductible for Class 4 purposes.

Example 20.4

John Smith is self employed and prepares his accounts to 31st March each year. For the tax year 2005/06 John's adjusted trading profit is £65,000.

John's Class 2 NICs = 52 x £2.10 = £109.20 per annum

John's Class 4 NICs =

8% x (£32,760 - £4,895) + 1% x (£65,000 - £32,760) = £2,229 + £322.40 = £2,551.40 per annum

---

Class 3

These are voluntary payments of NIC and are made at the weekly rate of £7.35.

Such payments may be made by employee or self employed where the individual's NIC contribution record may be insufficient in order to provide for full State benefits.

Tax deductibility of NICs

The self employed may *not* deduct either Class 2 or 4 NICs in arriving at taxable trading profit.

Similarly, an employee cannot deduct Class 1 NICs in arriving at net employment taxable income.

However, employers (sole trading or company) may deduct their (i.e. employer) contributions made on behalf of employees in arriving at taxable trading profit.

Administration

An employee's Class 1 NICs are collected by the employer by deducting the appropriate amounts from the employee's salary each week or month as appropriate.

The employer pays over these amounts together with its own NIC contribution to the Collector of Taxes no later than 14 days (i.e. by 19th) after the end of each PAYE month (which is 5th of every month).

In the case of Class 1A, however, the employer pays over the relevant amount to the Collector of Taxes in one lump sum by the 19th July after the end of the tax year.

Class 4 NICs are paid by the self employed at the same time as their income tax payments are due (see Chapter 21) which, in essence, means that Class 4 NICs due for a tax year are paid by way of two equal payments on account on 31st January within the tax year and on 31st July after the end of the tax year with a balancing payment due on the 31st January following the end of the tax year.

Contribution periods

For an employer and employee the Class 1 NICs are calculated for contribution periods.

A contribution period is either a week or a month depending upon how the employee is paid. Gross earnings for a contribution period then form the amount on which NIC is payable. Throughout the tax year each contribution period is treated separately i.e. gross earnings are not cumulated throughout the tax year.

In order to avoid abuse by directors of companies such individuals are deemed to have an *annual* earnings period (rather than a weekly or monthly period for employees) with:

- an annual earnings threshold of £4,895 and
- an upper earnings limit of £32,7600 (52 x £630)

The object is to stop directors paying themselves a low weekly/monthly salary and a large single bonus in one single week/month.

Example 20.5

John Smith is paid a monthly salary of £1,000. In March 2006 a bonus is paid to John of £10,000.

What are the primary Class 1 NICs payable by John if
(a) John is an employee?
(b) John is a director?

Answer

John therefore receives 11 monthly payments of £1,000 and one monthly payment of £1,000 plus the one-off bonus payment of £10,000.

(a) 11 x [1,000–4,895/12] x 11% + [2,730*–4,895/12] x 11% + [11,000–32,760/12] x 1% = £716 + £255 + £83 = £1,054

In March 2006 actual payment = £1,000 + £10,000 = £11,000

*However, monthly figure capped at 32,760/12 = £2,730 when subject to 11%

(b) 11% x [22,000 – 4,895] = £1,881.55

If John Smith's salary had been, say, £35,000 per annum as a director his Class 1 contributions would have been:
11% x [32,760 -4,895] + 1% x [35,000-32,760] = £3,065.15 + £22.40 = £3,087.55

SUMMARY

NICs are payments made by employees, employers and the self employed to the Government. In return employees and the self employed receive certain state benefits including a state retirement pension on reaching pensionable age (see Chapter 22).

NICs are not tax deductible either by employees or the self employed; however, NICs payable by employer's on behalf of employees are tax deductible in computing the trading profits of employers.

The rates of NIC are higher for the employee than for the self employed.

Whereas employee NICs were capped prior to 6th April 2004 this is no longer the case. Above £32,760 a rate of 1% applies to the excess.

CHAPTER 21

Tax Administration

INTRODUCTION

This chapter will look at the administrative provisions relating to individuals and companies.

Tax return

In early April each year the Inland Revenue issue tax returns to those taxpayers who are likely to need them (i.e. taxpayers who receive income which has not been taxed at source e.g. sole traders; those receiving rental income and/or capital gains).

The information requested in the return relates to the tax year just ended (e.g. tax returns issued in April 2006 require information concerning the taxpayer's income and gains for the tax year 2005/06 and in addition the return enables the taxpayer to claim allowances and reliefs for the same year i.e. 2005/06).

Annual filing date

The annual filing date by which a tax return needs to be filed is 31st January following the tax year to which the return relates. Thus, for the tax year 2005/06 the annual filing date is 31st January 2007.

In addition to preparing the tax return the taxpayer must also self assess. This means the taxpayer must work out for the tax year covered by the tax return his income and capital gains taxes payable. Such taxes are computed as set out below and are payable by the filing date (see below).

However, if the taxpayer lodges his tax return on or before 30th September following the tax year he no longer needs to self assess as the Inland Revenue will work out on his behalf any taxes due and payable by the filing date.

Where any tax return is filed late automatic penalties apply (see below).

Income tax

Payments on account

Two payments on account ("POA") of a tax year's income tax liability are required to be made on the *31st January in the tax year, and on the 31st July following the tax year.*

> **Example 21.1**
>
> John Smith in respect of the tax year 2005/06 will be required to make POA on 31st January 2006 and 31st July 2006.

Relevant amount

Each POA is normally equal to 50% of the aggregate of the income tax and Class 4 NIC liabilities of the *previous* tax year less any tax deducted at source.

Tax deducted at source includes PAYE, tax deducted at source on bank interest and tax credits on dividends.

The income tax liability for the previous tax year plus Class 4 NIC liability less tax deducted at source is referred to as the "relevant amount". Thus, each POA is equal to 50% of the relevant amount.

However, no POAs are required where:

- the relevant amount is less than £500; *or*
- if more than 80% of the taxpayer's income tax liability plus Class 4 NIC for the previous tax year is satisfied by deduction of tax at source; *or*
- if no relevant amount exists for the previous tax year.

Balancing payment

When the actual income tax payable for the tax year is finally known a balancing payment (or repayment) may be due on the 31st January following the tax year end equal to the income tax payable figure for the tax year less the total POAs which have been made.

Where any balancing payment and/or POA are paid late and/or are insufficient interest will be levied and surcharges (but not to POAs) may also apply.

Example 21.2

John Smith's income tax liability and Class 4 NICs for 2004/2005 was £20,500 of which £19,500 was paid at source.

For 2005/2006 his income tax and Class 4 NIC liability is £20,000 of which £16,000 was paid at source.

What amount of tax is John to pay and on what dates in respect of the 2005/2006 tax year?

Answer
2004/2005

More than 80% of John's income tax and Class 4 NIC liability for this tax year was paid by way of tax deducted at source, i.e. 19,500/20,500 = 91.2%.

Therefore no POAs are required for 2005/2006.

John's liability of £4,000 (£20,000 - £16,000) for 2004/05 is payable on 31st January 2007 in one lump sum.

Example 21.3

For the tax year 2004/2005 John Smith suffers income tax of £8,000 by deduction of tax at source and his total income tax and Class 4 NIC liability was £38,000.

For 2005/2006 his income tax and Class 4 NIC liability is £42,000 of which £5,000 is paid by way of deduction of tax at source.

State the dates on which he is required to pay his 2005/2006 income tax liabilities and in what amounts.

Answer

John's income tax and Class 4 NIC liability for 2004/05 is £38,000.

Relevant amount = (£38,000 - £8,000) = £30,000

2005/06

POA on 31st January 2006: £15,000 (i.e. 50% of 2004/2005 relevant amount)

POA on 31st July 2006:   £15,000 (i.e. 50% of 2004/2005 relevant amount)

Balancing payment on 31st January 2007: £7,000

(i.e. £42,000 - £5,000 - £30,000).

Interest

Interest is charged on all late payments of income tax, surcharges and penalties.

Interest is also charged where a claim to reduce POAs has been made and the POAs which in the event should have been paid are greater than those actually made following the claim (see below).

The interest charge is calculated from a time perspective as follows:

- on late POAs interest runs from the due date of payment to the date the POAs are actually paid
- on insufficient POAs, albeit paid on the correct dates, interest runs from the POA dates to 31st January following the tax year
- on surcharges (see below) interest runs from the due date of payment (i.e. 30 days after date of imposition) to date of actual payment.

The prescribed rate of interest which applies to the late payment of income tax and capital gains tax is 6.5% from 6th August 2003 and 7.5% from 6th September 2004.

Late payment of Classes 1, 1A and 4 NICs are also charged at these interest rates.

Example 21.4

John Smith made POA on 20.3.06 and 15.9.06 in respect of the tax year 2005/06 with a balancing payment on 15.6.07.

From and to what dates will interest be charged?

Answer

Interest will be charged for the following time periods:

1st POA	31.1.06 to 19.3.06
2nd POA	31.7.06 to 14.9.06
Balancing payment	31.1.07 to 14.6.07

(note the interest runs up to the day prior to the actual payment dates).

Claim to reduce POAs

Where a claim to reduce POAs is made (which must be made on or before the 31st January following the tax year) and the POAs which should have been made are greater than those which have in fact been paid interest is charged on the under-payments. The POAs which should have been made are the *lower* of:

- the POAs had no claim been made (i.e. 50% of previous tax year's relevant amount); and
- 50% of final total income tax payable.

Example 21.5

John Smith's relevant amount for 2004/05 is £6,000.

John Smith makes a claim to reduce the POA to £1,500 each for 2005/06.

These POAs are made on time.

His income tax and Class 4 NIC payable for 2005/06 is £4,000 and a balancing payment is made on 31.01.07 of £1,000 (i.e. £4,000 - £3,000).

How will interest be charged?

Answer

Each POA assuming no claim for reduction is made:
50% x £6,000 = £3,000   (1)

Each POA based upon actual income tax and Class 4 NIC payable for 2005/06:
50% x £4,000 = £2,000   (2)

Lower of (1) and (2): £2,000.

Each POA actually made: £1,500

Therefore interest will be charged on each under payment of POA as follows:

- (£2,000 – £1,500) = £500   from 31.1.06 to 30.1.07
- (£2,000 – £1,500) = £500   from 31.7.06 to 30.1.07

Surcharges on income tax paid late

Surcharges are payable *in addition* to any interest which may be charged.

Surcharges do not apply to POAs; only balancing payments.

Where all or part of a balancing payment remains unpaid for more than 28 days after the due date a surcharge of 5% of the unpaid tax applies.

Any tax that still remains unpaid more than six months after the due date (i.e. by 31st July) is subject to a further 5% surcharge.

Surcharges are payable 30 days after the date on which they are imposed.

Example 21.6

A balancing payment of £7,000 is due on 31.1.07 re 2005/06 but only £4,250 is actually paid.

What will be the interest charge and will any surcharge arise?

Answer

Interest will be charged at the rate of 7.5% (see above) on £2,750 (i.e. £7,000 - £4,250) from 31.1.07 to day before date of payment.

Surcharge of (5% x £2,750) = £137.50 will also be due if tax of £2,750 is not paid by 28.2.07

Further surcharge of £137.50 will be due if £2,750 is still not paid by 31.7.07

Interest on overpaid income tax

Repayments to a taxpayer of overpaid income tax attract interest calculated at a lower rate than the interest rate charged on overdue income tax (see above). This interest repayment (or more specifically repayment supplement) is calculated at a rate of 3.5% from 6th September 2004.

Interest on any repayment runs from the "relevant time" to the date on which the tax is repaid to the taxpayer. Relevant time is the date of payment as regards POAs and any other payments of income tax other than tax deducted at source; as regards income tax deducted at source the relevant time is 31st January following the tax year for which the tax is deducted.

Repayments of income tax for a year are attributed first to the balancing payment made for that year, secondly in two equal parts to the POAs for **that year and finally tax deducted at source for that year.**

Taxability of interest payments and repayment supplement

Any interest payable on late and/or underpayments of income tax etc. is not tax deductible nor is any repayment supplement itself subject to tax.

Penalties

Typically, the law specifies a maximum penalty which may be mitigated depending upon the seriousness of the offence and the degree of cooperation of the taxpayer.

Penalties include:

- failure to notify chargeability to tax
- late submission of tax return (i.e. £100 plus additional £100 if still not filed by 31st July after tax year end)
- submission of incorrect tax return
- fraud/negligence when claiming reduced POAs
- failure to keep required records

In every case the penalty is in addition to the tax itself and to any surcharges or interest charged in relation to that tax.

Administration of capital gains tax

The above discussion re income tax also applies to CGT.

On the tax return the *acquisition* of chargeable assets does not need to be entered.

Chargeable disposals similarly do not need to be entered where the total disposal proceeds for the tax year do not exceed twice the amount of the annual exemption (i.e. twice £8,500 for 2005/2006) *and* total gains for the year do not exceed the amount of the annual exemption *and* the taxpayer does not wish to notify the Inland Revenue that there are net losses for the year.

Any losses which are not notified to the Inland Revenue cannot be carried forward for offset against later capital gains. Thus to be able to utilise such losses the Inland Revenue need to be notified and the deadline for such notification is 31st January in the sixth year of assessment following the year in which the losses arose (e.g. losses arising in the tax year 2000/2001 must be notified by 31st January 2007).

CGT is normally payable on the 31st January following end of tax year to which the tax relates (e.g. 31st January 2007 for tax year 2005/2006).

POAs are never required for CGT.

Interest on late payments of CGT is charged at the rate of interest which also applies for income tax i.e. 7.5% from 6th September 2004 (see above) and the repayment supplement is also the same i.e. 3.5% (see above).

National Insurance Contributions

As indicated in Chapter 20, Class 4 NICs which are payable by the self employed are to be paid at the same time and in the same manner as an individual's income tax liability.

As a consequence, in any tax year POAs are required. They are payable at the same time as POA for income tax.

Interest on late payments and any repayment supplement are the same as those for income tax (see above).

Example 21.7

John Smith is self employed and his tax position for the tax year 2004/2005 is as follows:

Total income tax liability	£9,200
Tax deducted at source on savings income	£3,200
Class 4 NIC	£1,776
Class 2 NIC	£104
CGT	£4,800

How much are the payments on account for 2005/2006?

Answer

Income tax

Total income tax liability for 2004/2005		9,200
Less tax deducted at source 2004/2005		(3,200)
		6,000
Class 4 NIC		1,776
Relevant amount		7,776

Payments on account for 2005/2006:

31st January 2006	7,776* 50%	3, 888
31st July 2006	7,776* 50%	3, 888

Therefore two POAs need to be made each equal in total to: 3,888.

There is no requirement to make a POA for the CGT liability. Any CGT liabilities are due on 31 January following tax year in which capital gains are made; in the above example the CGT liability of 4,800 must be made on 31st January 2006.

Class 2 NICs are paid weekly.

Companies

Companies like individuals must compute their own corporation tax liability in respect of any accounting period.

Payment date

The self assessment corporation tax return must be submitted within twelve months of the end of the accounting period to which it relates although any corporation tax liability for the accounting period must be paid nine months after the end of the accounting period (see below for large companies).

The return must contain all information relevant to the accounting period. Accounts for the accounting period are also normally appended to the tax return.

Interest and penalties

Failure to submit the return by the due date gives rise to a penalty of £100 with an increase to £200 if the return is three months or more late. Where the return is more than six months late an additional tax geared penalty equal to 10% of the corporation tax unpaid is charged which rises to 20% if the return is more than twelve months late.

Instalment basis

As indicated above companies settle their corporation tax liability nine months after the end of the accounting period. However, where a company pays tax at the 30% rate then its corporation tax liability must be settled by the payment of four equal quarterly instalments payable on the 14th of months 7, 10, 13 and 16 following the start of the accounting period assuming a 12 month period.

Unlike the position for individuals the corporation tax instalments for an accounting period are based upon estimates of the corporation tax liability for the accounting period and not on the liability for the previous accounting period.

Example 21.8

JS Ltd a large company prepares its accounts to 31st March 2006.

Its corporation tax liability will therefore need to be settled in instalments payable on the 14th of months October 2005, January 2006, April 2006 and July 2006.

Where a company becomes a large company for an accounting period for the first time the instalment basis does not apply for that period if the company was not a large company for the previous accounting period *and* the profits for the current period do not exceed £10 million (or pro rata reduced if associated companies exist).

Interest is chargeable where corporation tax is paid late running from the date the liability was due to the date of actual payment and unlike the position for individuals any such interest is a deductible expense in arriving at any net interest income under the loan relationship rules; any interest paid to the company on overpayments of tax will similarly be treated as taxable interest income (see Chapter 16).

PAYE

Pay As You Earn (PAYE) is designed to enable employers to deduct from their employees' salary over a tax year the latter's income tax liability for a tax year.

PAYE applies to wages and salaries, round sum allowances and readily convertible assets (i.e. assets readily convertible into cash). It does not, however, apply to reimbursed business expenses.

PAYE does not normally apply to benefits. Benefits will, however, usually restrict the amount of the PAYE code.

PAYE Code

Thus, for example, if an employee's sole source of income in a tax year is salary, by applying the correct PAYE code (see below) to the employee's salary the employer by the end of the tax year will have deducted an amount of income tax from the salary which equals the employee's income tax liability. In principle, the employee will then have no further income tax liability.

An individual's PAYE code depends upon various factors. It will, thus, depend upon the level of personal allowances to which the individual may be entitled (e.g. personal allowance; married couple's allowance; etc); whether that individual receives any benefits (e.g. company car); whether that individual receives any untaxed income (e.g. interest on National Savings Bank investment accounts); and whether the individual has any unpaid income tax from prior tax years.

Example 21.9

John Smith, an employee, earns a salary of £20,000 for 2005/06. His company car is valued for tax purposes at £1,200. He owes £780 income tax from the previous tax year 2004/05.

John is single, aged 35, and a basic rate tax payer.

Show John's PAYE code for 2005/06.

Answer

Personal allowance	4,895
Benefits	(1,200)
Unpaid tax	(1,000)
	2,695

John's PAYE code is thus 269L

Notes

1. The 1,000 above represents 780/0.78. As John owes tax of £780 to collect this amount means a reduction in his PAYE code (i.e. the £4,895 personal allowance) of £1,000 not £780.

> 2. To obtain an individual's PAYE code it is usual simply to knock off the last digit. Thus to get John's code requires that the '5' be knocked off to get 269. However, John is still entitled to allowances in total of £2,695 (not just £269) (see below).

An employer is notified of an employee's PAYE code for a tax year but the employer does not know the breakdown of the code; just the final amount.

The employer then, each week or month (depending upon how an employee is paid), applies 1/52 or 1/12 of the employee's allowances (e.g. £2,695 for John in Example 21.9 above) against the weekly or monthly salary. In this manner over the tax year the employee will have discharged his income tax liability for that tax year.

It may be that for various reasons (e.g. an employee receives a company car for only part of the year) some sort of balancing amount of income tax may be due at the end of the tax year (or possibly a repayment of income tax).

Any income tax (and indeed NICs) collected by the employer in this way must be paid over to the Inland Revenue within 14 days of the end of each tax month.

Various letters are also typically added after an individual's PAYE code. For example, an 'L' means the individual simply receives the standard personal allowance of £4,895 (for 2005/06); a 'Y' applies where the individual receives the personal allowance for those aged over 75; and a 'P' if the individual is aged 65 to 74; etc.).

The application of the codes is on a cumulative basis. Thus, after the first three tax months of the tax year an individual would have received one quarter of his annual allowance entitlement. For an individual who starts to work for the first time, say from 6th September in 2005, then when he is paid on, say 30th September, he will receive six months' worth of his annual allowances as he had not prior to 6th September received any of them. Thereafter, he will simply receive as normal one month's allowance per month.

Forms/returns

A variety of information is required to be supplied by an employer to his employees each tax year. This information is supplied on various forms as follows:

- *Form P60* (deadline 31st May after end of tax year). This form shows the employee's total taxable earnings for the tax year, total tax deducted, code number, national insurance number, and employer's name and address.

- *Form P11D/9D* (deadline 6th July after end of tax year). This form shows the cash equivalent of all benefits provided to the employee; the P11D applies to those other than the lower paid who receive the P9D).
- *Form P45* (given to an employee who leaves his employer's employment. This form shows the employee's PAYE code, income of the employee to date of leaving and income tax paid to date of leaving. The form is in four parts, two parts being given to any new employer).

An employer must also complete various forms/returns which need to be supplied to the Inland Revenue. These, broadly, summarise the overall tax position for the employer with respect to all his employees for the tax year. These include end of year returns P14 and Form P35, both of which need to be submitted by 19th May after the end of the tax year. Forms P11D and P9D, completed for all relevant employees must also be submitted by 6th July following the end of the tax year.

SUMMARY

The self assessment system requires individuals (and companies) to not only file an annual tax return containing information about an individual's income and capital gains but to also calculate any income and capital gains tax liabilities.

Payments on account need to be made in respect of income tax liabilities for a tax year but are not required in respect of any capital gains tax liabilities. Payments on account are based upon the individual's income tax liabilities for the previous tax year. Class 4 NICs payable by the self employed are also paid at the same time as any POA of any income tax liability and calculated in the same manner.

Interest may be charged where tax liabilities are settled late and/or are of an insufficient amount.

Surcharges and penalties may also be levied in addition to any interest charged.

Companies also need to self assess and large companies must also pay their corporation tax liabilities in instalments. Companies which are not large pay their corporation tax liabilities in one lump sum nine months after the end of the accounting period.

PAYE codes are used by employers to collect, from an employee's monthly or weekly salary, the employee's income tax liability for the tax year.

Employers are required by deadline dates to file with the Inland Revenue certain Forms/Returns. In addition, again by deadline dates, employees must also receive from employers certain Forms.

CHAPTER 22

Pensions

INTRODUCTION

Pensions are taxable just the same as other forms of income. More specifically, pensions are taxed under the new Income Tax (Earnings and Pensions) Act 2003 (see Chapter 10).

There are three types of pension:

- State retirement pension
- occupational pension
- personal pension

State retirement pensions

The State retirement pension is payable to men on attaining the age of 65 and to women on attaining the age of 60 i.e. when basically retirement age is reached.

Currently for 2005/06 the basic State pension is £82.05 per week for a single individual and £131.20 per week for a married couple. The basic State pension is payable in full once an individual reaches pensionable age (see above) and assuming that sufficient national insurance contributions (see Chapter 20) have been paid during the individual's working life.

An additional pension referred to as the State second pension is also available in certain cases.

Occupational pensions

An occupational pension scheme is one which is run by an employer to provide its employees with a retirement pension on retirement. Invariably, the pension scheme will be approved by the Inland Revenue which means that a number of tax benefits accrue (see below).

Occupational schemes are of two types, namely, either final salary schemes otherwise known as defined benefit schemes or money purchase schemes otherwise known as defined contribution schemes.

Final salary scheme

The amount of pension payable on retirement to an employee depends upon the employee's final remuneration at retirement together with the employee's length of service. Basically, remuneration includes all the employee's taxable earnings (e.g. includes salary and benefits; see Chapter 10).

There is, however, an earnings cap (i.e. a maximum level of remuneration which may be taken into account) which applies when determining pension entitlement. This amount increases every tax year and for 2005/06 is £105,600.

A typical final salary scheme will require the employee to make contributions to the pension fund whilst working for the employer out of his salary. It is not unusual for a typical employee contribution to be set at 5% of salary (not remuneration). The employer will then deduct each month (or week) this level of contribution from the employee's salary. This deduction will be made at the same time as any income tax liability is deducted under the PAYE scheme (see Chapter 21).

The employer will also contribute to this fund on behalf of its employees at a rate normally of around 10% of its gross salary bill for all its employees.

An employee may commute a part of his pension entitlement into a tax free cash lump sum. The maximum cash lump sum which may be received is equal to 3/80ths of final remuneration for each year of service up to a maximum of 40 years.

After any commutation the remaining pension payable will, of course, be reduced.

Example 22.1

John Smith is a member of his firm's occupational pension scheme. He is about to retire after 35 years of pensionable service and his salary at retirement will be £45,000. Under the scheme he is entitled to 1/40th for every year of service.

Calculate John's pension and the maximum tax free lump sum to which he is entitled.

Answer

Pension	= 1/40 x 35 x £45,000 = £39,375 per annum
Maximum lump sum	= 3/80 x 35 x £45,000 = £59,063

Money purchase scheme

Unlike a final salary scheme under a money purchase scheme an employee does not know until retirement the level of his pension i.e. it is not geared to final level salary as occurs in a final salary scheme.

The employee makes contributions but such contributions are kept separate from those of other employees. In effect each employee has his own separate pool of funds which are invested and any investment returns credited to it. At retirement the aggregate pool is then used by the employee to purchase an annuity i.e. the money from the pool is used to buy from an insurance company an income for life (i.e. basically his pension). Thus, until the employee gets to retirement he does not know either the value of his pool of contributions plus investment returns or the amount of annuity the pool will purchase.

Other things being equal, from the employee's perspective a final salary scheme is the better option. However, from the employer's perspective the money purchase scheme is likely to be much cheaper.

Tax effects

Most occupational pension schemes are approved by the Inland Revenue; more specifically such schemes are approved by the Savings, Pensions, Share Schemes Office of the Inland Revenue.

Approval means that a number of tax advantages are available to both employer and employee. Unless a scheme is approved such tax advantages are not available.

For the employer any tax contributions made on behalf of employees are tax deductible in computing trading profits. There is also no upper limit on employer contributions.

For the employee the contributions made on their behalf by their employer are not taxable as benefits for income tax purposes (see Chapter 10). An employee's own contributions are tax deductible in arriving at taxable income (see Chapter 3) up to an amount of 15% of annual remuneration (excludes the taxable elements of any termination payements but include salary plus benefits) and assuming the £105,600 annual remuneration cap is not exceeded. For computational purposes it is normal to deduct the contributions to an occupational pension scheme by the employee from the aggregate of his salary plus benefits before including the net figure in the Non-savings income column (see Chapter 3).

At retirement, pensions are taxable (on an accruals not receipts basis; see Chapter 10) even when payable under an approved scheme. However, an employee may commute a part of his pension entitlement into a tax free cash lump sum. The maximum cash lump sum which may be received is equal to 3/80ths of final remuneration for each year of service up to a maximum of 40 years.

After any such commutation the remaining pension payable will, of course, be reduced.

Personal pensions

Personal pension schemes are primarily for those who are self employed. In addition, if an employee is not a member of an occupational pension scheme (whether by choice or because his employer provides no scheme) such an employee may take out a personal pension instead.

Any individual (self employed, employee or even someone not working), however, may contribute up to £3,600 gross per annum to a personal pension scheme, irrespective of the level of earnings (see below), unless the individual is an employee who is also a member of his employer's pension scheme and is earning more than £30,000 per annum.

Personal pension schemes are basically money purchase schemes i.e. the benefits payable on retirement are dependent upon the amount of the employee's contributions and any investment returns and not on the employee's final salary.

Similar to a money purchase scheme discussed above, at retirement, an annuity is purchased to provide the pension in retirement. This pension is taxable. A part of it may be commuted to provide a tax free lump sum.

As with occupational pension schemes there are tax benefits available for personal pension schemes assuming the scheme is approved by the Inland Revenue (see below).

Unlike occupational schemes, where an employee does take out a personal pension it is not unusual for an employer not to contribute to the personal pension scheme. However, where the employer does make a contribution a tax deduction in computing trading profits will normally be given. The employer's contribution will not be treated as a taxable benefit on the part of the employee.

In the case of the self employed (for whom personal pensions are primarily designed) of course only the self employed person himself may make contributions to a personal pension scheme.

Where contributions are made the contributions are made net of basic rate tax (i.e. net of 22%). In other words on making the contribution the self employed or employed person deducts income tax at source at the rate of 22%. The fund itself may then claim back from the Inland Revenue the tax so deducted which is then added to the fund.

However, the contributor is entitled to tax relief at his highest rate of tax i.e. 40%. Where a self employed or employee is liable to income tax at 40% the extra 18% of tax relief (i.e. 40% less 22%) is obtained by extending his basic rate of income tax (see Chapter 4).

Example 22.2

John Smith makes a gross contribution of £10,000 in tax year 2005/06 to a personal pension scheme.

On making the payment John is entitled to withhold income tax at the basic rate of 22% from the gross payment. Thus, John will withhold 22% x £10,000 = £2,200 and simply transfer the net amount of £7,800 to the pension scheme.

If John is a higher rate taxpayer (i.e. he pays tax at the 40% rate) then he will be entitled to higher rate tax relief which will be obtained by extending the basic rate band (see Chapter 4).

Contribution limits

There is a limit on the amount of contributions which a self employed/employee may make in a tax year. The limit depends upon the age of the person on 6th April of the relevant tax year and his net relevant earnings for that tax year.

Age at start of tax year	Maximum % contribution
16 to 35	17.5%
36 to 45	20%
46 to 50	25%
51 to 55	30%
56 to 60	35%
61 and over	40%

Net relevant earnings for the self employed are defined as the person's trading profit assessment for the tax year plus any income from furnished holiday lettings (see Chapter 5) less loss reliefs for the tax year set against trading income.

For the employee net relevant earnings are defined as the employee's earnings for the tax year (which includes benefits) less any allowable expenses.

In determining the maximum contribution for any tax year the net relevant earnings used may be the highest of the net relevant earnings for the tax year under consideration or those of any of the five previous tax years. However, the maximum amount for any tax year is still based upon age at the beginning of the tax year.

Example 22.3

John Smith is self employed. On 6th April 2005 John was aged 48. His net relevant earnings are as follows:

1999/00	£55,000
2000/01	£50,000
2001/02	£30,000
2002/03	£35,000
2003/04	£20,000
2004/05	£15,000
2005/06	£13,000

What are the maximum contributions John can make for the tax year 2005/06 to a personal pension scheme?

Answer

John's age at 6th April 2005 is 48 and in 2005/06 John's net relevant earnings are £13,000.

In the previous five tax years i.e. 2000/01 to 2004/05 the highest net relevant earnings are £50,000.

Therefore John can contribute a maximum amount = 25% x £50,000 = £12,500.

Note

It is John's age on 6th April 2005 that determines the maximum amount which may be contributed for tax year 2005/06 not his age for the tax year 2000/01.

Contribution carry-back

It is also possible for contributions made in one tax year to be carried back to the immediately preceding tax year for tax relief in that earlier tax year.

For premiums to be carried back they must be paid on or before 31st January in the tax year and an election must have been made to carry the contributions back on or before the actual payments are made. It is important, however, to ensure that the maximum limit of the prior tax year after the carry back is not exceeded.

Example 22.4

John Smith for the tax year 2004/05 has made personal pension contributions of £20,000.

John was 50 on 6th April 2004. His net relevant earnings for 2004/05 are £100,000.

What additional contributions may John make in tax year 2005/06 and relate back to 2004/05?

Answer

The maximum contributions for 2004/05 = 25% x £100,000 = £25,000.

Actual contributions made in 2004/05 = £20,000

£5,000 (i.e. £25,000 - £20,000) of contributions may be made in tax year 2005/06 (so long as made before 31st January 2006) and then treated as eligible for tax relief for the tax year 2004/05.

SUMMARY

Pensions, whether state, occupational and/or personal, are taxable on the recipient.

Contributions to occupational or personal pension funds are tax deductible on the part of the self employed or employee. The manner in which tax relief is granted, however, differs.

In the case of a personal pension contribution tax relief is obtained by way of tax deducted at source plus an extension of the basic rate. Tax relief for contributions to an occupational pension scheme is obtained by the employee deducting the contributions from salary.

Personal pensions are intended primarily for the self employed although an employee may also take out a personal pension where such employee is not a member of an occupational pension scheme or the employer does not provide an occupational scheme.

CHAPTER 23

Value Added Tax

INTRODUCTION

VAT is a tax on consumer expenditure; a so-called indirect tax. Prior to April 2005, VAT was administered by HM Customs & Excise. It is now administered by HM Revenue & Customs (HMRC). It is a tax which is totally different from income, capital gains and corporation tax.

Supplies

VAT is charged on a supply of goods and services when made in the UK where the supply is a *taxable supply* by a *taxable person* in the course of business carried on by him.

Output and input tax

Output tax

The VAT charged *by* a taxable person on supplies made *by* him to another person is called output tax. This output tax (less input tax; see below) is paid over to HMRC by the trader periodically.

Input tax

Input tax is the VAT charged *on* a taxable person on goods and services supplied *to* him by another taxable person.

Example 23.1

John Smith a taxable person over a three month period charges VAT of £3,500 on goods supplied by him and pays to his suppliers on purchases VAT of £1,500.

John will therefore need to account to HMRC for £3,500 (output) - £1,500 (input) = £2,000.

Example 23.2

John Smith a taxable person over a three month period charges VAT of £1,500 on goods supplied by him and pays to his suppliers on purchases VAT of £3,500.

John will therefore obtain a refund from HMRC for £1,500 (output) - £3,500 (input) = £2,000.

Supplies of goods

Goods are supplied in the UK if they are located here and are either removed to elsewhere in the UK (i.e. sold to a UK based customer).

In addition to a simple sale of goods a supply of goods also includes, for example, a supply of power or heat, the application of a treatment or process to another person's goods and the granting of a freehold interest in land.

A supply of goods also arises where a gift of goods is made or where goods are taken out of the business for private use.

Supplies of services

Supplies of services are supplied in the country where the service provider belongs; where they are performed is irrelevant. Thus a UK based accountant makes his supplies in the UK as he is based in the UK even if providing services to an overseas based client.

Supplies of services include anything done for consideration which is not a supply of goods.

Value of supply

VAT is charged on the value of the supply of goods or services which is generally the money paid for the goods or services.

In the case of gifts market value is used. However, where services are provided for no consideration no supply for VAT is assumed to have been made and thus no VAT is chargeable.

Standard rated, Zero rated and Exempt supplies

Supplies made by a taxable person may be standard rated and/or exempt and/or zero rated. Although generally speaking a taxable person will tend to make only one type of rated supply in a number of cases a mixture of the three different rated supplies may be made.

Standard rated

The general rule is that all supplies are subject to VAT at the standard rate; currently 17.5%. Input tax attributable to standard rate supplies is recoverable (ie offsettable).

However, a lower rate of 5% applies to a small number of supplies including supplies of domestic fuel and power.

Zero rated

Zero rated supplies are subject to VAT but at the zero rate (i.e. 0%).

Unlike exempt supplies (see below) they are not ignored and input tax is recoverable as in the case for standard rated supplies.

Examples of zero rated supplies are supplies of most food, books and newspapers and children's clothing and footwear.

Exempt

An exempt supply is one where no VAT is charged as the supply is not a taxable supply.

Input tax cannot be recovered where the input tax relates to the exempt supply.

Examples of exempt supplies include supplies of land, insurance, education and health.

Taxable supplies

Standard and zero rated (but not exempt) supplies are referred to as taxable supplies.

Example 23.3

John Smith makes the following supplies of goods VAT (excluded):

Standard rated	£30,000
Zero rated	£20,000
Exempt	£10,000

John's total output VAT is charged on his *taxable* supplies i.e. £30,000 x 17.5% + £20,000 x 0% = £5,250

Mixture of supplies

If a business makes a supply of taxable (i.e. standard and zero rated) and exempt rated supplies it is referred to as a partially exempt supplier. This means that input VAT which is directly attributable to taxable supplies is recoverable (i.e. off-settable) whereas that directly attributable to the exempt supplies is irrecoverable. If any input VAT cannot be directly attributable to a particular type of supply then it may be partially recoverable.

However, it should be noted that in any event not all input VAT is recoverable even if attributable to a taxable supply; for example, VAT attributable to client/customer entertaining is irrecoverable as is VAT charged on the purchase of a motor car.

Rates of VAT

A standard rate supply is one where 17.5% VAT is charged on the VAT exclusive value of the goods/supplies.

A supply taxed at the zero rate is still a taxable supply albeit at the rate of 0%.

VAT fraction

Where the total value of the supply includes VAT then to calculate the amount of VAT which has been included the VAT inclusive amount is multiplied by the so-called VAT fraction, currently 7/47ths.

Example 23.4

John Smith charges a customer £235 for a supply of goods which amount includes VAT charged at the standard rate.

The VAT included in this amount is therefore = 7/47 x £235 = £35.

i.e. £200 + (17.5% x £200) = £235

Registration

There are two types of registration: compulsory and voluntary.

Compulsory registration

Where a person makes supplies such that at the end of any month the value of the prior twelve months supplies ending on the last day of the month exceeds £60,000 (exclusive of VAT) then compulsory registration is required.

If at any time there are reasonable grounds for believing that in the next thirty days the value of supplies will exceed £60,000 (exclusive of VAT), effective 1st April 2005, then compulsory registration is required.

Under the former situation the person must notify HMRC within 30 days of the end of the relevant month. In this case registration is then effected from the start of the month following this 30 day period.

Under the latter situation HMRC must be notified by the end of the 30 day period. In this case registration is effected from the start of the month in which the grounds for registration arose.

Example 23.5

John Smith after a few months trading realises that his taxable supplies have exceeded £60,000 and that he will need to notify HMRC of his requirement to register by 30th April. His registration will then be effected from 1st May.

Even if the £60,000 limit has been exceeded in the previous twelve months if taxable supplies in the next twelve months are likely to be £58,000 or less registration can be avoided (see below).

Disposals of capital assets should be ignored in calculating the amount of taxable supplies for registration purposes.

It is the *person* who is liable to be registered, not the business, and therefore in ascertaining if the registration limits are exceeded by any person all taxable supplies made by the person in all his businesses must be aggregated.

A person making only exempt supplies cannot be required to be compulsorily registered because such a person is not making taxable supplies.

Example 23.6

John Smith makes has just started to trade and in the first few months made the following supplies:

January	£12,000
February	£13,000
March	£15,000
April	£33,000

The VAT limit of £60,000 is exceeded during the month of April (i.e. 12,000+13,000+15,000+33,000).

John is therefore required to compulsorily register and he must notify HMRC on or before 30th May, and will be registered from 1st June.

If a supply is made before a liability to registration arises but payment is made after registration, no VAT is due.

Voluntary registration

Where a person is not required to compulsorily register he may still register voluntarily if he is making taxable supplies in the course of a business or is carrying on activities with a view to then making taxable supplies.

Voluntary registration enables any input VAT to be recovered which otherwise would not be the case i.e. unless registration is effected no input VAT can be recovered because in this situation the person will not be making taxable supplies.

Deregistration

Where a person ceases to make taxable supplies, within 30 days of cessation HMRC must be notified.

Also, as indicated above, where a person expects taxable turnover to fall below £58,000 (the deregistration threshold) in the next 12 months voluntary deregistration may be effected (or initial compulsory registration may be avoided).

The effect of deregistration is that no further input VAT may be recovered and no further output VAT may be charged.

Penalties for late registration

Where a person has failed to notify HMRC of the need to compulsorily register a penalty based upon the amount of VAT that should have been paid had the registration been effected correctly may be charged.

The penalty is equal to a percentage of the VAT which was due, namely:
- 5% for notification up to 9 months late.
- 10% for notification over 9 up to 18 months late
- 15% for notification over 18 months late

There is a minimum penalty of £50.

If there is a delay of more than three years HMRC may apply for a civil penalty which could be as much as 100% of the VAT chargeable.

A person is liable to register from the date he should have registered rather than when he does in fact register.

Example 23.7

John Smith started to trade on 1st Febuary 2005 and over the first few months his supplies are as follows:

February	£13,000
March	£23,000
April	£20,000
May	£15,000
June	£5,000
July	£30,000
August	£10,000

He realises in late August that he should have notified HMRC of the requirement to register by 30th June as the £60,000 limit was exceeded during May (13,000 + 23,000 + 20,000 + 15,000) and notifies them on 1st September.

John is therefore two months late in notifying HMRC.

A penalty of 5% is thus leviable on VAT which should have been paid which is VAT on the July and August supplies (as the 1st July is the date from which his VAT registration should have been effected):

i.e. 5% x [(£30,000 + £10,000 =£40,000) x 17.5%] = £350

Transfer of a Business as a Going Concern

If a business is transferred as a going concern, the transfer is not a taxable supply and no VAT is charged.

For this to occur:

- the transferor and transferee must be VAT registered and the business concerned must be carried on as a going concern.
- the assets transferred must be used in the same kind of business as that of the transferor
- there must be no significant break in business activities

If the transferee takes over the VAT number of the transferor it also takes over any outstanding VAT compliance regulations and VAT liabilities of the previous owner.

Where the above conditions are not satisfied then VAT is due if the assets transferred are standard rated.

Pre Registration VAT

Where, prior to registration, VAT is incurred on the purchase of goods and/or services this VAT may be recoverable once the person registers. VAT is recoverable:

- on *goods* including capital goods and trading stock provided:
  - they are still owned at the date of registration, *and*
  - they were purchased within the three year period prior to registration

- on *services*, if they were supplied within six months of registration

and the goods or services must have been used for business purposes and invoices must be available to support the claim for VAT recovery.

Time of the supply: tax point

The time of a supply whether of goods or services, referred to as the tax point, determines both the rate of VAT to be charged and the period into which the supply falls (important for accounting for VAT purposes; see below).

The basic tax point for goods is when they are removed by the customer or made available to him.

The basic tax point for services is the time when they are performed.

The above general rules are overridden in the following situations:

- if an invoice is issued or payment received *before* either of the above dates; the tax point becomes the earlier of the date of invoice and receipt of payment.
- if an invoice is issued within 14 days after the basic tax point date the invoice date becomes the tax point, unless payment has already been received in which case the payment date remains the tax point.
- if goods are taken on sale or return, the tax point is the earlier of when the customer accepts them or 12 months after the date of despatch
- the tax point for goods taken for non business use is the date of taking.
- a continuous supplies of services (e.g. electricity; tax advice) paid for periodically have tax points on the earlier of receipt of such payments and the date of the invoice.

Example 23.8

John Smith in the course of his VAT quarter to 30th June sold one of his customers goods to the total value of £25,000. The goods were not in stock and John had to place an order on his suppliers. The customer was asked to leave a deposit of £4,700 on 25th June.

The goods arrived on 1st September and the customer picked them up on 2nd September. John raised an invoice on 30th September for the balance of the monies owed which the customer paid on 10th October.

Show John's VAT position.

Answer

Deposit monies

The tax point for the deposit monies is 25th June.

The deposit monies are assumed to include VAT.

Therefore John needs to account for output VAT for the quarter ended 30th June of 7/47 x 4,700 = 700.

Balance of payment

The goods were made available to the customer on 2nd September.

John issued an invoice on 30th September with payment by the customer on 10th October.

As the invoice was not issued within 14 days of the basic tax point (i.e. 2nd September) and payment was not made prior to 2nd September then 2nd September is the tax point.

John will therefore need to account for output VAT in the quarter ended 30th September of $17.5\% \times [(25,000 - (4,700 - 700)] = £3,675$

Miscellaneous matters
Discounts
Whether a cash or trade discount is offered VAT is chargeable on the discounted amount.

This applies even if in the case of a cash discount offered to a customer for prompt payment the customer does not take advantage of the discount.

Example 23.9

John Smith supplies goods for £300 (VAT excluded) offering his customer a 10% discount for settlement within 30 days.

John should charge VAT at 17.5% on the discounted figure of £300 – (10% x £300) = £ 270

i.e. $17.5\% \times £270 = £47.25$

Gifts/sales at less than full value
In the case of a gift of a business asset, VAT is due on the value of similar goods both in age and condition.

This rule also applies to goods taken for private use by the owner of the business or an employee thereof.

If goods are sold to employees at a discounted price VAT is due on the discounted price.

There is no VAT on gifts of services.

If goods or services are purchased specifically for private use, no VAT can be recovered (i.e. the VAT payable cannot be treated as input VAT). If, however, there is both business and private use of goods purchased *either* the input tax can be apportioned (i.e. only the business element is deducted) *or* all the input tax may be recovered (including the element attributable to private use) but account must then be taken of output tax on the non business use element.

Motor cars

No recovery of input tax can be made on the purchase of a motor car unless (which generally is most unlikely) the car is used wholly for business purposes (e.g. purchase of a car by a garage for resale).

As a consequence, on the sale of a used car (other than by a garage which buys and sells cars) no VAT is chargeable.

Accessories

VAT cannot be recovered on the cost of accessories fitted when the car is bought unless there is 100% business use. It is, however, normally possible to recover VAT on accessories fitted subsequently despite potential private use.

Repairs/maintenance

Provided that there is some business use, a taxable trader can recover *all* the VAT on repair and maintenance costs even if the car is used partly for private use.

Car fuel

If petrol is provided for a car which includes private use by an individual (i.e. proprietor, employee or director) at less than the cost of that fuel to the business providing the fuel (not applicable to a van; see below) then the business providing the fuel may recover the input VAT on the total cost of the petrol *if* it also accounts by way of *output* VAT an amount calculated according to the scale rate provided by HMRC.

The quarterly scale charges for periods beginning on or after 1.5.05 VAT *inclusive* are:

Engine size	Petrol	Diesel
cc	£	£
≤ 1400 cc	246	236
> 1400 cc ≤ 2000 cc	311	236
> 2000 cc	457	300

The amount of output VAT will be determined by taking 7/47ths of the appropriate scale charge.

Example 23.10

John Smith, a sole trader, has purchased a motor car, engine size 2,000cc, which he uses partly for business and partly for private purposes.

His anticipated fuel bill for the year is £950 (VAT inclusive).

If John wants to reclaim the input VAT (i.e. 7/47 x £950 = £141.49) then he must also treat as VAT output tax 7/47 x £1,245 = £185.43.

It would, therefore, not make sense for John to try to reclaim the input VAT, as he would end up having to pay to HMRC (£185.43 - £141.49) i.e. £43.94.

Vans

VAT can normally be recovered on the purchase of vans and lorries.

If the trader who sells a used vehicle has recovered input VAT on the cost price (e.g. on a van or haulage vehicle) VAT must be charged on the full selling price when it is disposed of.

Accommodation

No VAT can be recovered on costs of providing residential accommodation for a director or a person connected with him or her.

VAT on staff removal expenses is normally recoverable.

Bad debts

If a debt has become bad a claim for repayment of VAT can be made if the following conditions are satisfied:

- the debt has been written off as a bad debt, *and*
  at least six months has elapsed since the debt was due and payable, *and*
- the VAT charged on the supply has been paid to HMRC, *and*
- the appropriate accounting records have been maintained by the supplier.

If a payment on account of the debt has been made it will be allocated on a FIFO basis unless the debtor has attributed it to a specific debt or debts.

The claim for bad debt relief must be made within three years and six months from the later of the time of the supply or the due date of payment for it.

Prior to 1st January 2003 if the supplier claimed bad debt relief then the customer had to be notified of the claim for relief; this no longer applies. However, where the debt is outstanding for six months then the debtor must repay the VAT to HMRC.

Entertainment

VAT on business entertainment is not deductible whereas VAT on entertaining staff is recoverable.

Where spouses/partners of the employee and/or others attend (e.g. an employer's summer party) no VAT is recoverable on the element of costs attributable to their entertainment.

All VAT can be recovered on the costs of hotels and subsistence incurred by a taxable trader or its staff for business purposes.

Mixed and composite supplies

Where a mixed supply occurs it is necessary to break down the supply into its constituents and charge VAT accordingly (e.g. may partly be standard rated and partly zero rated or exempt).

Where the supply is a composite supply, i.e. cannot be split into its constituent parts, only one rate of VAT is applied to the full amount.

Administration and penalties

VAT Returns

VAT on the supplies of goods and services must be accounted for on a quarterly basis. However, the quarters which are relevant are determined by HMRC. Thus some traders will have quarterly return periods of, say, 31st March, 30th June, 31st October and 31st December; others may have 28th February, 31st May, 30th September and 30th November etc.

The return (Form VAT100) which is completed by the trader shows the total input and output VAT for the period and thus the VAT that needs to be accounted for. HMRC must receive the completed return and the VAT due by the end of the month following the relevant quarter period. Where a VAT refund is due this will normally be paid by HMRC within 10 days of receiving the return.

Where a trader is likely to receive VAT refunds rather than having to make VAT payments as may occur where a registered trader is making primarily zero rated supplies monthly returns may be submitted.

VAT invoices

If a taxable person makes a taxable supply, a VAT invoice must be issued to the purchaser. This enables the recovery of any input VAT by the purchaser. It must broadly contain the following:

- the supplier's name, address and VAT registration number
- the name and address of the customer
- the invoice number, its date of issue and the tax point
- the type of supply and a description of the goods supplied
- the VAT exclusive amount, the rate of VAT and any cash discount offered

Less detailed invoices can be issued where the VAT inclusive amount does not exceed £100.

VAT invoices are not needed for payments up to £25 each (including VAT) for car park fees, phone calls or which are made through cash machines but the input VAT is still recoverable as normal.

Default surcharge

If either a VAT return is not submitted by the due date or the tax due with the return is paid late, it will trigger a default surcharge.

On the occasion of the first default a surcharge liability notice is issued covering a period of 12 months from the end of the quarter in respect of which the default has arisen. If any further default occurs during this 12 month period of the notice a penalty surcharge of 2% of the VAT due for the quarter is levied. Furthermore, the surcharge notice period is extended by a further 12 months from the end of the quarter in respect of which the latest default occurred.

Further defaults will similarly lead to additional surcharges and further extensions of the notice period. Thus, for the second default within a notice period the surcharge rises to 5%; 10% for the third; and a maximum of 15% for the fourth and subsequent defaults within the period of a notice.

The default surcharge payable is the greater of £30 and the amount calculated using the appropriate percentage.

There will be no surcharge levied where the return is late but the VAT is paid on time or a nil return is submitted late. This default will, however, extend the period that a surcharge liability notice is in force but not the percentage rate of a surcharge.

Where the VAT returns and VAT payments are completed satisfactorily for four subsequent VAT quarters the surcharge regime recommences i.e. any subsequent failing to file a return on time and/or pay VAT due late will constitute the first default giving rise to a new surcharge liability notice but no default surcharge unless and until a further default arises within the surcharge notice period.

A default surcharge will not apply if the trader can show that the return or payment was posted on time or that there was a reasonable excuse as to why the failure arose.

Example 23.11

John Smith's VAT quarters are calendar quarters. He has always submitted his VAT returns on time. However, three returns and accompanying payments were submitted late as follows:

Quarter to 31st March 2005 was submitted on 10th May 2005

Quarter to 30th September 2005 was submitted on 10th December 2005

Quarter to 31st December 2005 was submitted on 10th January 2006

What is the position with respect to any VAT surcharges?

Answer

Quarter to 31st March 2005

This was John's first late submission. No penalty will arise but a surcharge notice will be issued covering the period 1st April 2005 to 31st March 2006.

Quarter to 30th September 2005

This is John's *first* default *within* the surcharge notice period. A penalty surcharge of 2% of the VAT due for the quarter will be levied.

In addition, a second surcharge notice will be issued extending the surcharge notice period to 30th September 2006.

Quarter to 31st December 2005

This is John's *second* default *within* the surcharge notice period. A penalty surcharge of 5% of the VAT due for the quarter will be levied.

In addition, a third surcharge notice will be issued extending the surcharge notice period to 31st December 2006.

Misdeclarations

A penalty of 15% of the underpaid/over-claimed VAT can be imposed if there is a misdeclaration in respect of VAT. A misdeclaration arises where:

- there is a mistake in a VAT return resulting in an underpayment of tax, *or*
- a trader obtains a repayment to which it is not entitled, *or*
- an assessment is made on a trader which understates its liability and the trader does not take all reasonable steps to draw this to the attention of HMRC within 30 days of receiving it.

If a misdeclaration is discovered by HMRC in a VAT return there will only be a penalty if the error equals or exceeds the lower of £1,000,000 or 30% of the gross *amount of tax for that period*. Broadly, the gross amount of tax for a period is the correct total of input and output tax that should have been shown on the tax return for that period.

Interest

Interest is chargeable on assessments for late VAT and where there has been an over declaration of input tax or under declaration of output tax. It runs from the date VAT should have been paid (i.e. one month after end of return period) to the date of actual payment.

However, it will not normally be charged where there is no VAT loss to HMRC as would occur where one business has failed to charge VAT that another business could have recovered if it had been charged.

HMRC will pay interest on VAT repayments when the tax return was submitted on time but an instruction for repayment was not issued within 30 days from the end of the relevant return period. It is the greater of £50 or 5% of the tax due.

Small businesses

VAT for small businesses is a burden because of the administration that it requires. As a consequence, some reduction in the administrative burden is sometimes possible.

Three particular schemes in this regard are:
- annual returns
- cash accounting
- flat rate

Annual accounting

Where a business has an anticipated annual taxable turnover (i.e. standard plus zero rated supplies excluding the VAT) not exceeding £660,000 (excluding VAT) then instead of being required to complete four quarterly returns each twelve months such a business may make a single annual return for the previous 12 months.

The above applies to a business which has been registered for at least 12 months. For businesses which are about to register or have been registered for less than 12 months, and anticipated annual taxable turnover is £150,000 or less, application to join the scheme may still be made.

Although only one return is necessary, the business is required to make nine equal monthly payments of VAT based upon the net VAT liability for the previous year (i.e. each payment equals 10% of the previous year's net VAT liability). These payments are due in months 4 to 12 inclusive.

A final balancing payment for the year must be made within two months of the end of the year at which time the annual return must also be lodged.

Even the above nine instalments can be reduced to just three quarterly instalments (25% each) where the turnover of the business does not exceed £100,000 and the previous year's net VAT liability was less than £2,000. The three payments are made at the end of months 4, 7 and 10.

A trader must leave the scheme where his taxable turnover for the last annual accounting period exceeded £825,000. The trader must notify HMRC with a view to leaving the scheme where it anticipates that its turnover will exceed these limits in the current accounting period.

Cash accounting

As discussed above VAT is calculated for each quarter on the basis of invoices issued and received; basically the accruals basis.

However, where annual taxable turnover is not anticipated to exceed £660,000 a trader may elect to lodge returns on the cash basis. This basis simply requires that output and input VAT for a quarter is calculated on a cash received and cash paid basis.

This basis has the advantage that any output VAT which is normally accounted for in the quarter in which an invoice has been raised need not be so accounted for until the trader actually receives settlement of the invoice. Inter alia, this means that automatic relief for bad debts is obtained.

On the other hand, until the trader settles invoices raised on purchases no input VAT can be recovered.

A trader must leave the scheme if annual taxable turnover has exceeded £825,000 at the end of a VAT period.

Optional flat rate scheme

Under the flat rate scheme small businesses may calculate their VAT liability as a flat rate percentage of total turnover (i.e. inclusive of VAT, and including standard, zero rated and exempt supplies) thus avoiding the need to keep detailed records of input and output tax.

The scheme is available to small businesses with a taxable turnover which is not anticipated to exceed £150,000 in the next 12 months and total turnover (i.e. standard plus zero rated supplies (excluding VAT) plus exempt supplies and plus other non-business income) of up to £187,500 in the next 12 months.

Under the scheme a trader charges customers the normal amount of VAT (i.e. output VAT) on sales and is charged on purchases normal amounts of VAT (i.e. input VAT). However, the output VAT is not paid over to HMRC nor is the input VAT recoverable. Instead, in each VAT period a flat rate is charged to the VAT inclusive turnover plus any exempt supplies and this amount of VAT is then payable to HMRC as normal.

The flat rate varies according to the type of business or trade sector. Rates vary, and by way of example the flat rate percentage for accounting is 13%; for advertising 9.5%; estate agency 11%; legal services 13%; food manufacturing 7.5%; and tobacco or newspaper retailing 2%.

This scheme, however, cannot be used in conjunction with the cash accounting scheme (see above) but can be used with the annual return scheme (see above).

Example 23.12

John Smith uses the flat rate scheme (applying a flat rate of 13%) and makes annual sales (VAT excluded) of £80,000. John's purchases amount to £5,000 (VAT excluded).

Compare the flat rate method with the normal method.

Answer

Under the flat rate scheme John will account for:

Output VAT =	13% x (80,000 + 14,000)	= £12,220

If John used the normal method:

Output VAT =	7/47 x (80,000 + 14,000)	= 14,000
Input VAT =	7/47 x (5,000 + 875)	= (875)
Net output VAT		= £13,125

By using the flat rate scheme John saves VAT of:

£905 (i.e. £13,125 – £12,220)

Substantial traders

If a trader has an annual VAT liability exceeding £2,000,000 then monthly payments on account of each quarter's liability must be paid over to HMRC thereafter.

These monthly payments on account in each quarter are taken into account when calculating the net VAT payable for the quarter. Each monthly payment is based on the previous year's VAT liability and equals 1/24th of this annual amount.

Interaction of VAT and the other taxes

Generally speaking, VAT is excluded from tax calculations.

Thus, all calculations are performed net of VAT. The simple reason is that in the majority of cases VAT is charged as output on sales and input VAT payable on purchases is then offset giving rise to a VAT net payment or net recovery. In other words VAT does not impact upon the business other than from a cash flow perspective.

However, sometimes VAT may not be irrecoverable by a trader (e.g. on the purchase of motor cars; if only exempt supplies are made). In such cases some form of relief is in principle available as follows:

Income and corporation tax

Irrecoverable VAT may be deducted as a business expense in computing trading profit.

However, if such VAT relates to the purchase of a capital item and is irrecoverable it may form part of the cost of the item for capital allowance purposes instead.

Capital gains tax

VAT paid on the purchase of a chargeable asset is excluded form any subsequent capital gain computation if the VAT is recoverable. However, where the VAT is irrecoverable the purchase price will be the VAT inclusive price.

Note, however, that on a future sale any VAT that may be charged on the sale price should be excluded in computing any capital gain.

SUMMARY

VAT is a tax on consumption. Other than from a cash flow perspective VAT is generally neutral for businesses except if the business makes exempt supplies.

VAT charged on sales (output VAT) is offset against VAT paid on purchases (input VAT) over a three months period and VAT either paid over or recovered from HMRC who are responsible for administering VAT.

Failure to file a VAT return and/or make the appropriate payment in a timely manner will lead to default surcharges and interest charges.

For small businesses certain reliefs to make the administration of VAT easier are available including annual rather than quarterly returns, cash accounting and the flat rate scheme. Various conditions need to be satisfied before any of these options may be adopted.

APPENDIX 1

How to Study Taxation: Some Pointers

INTRODUCTION

Studying UK taxation requires commitment. This is because the subject matter is involved and at times complex. However, this book has simplified the tax law as much as possible.

To some extent UK taxation is logical but often it is not. Don't worry therefore if you have difficulty understanding a particular issue because it doesn't seem logical; it probably isn't!

For example, the UK's income tax year runs from the 6th April to the next 5th April (e.g. 6th April 2005 to 5th April 2006). It does *not* operate on a calendar year i.e. 1st January to 31st December basis.

The taxes which you will generally study as part of your course are:
- income tax;
- capital gains tax;
- corporation tax; and
- value added tax.

Inheritance tax (levied on death) is normally studied only at the advanced level (e.g. Paper 3.2 ACCA).

Income tax: the basis

Income tax is **very** *important* and an understanding of income tax (the tax paid by individuals) is necessary before it is possible to understand corporation tax (the tax paid by companies).

An understanding of capital gains tax and value added tax does not, however, require knowledge of either income or corporation tax.

Computational approach

The tax syllabus, whether for ACCA, CAT, ATT or CIMA, primarily involves the ability to perform computations i.e. working out an individual's income tax liability or a company's corporation tax liability.

There is no real need to be able to write letters of advice, memoranda or other types of written document. This makes taxation, for those who may have difficulty with the English language, a relatively easier subject to study.

Virtually no understanding of the UK's tax case law or its legislation is needed. Students do not therefore need to be able to recite details of tax cases heard by the courts or section numbers from the tax legislation (i.e. the various Acts of Parliament).

As the approach is computational without doubt one of the keys to passing the examinations is to understand and remember the various pro-forma layouts adopted in doing the various types of computation.

Pro-formas

A pro-forma is simply a standard layout of how a particular computation should be carried out.

The pro-forma layout not only reflects the order in which a computation needs to be performed but can also effectively be used as a revision aid with the simple addition of your own detailed notes.

One approach to studying tax is therefore to ensure that you know the pro-forma for a particular purpose and to make your own notes for each pro-forma highlighting associated key points. For example, let us look at calculating an individual's income tax liability; one of the first things you will be taught on your course:

The pro-forma is as follows:

	Non-Savings Income	Savings Income	Dividend Income

Income (1)

Less: Charges on income (2)

STI (Statutory Total Income)

Less: Personal allowance (3)

Taxable income (4)

Having then worked out the **Taxable Income** for each category of income (i.e. Non-savings, Savings and Dividend income) the individual's income tax liability can then be worked out as follows.

Income tax liability on:
Non-savings income (5)
Savings income
Dividends
Total income tax on all income
Less: Tax reducers (Paper 3.2 only) (6)
Plus: Basic rate tax withheld on charges on income (7)
Income tax liability (8)
Less: Income tax suffered at source on following income:
Tax credit on UK dividends (9)
PAYE on salary
Tax on bank deposit interest
Tax on building society deposit interest

Income tax payable (10)

Notes

1. *Income* identifies the individual's income which comprises, for example, trading profit, property business profit, employmenet earnings etc.
2. *Charges on income* are of two types: qualifying interest payments (paid gross) and patent royalties (paid net)
3. Each individual is entitled to an annual PA which is £4,895 for 2005/06
4. Taxable income = STI − PA
5. Income tax is levied first on Non-savings, then Savings and finally Dividend income
6. Tax reducers are:
7. EIS (20%) and VCT schemes (40%)
8. Marriage couple's allowance (10%)
9. The only charge on income included here is a patent royalty payment
10. This is the income tax liability of the individual after taking into account all categories of income and all deductions
11. Tax credit on dividends are offset first as these are not reclaimable whereas the tax deducted on the other items is reclaimable.
12. *Income tax payable* = Income tax liability minus tax already paid

Now don't worry if at this stage you do not follow or understand the above.

I have included it simply to try and illustrate what a pro-forma looks like and how you can eventually use it together with your own notes as a revision aid.

Repetition

Because of the volume of material covered in a taxation course there is often little time to revise bits of the course as you go along which is, of course, the ideal way to study. The pro-forma plus notes should help in this regard.

Doing questions

When starting to study a new tax (e.g. capital gains tax) or aspect of it (e.g. use of capital losses) the starting point should be for you to try to understand the theory i.e. an explanation of the underlying concepts. Simply doing questions is *not* the answer.

Try to understand the underlying concepts *before* turning to try any questions yourself. In this book I have included worked examples in the text which illustrate the points under discussion. Read the text and together with the examples try to understand what is happening. Do not simply try to follow the example without having first tried to understand the theory.

Only when you think you have understood the theory and any related examples does it make sense to try some questions for yourself.

In trying questions the more you can try the better. If you find difficulty in answering a particular question then *before* looking at the answer reread the theory and try the question again. Do not simply and immediately look at the answer; this should only be done as a last resort when you have really tried to answer the question.

When looking at an answer, do not simply check the numbers; note, in particular, the layout and order in which the various issues are tackled.

Common parts of the syllabus

Some tax topics are inevitably relevant to more than one type of tax and certainly some are, relatively speaking, more important than others.

For example, capital allowances (basically tax depreciation) are relevant to both income and corporation taxes. Therefore by studying this particular topic means that you will be able to attempt more questions in the exam than where a particular topic can only appear once (e.g. VAT cash accounting scheme).

Similarly the adjustment of accounts profits (i.e. converting accounts profits in to taxable profits) is highly relevant to both income and corporation taxes. It is therefore a good idea when you see that a topic appears relevant to more than one type of tax or situation to make sure you fully understand it. This will enhance your ability to pass the exam.

SUMMARY

The most important point is to really try to understand the underlying concepts.

Simply doing lots and lots of questions without attempting to understand the underlying theory is not a good idea.

Only when you feel you have a reasonable understanding of an area should you then attempt a variety of questions.

When looking at model answers to questions take serious note of how the answer is laid out and the order in which it's presented.

When you have finished a particular tax, e.g. income tax, it is a good idea to try to find time to look through the material again before starting the next tax. Your pro-forma plus attaching notes should be of immense help in this regard.

Don't be frightened to look at other tax sources which may also help.

You can email me at my website www.mgtdynamics.co.uk if you have any questions on any part of my book. Also feel free to offer any suggestions for improving it.

You might also look at another tax textbook. Or, you might like to look at the web-sites www.taxationweb.co.uk and www.accountingweb.co.uk to check if you can find anything there of help by using the search function.

Although not the easiest of websites for the newcomer to UK tax the official HM Revenue & Customs site www.hmrc.gov.uk may also sometimes be of help.

Identify in particular those areas which are relevant to more than one type of tax or situation.

Finally, try to enjoy your studies.

Good luck with your exams!

APPENDIX 2

Questions for Students

Answers can be found at www.spiramus.com/uk_taxation_for_students.htm

Chapters 1 to 5

Question 1

James Brown has the following income:

Employment income	15,000
Bank interest (received)	800
Dividends (received)	900

Income tax of 1,000 was deducted under the Pay As You Earn (PAYE) regulations from James' employment earnings of 15,000.

Calculate the income tax payable for 2005/06.

Question 2

James Brown has the following income:

Employment income	25,000
Bank interest (received)	1,600
Dividends (received)	1,800

Income tax of 2,000 was deducted under the Pay As You Earn (PAYE) regulations from James' employment earnings of 25,000.

Calculate the income tax payable for 2005/06.

Question 3

James Brown has the following income:

Employment income	45,000
Bank interest (received)	1,600
Dividends (received)	1,800

Income tax of 6,000 was deducted under the Pay As You Earn (PAYE) regulations from James' employment earnings of 45,000.

Calculate the income tax payable for 2005/06.

Question 4

James Brown has the following income:

Employment income	35,000
Rental income	5,000
Bank interest (gross)	1,600
Dividends (received)	1,800

Income tax of 5,000 was deducted under the Pay As You Earn (PAYE) regulations from James' employment earnings of 35,000.

In addition, James paid a patent royalty of 5,000 (gross).

Calculate the income tax payable for 2005/06.

Question 5

James Brown has the following income:

Employment income	35,000
Rental income	15,000
Bank interest (received)	1,600
Dividends (received)	1,800

Income tax of 5,000 was deducted under the Pay As You Earn (PAYE) regulations from James' employment earnings of 35,000.

In addition, James paid a patent royalty of 5,000 (gross).

Calculate the income tax payable for 2005/06.

Question 6

James Brown has the following income:

Employment income	35,000
Rental income	15,000
Bank interest (gross)	1,600
Dividends (received)	1,800

Income tax of 5,000 was deducted under the Pay As You Earn (PAYE) regulations from James' employment earnings of 35,000.

In addition, James paid interest of 5,000 on a qualifying loan.

Calculate the income tax payable for 2005/06.

Question 7

In setting off charges on income paid against an individual's income subject to income tax why is it the most tax efficient to offset such charges against non-savings income followed by savings income followed by dividend income?

Question 8

Give two examples of qualifying interest payment.

Question 9

James Brown has the following income:

Employment income	35,000
Rental income	15,000
Bank interest (gross)	1,600
Dividends (received)	1,800

Income tax of 5,000 was deducted under the Pay As You Earn (PAYE) regulations from James' employment earnings of 35,000.

In addition, James paid interest of 5,000 on a qualifying loan and made personal pension contributions of 1,560 (gross).

Calculate the income tax payable for 2005/06.

Question 10

James Brown has the following income:

Rental income	33,000
Bank interest (gross)	1,600
Dividends (received)	1,800

In addition, James paid interest of 1,000 on a qualifying loan and made personal pension contributions of 1,560 (gross).

Calculate the income tax payable for 2005/06.

Chapters 6 to 7

Question 11

James Brown carried on his trade as a sole trader. He made up his accounts to 30th September each year having started to trade on 1st October 2003.

His tax adjusted profits were:

Year ended 30th September 2004 12,000
Year ended 30th September 2005 24,000
Year ended 30th September 2006 36,000

Calculate James' assessments for each of the first three tax years of trade identifying the appropriate basis periods for each tax year and identify any overlap profits.

Question 12

James Brown carried on his trade as a sole trader. He made up his accounts to 30th June each year having started to trade on 1st October 2003.

His tax adjusted profits were:

Year ended 30th June 2004 18,000
Year ended 30th June 2005 27,000
Year ended 30th June 2006 36,000

Calculate James' assessments for each of the first three tax years of trade identifying the appropriate basis periods for each tax year and identify any overlap profits.

Question 13

James Brown carried on his trade as a sole trader. He made up his accounts to 30th June each year having started to trade on 1st May 2003.

His tax adjusted profits were:

Period ended 30th June 2004 30,000
Year ended   30th June 2005 27,000
Year ended   30th June 2006 36,000

Calculate James' assessments for each of the first three tax years of trade identifying the appropriate basis periods for each tax year and identify any overlap profits.

Question 14

James Brown carried on his trade as a sole trader. He made up his accounts to 30th April each year having started to trade on 1st December 2003.

His tax adjusted profits were:

Period ended 30th April 2005 30,000
Year ended   30th April 2005 27,000
Year ended   30th April 2006 36,000

Calculate James' assessments for each of the first three tax years of trade identifying the appropriate basis periods for each tax year and identify any overlap profits.

Question 15

James Brown a sole trader started carrying on his trade as a sports retailer (under the trading name of "Sports for All") on 1st May 2004 and his first set of accounts were prepared to 30th April 2005. His accounts prepared by his accountant for the year ended 30th April 2005 showed the following:

Income

Gross profit	100,000
Rental income	15,000
Building society interest received	16,000
Dividends received	900
	131,900

Expenses

Provisions	1,200
Depreciation	3,500
Salaries	39,000
Rent and rates	10,000
Light and heat	4,000
Repairs and maintenance	2,500
Advertising	25,000
Motor expenses	10,000
Sundry expenses	8,000
	103,200
Net profit	28,700

Notes

1. Salaries included a salary to James' wife of 15,000 as she works in the shop as a sales assistant. The other sales assistants doing the same job receive a salary of 12,000.

2. James and his wife live in a flat above the shop. The figures for "rent and rates" and "light and heat" are for both the shop and the flat. The accountant has agreed with the tax authorities that 30% of these expenses relate to the flat.

3. Of the "repairs and maintenance" 250 related to the decoration of the flat and 1,250 related to some improvements to the shop.

4. Included in the figure of 25,000 for advertising was 5,000 which related to Christmas presents to his customers of various wines and spirits; and 4,000 which related to diaries sent out to customers which had cost James 10 each and had on the front of them James' logo and the name of his business "Sports for All". The rest of the expenditure related to advertisements which James had placed in newspapers and trade magazines.

5. James decided to lease a new car (rather then buy it outright). The car had a retail price of 20,000 and James' annual leasing charge is 6,000. The balance of the expenditure related to normal running costs (eg petrol, repairs etc). The tax authorities have agreed that 60% of James' usage relates to private usage with 40% representing business usage. The car does not qualify as a low CO_2 emission car.

6. Sundry expenses included client entertaining of 2,000; staff entertaining of 450 on a day out in London; a fine of 500 for breach of health and safety regulations; a car park fine of 50 incurred by one of the sales assistants when on business for James; a donation to a local charity of 75 and a donation of 50 to his local political party; a subscription of 80 to the Sports Retailers Association; legal fees of 375 in connection with the granting of a brand new lease on the shop; and accountancy fees for accounts preparation of 500.

7. The figure for provisions comprised 800 in respect of a specific trade debt and the balance was a general provision.

8. James' son had always wanted a pair of trainers for Christmas. James therefore took a pair from the shop for his son but did not pay for them. The trainers if they had been sold to a member of the public would have a retail price of 135 but their cost to James had been 100.

Calculate James' trading profit for tax purposes.

Question 16

James Brown a sole trader bought various capital items all of which qualified for capital allowances.

He prepared his accounts to 31st December each year. His purchases were as follows:

Purchases

Fixtures and fittings	16,000	on 1st September 2004
Motor car:	15,000	on 1st August 2004 (for himself; not a low emission car)
Van	8,000	on 30th January 2005

James' business is considered to be small business for capital allowance purposes

Calculate James' capital allowances for the periods ended 31st December 2004 and 2005.

Question 17

James Brown a sole trader bought various capital items all of which qualified for capital allowances.

He prepared his accounts to 31st December each year. His purchases were as follows:

Purchases

Fixtures and fittings	16,000 on 1st September 2003
Motor car:	8,000 on 1st August 2004 (for an employee; not a low emission car)
Motor car:	7,000 on 1st August 2005 (for an employee; a low emission car)

James' business is considered to be small business for capital allowance purposes

Calculate James' capital allowances for the periods ended 31st December 2003, 2004 and 2005.

Question 18

James Brown a sole trader bought various capital items all of which qualified for capital allowances.

He prepared his accounts to 31st December each year. His purchases were as follows:

Purchases

Fixtures and fittings	16,000 on 1st September 2004
Motor car:	8,000 on 1st August 2004 (for an employee; not a low emission car)
Motor car:	7,000 on 1st August 2005 (for an employee; a low emission car)

Sales

Fixtures and fittings 3,000 on 31st October 2005 (all at below original cost)

James' business is considered to be medium business for capital allowance purposes.

Calculate James' capital allowances for the periods ended 31st December 2004 and 2005.

Question 19

James Brown commenced to trade on 1 August 2003. His adjusted profits for tax purposes before capital allowances were:

Year ended 30 July 2004	60,000
Year ended 30 July 2005	120,000

APPENDIX 2

Year ended 30 July 2006   180,000

James purchased and sold various assets all of which qualified for capital allowances. His purchases and sales were as follows:

Purchases

Fixtures and fittings	16,000 on 1st September 2003
Motor cars:	15,000 on 1st August 2003 (for himself; not a low emission car)
	10,000 on 1st August 2003 for one of his employees
Van	8,000 on 30th January 2004
Computers	3,000on 1st December 2004
Fixtures and fittings	7,000 on 18th May 2005
Motor cars:	20,000 on 1st June 2006 (for himself; not a low emission car)

Sales

Van	2,000 on 20th February 2005
Fixtures and fittings	2,000 on 30th April 2006 (all at below original cost)
Motor car	9,000 on 31st May 2006 (sale of James original car)

James has agreed with the tax authorities that his private use of his cars is 30% and that of his employee 25%.

James' business is considered to be small business for capital allowance purposes.

Calculate James' adjusted tax profits for each of the tax years 2003/04, 2004/05 and 2005/06.

Question 20

James incurred the following construction costs in building an industrial building:

Purchase price of land (including 3,000 professional legal costs)	45,000
Buildings (including drawing office 35,000, staff canteen 25,000, general office 80,000)	500,000
Cutting and levelling land	20,000
Total cost	565,000

Identify the cost which will be eligible for industrial buildings allowances.

Question 21

James incurred the following construction costs in building an industrial building:

Purchase price of land (including 5,000 professional legal costs)	40,000
Architects and surveyors fees	12,000
Buildings (including drawing office 35,000, staff canteen 25,000, general office 145,600)	500,000
Cutting and levelling land	20,000
Total cost	572,000

Identify the cost which will be eligible for industrial buildings allowances.

Question 22

James Brown a sole trader prepares his accounts to 31st May each year.

On 1st June 2002 he began to use a newly constructed factory to manufacture desks. The cost of the factory was 375,000 which included 45,000 for the land cost.

Calculate the allowances which James may claim for the years ended 31st May 2003, 2004 and 2005.

Question 23

James Brown a sole trader prepares his accounts to 31st May each year.

On 1st June 2002 he began to use a newly constructed factory to manufacture desks. The cost of the factory was 375,000 which included 45,000 for the land cost.

On 30th June 2005 James sold the factory to Mary Smith for a sales price of 400,000 which included 50,000 for the land cost.

Calculate the allowances which James may claim for the years ended 31st May 2003, 2004 and 2005. Show the balancing allowance or balancing charge for James in the year ended 31st May 2006 and identify the capital allowances which Mary may claim. She prepares her accounts to 31st December each year.

Chapter 8

Question 24

James Brown a sole trader has been trading for many years and makes up his accounts to 31st January each year.

His adjusted trading results for the past few years are as follows.

Year ended 30 April 2003	70,000
Year ended 30 April 2004	(50,000)
Year ended 30 April 2005	125,000

Calculate James' assessments for each relevant tax year assuming he makes a claim only under section 385.

Question 25

James Brown a sole trader has been trading for many years and makes up his accounts to 31st January each year.

His adjusted trading results for the past few years are as follows.

Year ended 30 April 2003	70,000
Year ended 30 April 2004	(50,000)
Year ended 30 April 2005	125,000

His other income for the tax years 2003/04, 2004/05 and 2005/06 is 10,000, 5,000 and 20,000.

Calculate James' assessments for each relevant tax year assuming he makes a claim only under section 380 and identify the amount of the trading loss of 50,000 (if any) which remains available for carry forward under section 385.

Question 26

James Brown a sole trader started to trade on 1st July 2002 and prepared his accounts to 30th June. His results were as follows:

Year ended 30th June 2003   (24,000)
Year ended 30th June 2004   36,000
Year ended 30th June 2005   48,000

Calculate James' assessments for the tax years 2003/04, 2004/05 and 2005/06 and identify any overlap profits. Assume he makes a claim under section 385 only.

Question 27

James Brown started in business on 1st July 2003 and prepares his accounts to 30th June each year.

His results were as follows:
Year ended 30th June 2004   (24,000)
Year ended 30th June 2005   5,000

Before he set up in business James was an employee and received the following salaries:
2002/03   7,000
2001/02   6,000
2000/01   5,000

James also received other income in each of these three tax years of 4,000 in 2002/03, 3,000 in 2001/02 and 1,000 in 2000/01.

Calculate James' taxable income for the tax years 2000/01, 2002/03, 2003/04, and 2005/06 assuming that James makes a claim under section 381 (assume also a personal allowance of 4,895 for each tax year).

Question 28

For the tax year 2005/06 James Brown, a sole trader, made a trading loss of 40,000.

He also had chargeable gains of 45,000 and a capital loss of 25,000. James also had a capital loss available for carry forward from prior tax years of 12,000.

James' STI for 2005/06 was 25,000.

Calculate the amount of James' chargeable gains after the annual exemption of 8,500 and after electing to also use section 380. Quantify also the amount of capital loss (if any) available for carry forward to future tax years.

Chapter 10

Question 29

James Brown was an employee of ABC Ltd.

His salary for the tax year 2005/06 was 100,000. James was also provided with a company car with a list price of 25,000 and CO_2 emissions of 222 grams/km.

The car was however only provided from the 6th December 2005.

Calculate the assessable benefit in respect of the car for 2005/06.

Question 30

James Brown was an employee of ABC Ltd.

His salary for the tax year 2005/06 was 100,000. James was also provided with a company car with a list price of 25,000 and CO_2 emissions of 222 grams/km.

The car was provided from the 6th April 2005 until 6th December 2005 when it was replaced with a new car list price 30,000 and CO_2 emissions of 265 grams/km.

Calculate the assessable benefit in respect of the cars for 2005/06.

Question 31

James Brown was an employee of ABC Ltd.

His salary for the tax year 2005/06 was 100,000. James was also provided with a company car with a list price of 25,000 and CO_2 emissions of 222 grams/km.

The car was provided from the 6th April 2005 until 6th December 2005 when it was replaced with a new car list price 30,000 and CO_2 emissions of 265 grams/km.

In respect of the first car James made a contribution towards its running costs of 50/month. In respect of the second car the company paid all of James' fuel both business and private and James was not asked to make any contributions.

Calculate the assessable benefit in respect of the cars and car fuel for 2005/06.

Question 32

James Brown accepted a job with XYZ Ltd. His salary was 40,000 but his employer did not provide him with a company car.

Instead James was expected to use his own car and the company agreed to pay him expenses when on business of 40p for the first 5,000 business miles and 50p per mile thereafter. In the tax year 2005/06 James did 30,000 business miles.

Calculate the amount of the assessment on James for 2005/06.

Question 33

James Brown accepted a job with ABC Ltd. His salary was 40,000 but his employer did not provide him with a company car.

Instead James was expected to use his own car and the company agreed to pay him expenses when on business of 20p for the first 5,000 business miles and 25p per mile thereafter. In the tax year 2005/06 James did 30,000 business miles.

Calculate whether James will be assessed on the payment of expenses from his employer or whether he will be entitled to make a claim for expenses when calculating his taxable income from the employment for 2005/06.

Question 34

James Brown is employed by XYZ Ltd and as part of his remuneration package is provided with accommodation.

The house in which he lives was purchased by his employer in January 2004 for 450,000. The annual value of the house is 1,500.

Calculate the assessable benefit for 2005/06 using the official rate of interest of 5%.

Question 35

James Brown is employed by XYZ Ltd and as part of his remuneration package is provided with accommodation.

The house in which he lives was purchased by his employer in January 2004 for 450,000. The annual value of the house is 1,500. John contributes 100 per month to his employer in respect of the provision of the accommodation.

Calculate the assessable benefit for 2005/06 using the official rate of interest of 5%.

Question 36

James Brown is employed by XYZ Ltd and as part of his remuneration package is provided with accommodation.

The house in which he lives was purchased by his employer in January 1998 for 450,000. The annual value of the house is 1,500.

The house was first made available to James on 6th April 2005. John contributes 100 per month to his employer in respect of the provision of the accommodation.

Calculate the assessable benefit for 2005/06 using the official rate of interest of 5%.

Question 37

James Brown is employed by XYZ Ltd and as part of his remuneration package is provided with accommodation.

The house in which he lives was purchased by his employer in January 1998 for 450,000. Further expenditure was incurred by XYZ Ltd in improving the house including 50,000 in March 2000, 15,000 in July 2004 and 34,000 in May 2005.

The annual value of the house is 1,500.

The house was first made available to James on 6th April 2005. John contributes 100 per month to his employer in respect of the provision of the accommodation.

Calculate the assessable benefit for 2005/06 using the official rate of interest of 5%.

Question 38

If the accommodation referred to in Question 37 above was job related accommodation what would then be the benefit taxable on James for 2005/06?

Question 39

Assuming the same circumstances as set out in Question 37, if in addition XYZ Ltd paid various running expenses of the house as set out below, calculate the benefit on which James will be taxed for 2005/06:

Heating	1,550
Cleaning and maintenance	1,000
Telephone	675*
Structural repairs	7,500
Council tax	1,100

*the telephone costs are made up of 250 for the line rental, business costs 350 and private calls of 75.

Question 40

How would your answer differ if in Question 39 you were told the accommodation was job related and if you were also told that James' net emoluments were, for the tax year, 2005/06 25,000?

Question 41

James Brown is employed by ABC Ltd who has allowed him the use of some photographic equipment which had a market value of 4,500 at the date it was first provided to James on 6th July 2005.

Calculate the benefit on which James will be taxed for the tax year 2005/06.

Question 42

James Brown is employed by ABC Ltd who has allowed him the use of some photographic equipment which had a market value of 4,500 at the date it was first provided to James on 6th July 2005.

John contributes 5 per month to his employer for the use of the equipment.

Calculate the benefit on which James will be taxed for the tax year 2005/06.

Question 43

James Brown is employed by ABC Ltd who has allowed him the use of some photographic equipment which had a market value of 4,500 at the date it was first provided to James on 6th April 2003.

On 6th December 2005 James' employer gave the equipment to James which at that time had a market value of 2,000.

Calculate the benefit on which James will be taxed for the tax year 2005/06.

Question 44

How would your answer differ to Question 43 if instead of the asset concerned being photographic equipment it was a computer?

Question 45

Identify which of the following items would be tax free to James, an employee of XYZ Ltd, where the goods/services were provided by his employer in the course of his employment:

1. removal expenses of 7,500
2. a car park space near to where James works
3. use of a mobile telephone
4. a loan of 6,000
5. job related accommodation
6. company car
7. luncheon vouchers of 15p per day

Chapters 12 to 15

Question 46

James Brown bought a non-business chargeable asset on 1st May 1992.

How many years qualify for taper relief if James sells the asset on or after 10th July 2005?

Question 47

How would your answer for Question 46 be different (if at all) if the asset concerned had been a business asset?

Question 48

How would your answer to Question 46 differ (if at all) had James Brown bought the non-business asset on 1st April 1998?

Question 49

Are indexation allowances computed to three decimal places? When is this not the case?

Question 50

Are capital losses offset against capital gains before or after taper relief?

Question 51

James Brown would like to carry forward to 2006/07 the unused element of his annual exemption for 2005/06. Is he permitted to do this?

Question 52

James Brown bought a business asset in May 2000 for a gross cost of 4,500. The incidental costs of the purchase amounted to 750.

James sold the asset for 8,250 in June 2005 which proceeds included 250 of incidental costs of sale.

Calculate James' taxable amount after annual exemption for the tax year 2005/06.

Question 53

James Brown bought a non-business asset in May 2000 for a gross cost of 4,500. The incidental costs of the purchase amounted to 750.

James sold the asset for 8,250 in June 2005 which proceeds included 250 of incidental costs of sale.

Calculate James' taxable amount after annual exemption for the tax year 2005/06.

Question 54

James Brown bought a non-business asset in January 1992 for 30,000. He sold the asset in October 2005 for 100,000.

The indexation allowance for the relevant period is 5,970.

James' taxable income for 2005/06 was 15,000.

Calculate James' taxable amount after annual exemption for the tax year 2005/06 and his tax liability on this taxable amount.

Question 55

James Brown bought a business asset in July 1995 for 45,000 and sold it in November 2005 for 75,000.

The RPI for July 1995, April 1998 and November 2005 were respectively 149.10, 162.6, and 195.8.

Calculate James' taxable amount after annual exemption for the tax year 2005/06

Question 56

James Brown bought a non-business asset in January 1992 for 30,000. He sold the asset in October 2005 for 100,000.

The indexation allowance for the relevant period is 5,970.

James brought forward from 2004/05 capital losses of 12,000.

Calculate James' taxable amount after annual exemption for the tax year 2005/06.

Question 57

James Brown sold the following three chargeable assets in 2005/06:

Asset 1   Gain 35,000
Asset2   Gain 7,500
Asset 3   Loss 10,000

The gains are after indexation allowance.

Calculate James' taxable amount after annual exemption for 2005/06.

John has taxable income (none of which is savings or dividend income) of 30,000 for 2004/05.

Question 58

James Brown sold the following chargeable assets in 2005/06:
Asset1 (a business asset)

| | acquired | 1 June 2004 | for | 50,000 |
| | sold | 1 April 2006 | for | 70,000 |

Asset2 (a non-business asset)

| | acquired | 1 October 1988 | for | 100,000 |
| | sold | 1 February 2006 | for | 150,000 |

Asset3 (a business asset)

| | acquired | 1 August 1996 | for | 40,000 |
| | sold | 1 April 2006 | for | 70,000 |

Indexation allowances are:

October 1988 – April 1998   48,500

August 1996 – April 1998   2,480

Calculate James' capital gains tax liability for 2005/06 assuming that his taxable income for 2005/06 was 26,000

Question 59

James Brown made the following indexed gains/losses on sales in 2005/06:

business asset sale in July 2005 making an indexed gain of 100,000

non-business asset sale in November 2004 making an indexed gain of 40,000

non-business asset sale in December 2004 making a loss of 40,000

In addition, James had a capital loss brought forward from 2004/05 of 20,000.

All assets had been acquired before 17th March 1998.

James had taxable income (none of which is either dividends or savings income) for 2004/05 of 27,500.

Calculate the capital gains tax liability of James having used the capital losses in the most tax efficient manner for 2004/05.

Question 60

James Brown bought a business asset in September 1994 for 12,000. He gave it to his daughter Mary in July 2005 when it was worth 40,000. Gift relief was claimed.

Indexation allowance: September 1994 – April 1998 = 1,452

Calculate for the tax year 2005/06:
   1.   the amount assessable on James and
   2.   Mary's base cost for capital gains tax purposes.

Question 61

James Brown bought a business asset in September 1994 for 12,000. His daughter Mary purchased the asset in July 2005 for 18,000 when it was worth 40,000. Gift relief was claimed.

Indexation allowance: September 1994 – April 1998 = 1,452

Calculate for the tax year 2005/06:
   1.   the amount assessable on James and
   2.   Mary's base cost for capital gains tax purposes.

Question 62

James Brown bought a business asset in September 1994 for 12,000. His daughter Mary purchased the asset in July 2005 for 18,000 when it was worth 40,000. Gift relief was claimed.

Mary subsequently sold the asset for 65,000 in March 2006.

Indexation allowance: September 1994 – April 1998 = 1,452

Calculate for the tax year 2005/06:

1. the amount assessable on James
2. Mary's base cost for capital gains tax purposes and
3. the amount on which Mary will be subject to capital gains tax on her sale.

Question 63

James Brown, a sole trader, sold the goodwill of his business in May 2005 for 2 million. The goodwill had a base cost of nil.

In July 2004 James had bought a new factory for his business at a cost of 2.5 million.

Calculate James' chargeable gain on the sale of the goodwill after claiming rollover relief and identify the base cost of the factory.

Question 64

James Brown decided that his business needed a new factory. He sold his existing factory for 900,000 in June 2006 having acquired it in February 1995 for 300,000.

His new factory cost 1.2 million acquired in March 2005.

Calculate James' chargeable gain (pre annual exemption) on the sale of the factory and inform him whether he is entitled to claim roll-over relief on this gain and if not why not.

Question 65

Assume that in Question 64 James Brown had purchased his new factory in August 2005.

How would your answer and advice be different (if at all)?

Question 66

James Brown decided that his business needed a new factory. He sold his existing factory for 900,000 in June 2006 having acquired it in February 1995 for 300,000.

His new factory cost 1.2 million acquired in March 2005 which he then sold on 5th April 2006 for 1.5 million.

Calculate James' chargeable gains (pre annual exemption) on each sale identifying the amount of any gains eligible for roll-over relief.

Question 67

James Brown decided that his business needed a new factory. He sold his existing factory for 900,000 in June 2006 having acquired it in February 1995 for 300,000.

His new factory cost 800,000 acquired in March 2005 which he then sold on 5th April 2006 for 1.5 million.

Calculate James' chargeable gains (pre annual exemption) on each sale identifying the amount of any gains eligible for roll-over relief.

Question 68

James Brown sold his existing factory for 900,000 in June 2006 having acquired it in February 1995 for 300,000.

Instead of purchasing a replacement factory (as in Question 66) he decided to purchase some new fixed plant and machinery at a cost 1.2 million acquired in March 2005. James then sold the plant and machinery on 5th April 2006 for 1.5 million.

Show how your answer will differ from the answer to Question 66 including carrying out all relevant calculations.

Question 69

James Brown decided that it was time to transfer his business to his son Matthew who unfortunately did not have sufficient monies to effect the purchase. James therefore decided to simply give all the shares in his company, James Brown Ltd, to Matthew.

The gift comprised 100,000 ordinary shares (100% of the company) worth 750,000 and the gift was effected in October 2005. The shares had cost James 25,000 in July 1994.

Indexation allowance July 1994 to April 1998 £3,225.

The company's net worth at the date of the gift was as follows:

Freehold factory	500,000
Goodwill	150,000
Investments	50,000
Current assets	100,000
	800,000
Current liabilities	(50,000)
Net worth	750,000

Calculate James' chargeable gain and identify how much (if any) of the gain may be rolled-over if gift relief is claimed. Assuming gift relief to have been claimed as appropriate identify the base cost of the shares for Matthew.

Question 70

James Brown sold 150,000 shares on 21st May 2005 for a net sales consideration of £450,000 in a company which qualified for business asset treatment.

He had acquired the shares as follows:

	Shares	Cost	Indexed cost
Indexed pool @ 5th April 1998	100,000	£40,000	£50,000
1st January 2001	10,000	£10,000	
3rd May 2002	15,000	£18,750	
17th October 2000	20,000	£35,000	
6th April 2005	5,000	£10,000	

Calculate James' taxable amount after annual exemption for 2005/06.

Question 71

In Question 70 what would have been James Brown's capital gains tax liability if his taxable income for 2005/06 had been £17,750?

Question 72

In Question 70 what would have been James Brown's capital gains tax liability if his taxable income for 2005/06 had been £17,750 and as at 6th April 2005 James had capital losses brought forward of £45,000?

Question 73

In Question 70 how would your answer differ (if at all) if the shares had not · qualified as business assets?

Chapters 16 to 19

Question 74

James Brown Ltd's accounting period for the year ended 31st March 2006 shows the following results:

Trading profit	45,000
Interest income	4,000
Rental income	6,000
Chargeable gain	5,000
	60,000
Less: Charges on income	(15,000)
PCTCT	45,000

Calculate James Brown Ltd's corporation tax liability for the accounting period ended 31st March 2006.

Question 75

If in Question 74 James Brown Ltd also received FII of 5,000 how would this affect your answer (if at all).

Question 76

If in Question 74 James Brown Ltd's accounting period was 31st December 2005 how would this affect your answer (if at all).

Question 77

James Brown Ltd prepares its accounts to 31st March each year.

For the year ended 31st March 2006 the company's net profit was 3 million.

This figure of 3 million was arrived at after the following adjustments:

	Deducting	Crediting
Dividends net from UK resident companies (non-group)		9,000
Dividends net fromm group companies		3,000
Building society interest accrued		40,000
Patent royalties accrued		70,000
Profit on sale of an office block		350,000
Entertaining (clients)	15,000	

Accountants fees for preparing accounts	19,000
Legal fees on a failed attempt	
to obtain a trading loan	5,000
Depreciation	300,000
Debenture interest payable (gross)	400,000
Gift aid payment to charity	20,000

Capital allowances of 100,000 have been claimed (not included in the above) and whilst the office block sale produced a capital profit of 350,000 computed on accounting principles for tax purposes it produced a chargeable gain of 570,000.

Calculate James Brown Ltd's PCTCT for the accounting period 31st March 2006 and its corporation tax liability for the year ended 31st March 2006.

Question 78

James Brown Ltd has four associated companies and for the twelve month period ended 31st March 2006 has a PCTCT of 10,000.

Identify the "Profit" limits which will be used to determine the rate of corporation tax to be applied to James Brown Ltd's PCTCT, the rate which will apply and the corporation tax liability.

Question 79

In Question 78 if James Brown Ltd also had FII of 50,000 identify the "Profit" limits which will be used to determine the rate of corporation tax to be applied to James Brown Ltd's PCTCT, the rate which will apply and the corporation tax liability.

Question 80

James Brown Ltd's accounting period for the year ended 31st March 2006 shows the following results before taking into account rental income and capital allowances:

Trading profit	45,000
Chargeable gain	5,000
	50,000
Less: Charges on income	(5,000)
PCTCT	45,000

On the 1st December 2005 James Brown Ltd granted a 40 year lease on a commercial property to a third party for a premium of 50,000.

As at 1st April 2005 the plant and machinery pool had a tax written down value of 60,000. On 3rd May 2005 plant of 16,000 was sold (original cost 25,000) and on 1st November 2005 a motor car was purchased for 20,000 and was used by James Brown the managing director 20% for private purposes.

Calculate James Brown Ltd's corporation tax liability for the accounting period ended 31st March 2006 including the appropriate element of the premium.

Question 81

Identify the accounting periods of James Brown Ltd in respect of which corporation tax will be charged given that it has prepared a set of accounts for the period 1st January 2005 to 30th April 2006.

When will the corporation tax liabilities have to be settled and when will the relevant returns need to be filed.

Confirm whether each of the following statements is true or false:
Rental income is apportioned on a time basis

Trading income is apportioned on a time basis

Interest income is apportioned on a time basis

Dividend income is taxable when received.

Question 82

James Brown Ltd's results for the accounting period ended 31st December 2005 were as follows:

Trading profit	1,500,000
Rental income	500,000
Chargeable gain	350,000
Gift aid payment to charity	25,000

For the accounting periods ended 31st December 2004 and 31st December 2006 trading losses of 175,000 and 425,000 respectively arose.

Calculate James Brown Ltd's corporation tax liability for the period ended 31st December 2005 after the earliest relief for any losses has been claimed identifying the sections under which any loss relief has been claimed.

Question 83

James Brown Ltd's results were as follows:

	Year ended 31.12.04	3 months ended 31.03.05	Year ended 31.12.03.06
Trading profit	150,000	250,000	(850,000)
Rental income	150,000	140,000	130,000
Interest income	125,000	115,000	140,000
Charges on income	112,000	103,000	115,000

Calculate James Brown Ltd's PCTCT for each of the above periods utilising the trading loss of 850,000 in the most tax efficient manner and identify (if any) the amount of trading loss remaining for carry forward under section 393(1).

Question 84

James Brown Ltd, Matthew Brown Ltd and Nicholas Brown Ltd form a group for group relief purposes. Their results were as follows for the accounting period ended 31st March 2006:

	JB Ltd	MB Ltd	NB Ltd
Trading profit	150,000	(200,000)	13,000
Rental income	5,000	15,000	10,000
Interest	20,000	2,500	5,000
Chargeable gains	30,000	4,000	2,000
Charges on income	5,000	2,000	15,000

Calculate the PCTCT for each company assuming optimum group relief is claimed and explain how the allocation of MB Ltd's trading loss was arrived at.

Question 85

James Brown Ltd, Matthew Brown Ltd and Nicholas Brown Ltd form a group for chargeable gain purposes. Each company prepares its accounts to 31st March 2006.

JB Ltd transferred a factory which it no longer wished to use to NB Ltd in November 2005 when its market value was 750,000. JB Ltd had originally paid 350,000 for the factory in August 1997.

NB Ltd subsequently sold the factory for 900,000 in July 2006.

MB Ltd having acquired some land for 150,000 in February 1999 transferred it to JB Ltd in December 2005 when its market value was 650,000.

Indexation allowances:

August 1997 to April 1998	9,100
August 1997 to November 2005	89,600
November 2005 to July 2006	1,000
February 1999 to December 2005	33,300

Calculate the chargeable gains (if any) arising on the transfers of the factory and land to NB Ltd and JB Ltd respectively and the chargeable gain arising on the sale of the factory by NB Ltd in July 2006. Identify relevant base costs on the intra-group transfers.

Question 86

James Brown Ltd had acquired a factory in March 1995 and sold it in April 2005.

How long for taper relief purposes has James Brown Ltd held the factory?

Question 87

If a number of companies form a group for group relief purposes they will automatically form a group for chargeable gains purposes. True or false?

Question 88

If a number of companies form a group for chargeable gains purposes they will automatically form a group for group relief purposes. True or false?

Question 89

Companies which form a group for group relief purposes are automatically associated companies.

Question 90

Companies which form a group for chargeable gains purposes are automatically associated companies.

Question 91

James Brown Ltd has a shareholding in an overseas resident company Karen Brown Inc from which, in its accounting period ended 31st December 2005, it received a net dividend of 315,000 after a local 10% dividend withholding tax had been levied.

JB Ltd's shareholding in KD Inc was 100%.

JB Ltd's results for the accounting period ended 31st December 2005 were as follows:

Trading profit	1,200,000
Chargeable gains	225,000
Charges on income	275,000

KD Inc's results for the year ended 31st December 2005 were as follows:

Profit before tax	1,100,000
Tax charge	(130,000)
Current provision	(85,000)
Deferred tax	(135,000)
Profit after tax	750,000
Dividend (before withholding tax)	300,000

The foreign corporation tax actually paid by KD Inc on its profit was 125,000.

Calculate the corporation tax liability of JS plc for the year ended 31st December 2005.

Chapters 20 to 23

Question 92

James Brown is a sole trader and his accounts are prepared to 30th June each year.

For the tax year 2005/06 James' trading profit is 25,000.

Identify which Class(es) of National Insurance Contributions (NIC) apply to James and calculate the amount payable for 2005/06.

Question 93

James Brown is an employee of James Brown Ltd. The company prepares its accounts to 30th June each year.

For the tax year 2005/06 James' salary is 25,000.

Identify which Class(es) of National Insurance Contributions (NIC) apply to James and James Brown Ltd and calculate the amount(s) payable for 2005/06.

APPENDIX 2

Question 94

James Brown is an employee of James Brown Ltd. The company prepares its accounts to 30th June each year.

For the tax year 2005/06 James' salary is 25,000 and his benefits (including a company car and an interest free loan) amount to a taxable benefit of 7,000.

Identify which Class(es) of National Insurance Contributions (NIC) apply to James and James Brown Ltd and calculate the amount(s) payable for 2005/06.

Question 95

Would your answer to Question 94 differ if James Brown informed you that he was a member of the James Brown Ltd approved pension scheme and his personal contribution during 2005/06 was 1,250?

Question 96

Identify the dates on which Classes 1, 1A, 2 and 4 are payable.

Question 97

In the tax year 2004/05 James Brown's income tax payable amounted to 10,000. 2,500 of his income tax liability had been deducted at source.

In the tax year 2005/06 the corresponding figures were 15,000 and 3,000 respectively.

Calculate the payments on account (if any) James would have been required to make on behalf of his income tax liability for the tax year 2005/06 and the amount of any balancing payment. State the dates on which these payments were due to be paid.

Question 98

In the tax year 2004/05 James Brown's income tax liability amounted to 12,000. 10,000 of his income tax liability had been satisfied by way of tax deducted at source.

In the tax year 2005/06 the corresponding figures were 15,000 and 3,000 respectively.

Calculate the payments on account (if any) James would have been required to make on behalf of his income tax liability for the tax year 2005/06 and the amount of any balancing payment. State the dates on which these payments were due to be paid.

Question 99

James Brown is a sole trader and is due to make payments on account of his income tax liability for the tax year 2005/06 of 2,500 on 31st January 2006 and 2,500 on 31st July 2006.

However, he actually makes these payments on 31st May 2006 and 30 September 2006.

Calculate any interest payments which may arise due to these late payments and confirm whether any surcharges may also be levied.

Question 100

James Brown submitted his tax return for the tax year ended 5th April 2005 on 31st March 2006. What penalty (if any) may be levied? If James has still not submitted the return by 31st July 2006 will any additional amount of penalty be levied and if so how much?

Question 101

James Brown Ltd for its accounting period ended 31st December 2005 was liable to corporation tax at 30%. State the payment dates on which its corporation tax liability has to be settled.

Question 102

In Question 101 if the accounting period specified therein was the first period in which the 30% rate had been applicable what (if any) difference to your answer would this information have made.

Question 103

James Brown is a sole trader. On the 6th April 2004 James was 52 years old.

His trading profit for the tax year 2004/05 was 45,000. He made personal pension contributions in respect of the tax year 2004/05 of 10,000.

Calculate the amount of personal pension contributions James may make in the tax year 2005/06 and elect to carry them back to the prior tax year 2004/05. State the date by which these payments must be made if they are to be allowed to be carried back.

Question 104

Explain the difference in the manner in which an employee obtains tax relief for pension contributions he may make to a company pensions scheme as compared to the manner in which a sole trader obtains relief for personal pension contributions. Confirm also whether or not an employee who is a member of a company pension scheme may still make personal pension contributions to a personal pension scheme.

Question 105

James Brown prepared his VAT returns to 31st March, 30th June, 30th September and 31st December. However, three of them as indicated below, were submitted late as were the accompanying payments:

	Date of payment	VAT due
31st March 2005	10th May 2005	7,000
30th June 2005	7th August 2005	15,000
31st September 2005	18th December 2005	12,000

Describe the consequences for James.

Question 106

James Brown a sole trader believes that the tax point on his sales is always the date of the invoice he raises; that he cannot claim any VAT relief for any of his trade debts which turn bad; and VAT must be charged on the discounted amount shown in his invoices.

Advise James as to whether his understanding is correct.

Question 107

James Brown started to trade as a sole trader on the 1st August 2004 preparing his accounts to 30th April each year.

He realises in January that his turnover exceeded 58,000 in November. He accordingly notified HMRC on 1st December.

Explain the consequences to James including informing him of the date he should have notified HMRC and any penalties which may now arise.

Question 108

James Brown charged a customer 475 inclusive of VAT. The customer asked James how much of this amount represented VAT.

Advise James of this amount.

Question 109

Michael Chin made the following gifts of assets to his daughter, Mika, during 2005–06:

(1) On 30 June 2005 Michael gave Mika a business that he had run as a sole trader since 1 January 2001. The market value of the business on 30 June 2005 was £250,000, made up as follows:

	£
Goodwill	60,000
Freehold property	150,000
Net current assets	40,000
	250,000

The goodwill has been built up since 1 January 2001, and had a nil cost. The freehold property had cost £86,000 on 20 May 2003. Michael used 75% of this property for business purposes, but the other 25% has never been used for business purposes.

(2) On 8 December 2005 Michael gave Mika his entire holding of 50,000 50p ordinary shares (a 60% holding) in Minnow Ltd, an unquoted trading company. The market value of the shares on that date was £180,000. Michael had originally purchased the shares on 5 January 2005 for £87,500. On 8 December 2005 the market value of Minnow Ltd's chargeable assets was £250,000, of which £200,000 was in respect of chargeable business assets.

(3) On 15 February 2006 Michael gave Mika 18,000 £1 ordinary shares in Whale plc, a quoted trading company.

On that date the shares were quoted at £6·36 – £6·52. Michael had originally purchased 15,000 shares in Whale plc on 7 December 2004 for £63,000, and he purchased a further 12,000 shares on 21 August 2005 for £26,400. The total shareholding was less than 1% of Whale plc's issued share capital.

Where possible, Michael and Mika have elected to hold over any gains arising.

Michael incurred a capital loss of £17,300 during 2003–04, and made a capital gain of £10,600 during 2004–05.

His statutory total income for 2005–06 is £5,945.

Required:

Calculate Michael's capital gains tax liability for 2005–06, clearly showing the amount of any gains that can be held over. You should assume that the rate of annual exemption for 2005–06 applies throughout.

Taper relief is not available in respect of any of Michael's disposals, and so can be ignored.

(The author and publisher gratefully acknowledge the ACCA's permission to reproduce this question (adjusted for 2005/06) which first appeared in the Paper 2.3 Business Taxation June 2005 examination).

APPENDIX 2

Question 110

On 5 July 2005 Dee Zyne resigned as an employee of Trendy-Wear plc. The company had employed her as a fashion designer since 1998. On 6 July 2005 Dee commenced self-employment running her own clothing business, preparing accounts to 5 April. The following information is available for 2005–06:

Employment

(1) During the period 6 April 2005 to 5 July 2005 Dee's total gross salary from her employment with Trendy-Wear plc was £26,000. Income tax of £8,530 was deducted from this figure under PAYE.

(2) During the period 6 April 2005 to 5 July 2005 Trendy-Wear plc provided Dee with a petrol powered company motor car with a list price of £17,500. The official CO2 emission rate for the motor car was 223 grams per kilometre. Trendy-Wear plc also provided Dee with fuel for private journeys. Dee paid £100 per month to Trendy-Wear plc for the use of the motor car, and she also made a capital contribution of £1,500 towards the cost of the motor car when it was first provided to her. The motor car was not available to Dee after 5 July 2005.

(3) On 1 January 2004 Trendy-Wear plc had provided Dee with an interest free loan of £60,000 so that she could purchase a yacht. Dee repaid £45,000 of the loan on 5 May 2005, and repaid the balance of the loan of £15,000 on 6 July 2005.

(4) During the period from 6 April 2005 to 5 July 2005 Dee was provided with free meals in Trendy-Wear plc's staff canteen. The total cost of these meals to the company was £350.

Self-employment

(1) Dee's tax adjusted trading loss for the period 6 July 2005 to 5 April 2006 was £12,900. This figure is before taking account of capital allowances.

(2) Dee purchased the following assets during the nine-month period ended 5 April 2006:

		£
10 July 2005	Computer	1,200
16 August 2005	Office furniture	1,500
13 November 2005	Motor car (1)	10,400
21 January 2006	Motor car (2)	17,800

Motor car (1) purchased on 13 November 2005 is used by an employee, and 15% of the mileage is for private purposes. Motor car (2) purchased on 21 January 2006 is used by Dee, and 20% of the mileage is for private purposes.

Other information

(1) During the period 6 April 2005 to 5 July 2004 Dee paid interest of £110 (gross) on a personal loan taken out on 1 August 2004 to purchase a computer for use in her employment with Trendy-Wear plc.

(2) During the period 6 July 2005 to 5 April 2006 Dee paid patent royalties of £390 (net) in respect of specialised technology that she uses in her clothing business.

(3) Dee's statutory total income for each of the years 1999–00 to 2004–05 was £80,000.

Required:

(a) Calculate Dee's trading loss for 2005–06.

(b) Assuming that Dee claims loss relief against her statutory total income for 2005–06 (under s.380 ICTA 1988), calculate the income tax repayable to her for 2005–06.

(c) Describe the alternative ways in which Dee could have relieved her trading loss for 2005–06 against statutory total income, and explain why these claims would have been more beneficial than the actual claim made in (b) above. You should assume that the tax rates for 2005–06 apply throughout.

(The author and publisher gratefully acknowledge the ACCA's permission to reproduce this question (adjusted for 2005/06) which first appeared in the Paper 2.3 Business Taxation June 2005 examination).

APPENDIX 3

True and False Question and Answer Quiz

This Appendix is intended to be a bit of fun whilst at the same time testing your knowledge.

I would suggest that you answer, say, 10 questions at a time before checking the answers. Think carefully also about each question; they are not always perhaps as easy as at first sight they may seem.

If having checked an answer you are still not sure then re-read the relevant section of the book.

The questions have been written in a form such that the answer is either "true" or "false". However, before checking any answers think a little more deeply about the question.

Thus, for example:

Question

A sole trader can claim a first year capital allowance on a motor car purchased for his sole business use.

Answer

False

A claim for first year capital allowances is possible only where the motor car is a low emission motor car

Otherwise motor cars are never entitled to a first year capital allowance irrespective of their use, business or private

Writing down allowances at the rate of 25% per annum (capped at £3,000 p.a.) are available for any period of account where the motor car is not a low emission motor car

First year capital allowances can be claimed for vans and lorries

Try the following:

Question

Savings income of an individual is subject to income tax at rates of 10% and 32.5% only.

[Think about the answer and then turn over for the answer].

Answer

False.

The rates given in the question apply to dividend income only not savings income in general

Savings income (other than dividend income) is taxed at rates of 10%, 20% and 40%

Savings income comprises, for example, interest earned on cash deposits with banks and building societies.

QUESTIONS

Income Tax

Q1

Statutory total income is total income *before* charges.

Q2

Savings income is subject to income tax at rates higher than Non-savings income.

Q3

Dividend income may be subject to income tax at 40%.

Q4

Children under the age of sixteen are not entitled to a personal allowance.

Q5

Students do not pay income tax on their earnings.

Q6

All charges on income are paid under deduction of basic rate income tax.

Q7

Savings income is never taxed at the basic rate of 22%.

Q8

From 6th April 2005 Schedule A taxes rental income from land and buildings situated in the United Kingdom.

Q9

A premium paid by a tenant to a landlord under a lease is subject to income tax on the part of the landlord.

Q10

Schedule E taxes employment income for the tax year 2005/06.

Q11

A tax credit of 10% is available in respect of a net dividend on shares paid by a United Kingdom based company.

Q12

Rental income on is taxed on an accruals basis.

Q13

A sole trader is subject to income tax on his/her profits under Schedule D Case I or II.

Q14

Client entertaining expenses are deductible in computing a sole trader's taxable trading profit.

APPENDIX 3

Q15
Capital allowances are available as a deduction in computing the rental profit from the renting out of residential accommodation.

Q16
Income tax at the basic rate of 22% is deducted by banks when crediting interest on an individual's deposit account.

Q17
Income tax at 40% is payable on an individual's taxable income above £32,400 for the tax year 2005/06.

Q18
Any income tax withheld on the making of a charge on income payment cannot be reclaimed by the tax authorities.

Q19
Unused Personal allowances for a tax year can be carried forward to be offset against an individual's statutory total income in future tax years.

Q20
The income tax year is from 5th April to the following 6th April.

Q21
Payments on account of an individual's income tax liability for a tax year are due on the 31st July in the tax year and on the 31st January after the tax year.

Q22
Payments on account of an individual's income tax liability for a tax year are based upon the individual's prior tax year's income tax liability.

Q23
Losses arising from a property business can be carried both forward and backward against future and earlier property business profits.

Q24
Reverse premiums paid by a landlord to a tenant are not taxable on the part of the tenant.

Q25
The rent a room schemeoes not apply where more than one room in an individual's main residence is let out.

Q26
An individual's income tax liability for a tax year is minimised if his/her personal allowance is offset against dividend income before being offset against either Savings or Non-savings income.

Q27
Savings income may be subject to income tax at the basic rate of 22%.

Q28

The 40% rate of income tax can in certain cases apply to dividend income.

Q29

Dividend income is treated as an individual's highest slice of taxable income.

Q30

Dividend income from shares in United Kingdom based companies is not liable to income tax.

Q31

Tax credits attaching to dividends on shares in United Kingdom based companies are reclaimable.

Q32

In calculating an individual's income tax liability for a tax year, earned income from employment taxed under ITEPA 2004 is included only after allowing for any income tax which has been deducted under the Pay As You Earn Scheme.

Q33

The business profits of a sole trader are taxed under ITEPA 2004.

Q34

Earned income from employment taxed under ITEPA 2004 is treated as Non-savings income when working out an individual's income tax liability.

Q35

The basis of assessment for earned income from employment taxed under ITEPA 2004 is the receipts basis.

Q36

Dividend income from UK companies is taxable on a receipts basis.

Q37

Relevant foreign income includes rental income from overseas based properties.

Q38

Rental income from UK property is treated as Savings income when working out an individual's income tax liability.

Q39

Any payment of interest on a borrowing is a tax deductible expense when calculating an individual's income tax liability.

Q40

Interest paid by an individual to a bank on a bank borrowing is paid under deduction of income tax at the basic rate of 22%.

Q41

Patent royalty payments are an example of a charge on income payment.

Q42

Income tax at 20% is deducted at source when making patent royalty payments.

Q43

The accounts profit of a sole trader for a period of account is always equal to the taxable profit for the period of account.

Q44

On a change of his accounting date a sole trader may obtain overlap profit relief.

Q45

The taxable profit for a sole trader's first tax year of trading is based upon the period from the date of starting to trade to the end of the tax year in which the trade started.

Q46

In the tax year of cessation of a sole trader's business the taxable profit is based upon the period from the start of the tax year of cessation to the date of the cessation.

Q47

A sole trader's trading profit is treated as Non-savings income when computing an individual's income tax liability.

Q48

A first year capital allowance of 50% is available to a sole trader who qualifies as a medium sized business on expenditure on plant and machinery incurred between 6th April 2004 and 5th April 2005.

Q49

The payment of a personal pension contribution by a sole trader is eligible for tax relief at the individual's marginal rate of income tax.

Q50

The level of tax relievable personal pension contributions which can be made in any tax year is determined by the age of the taxpayer at anytime in the tax year.

QUESTIONS

Capital Gains Tax

Q1

In working out an individual's capital gains tax liability any capital gains are treated as the top slice of an individual's income.

Q2

Capital gains are subject to capital gains tax at the rates of 10%, 20% and 40%.

Q3

Capital losses brought forward are deducted from current year capital gains before current year capital losses.

Q4

Capital losses can be carried back and offset against the prior tax year's capital gains.

Q5

Taper relief reduces capital gains before any indexation allowance.

Q6

Indexation of capital gains ceases on 5th April 1999.

Q7

The indexation allowance can increase the amount of a capital loss.

Q8

The indexation allowance can turn a capital gain into a capital loss.

Q9

The indexation allowance is calculated before taper relief is obtained.

Q10

Taper relief is obtained before capital gains and capital losses are offset.

Q11

Enhancement expenditure on a chargeable asset is always deductible in computing the capital gain on a disposal.

Q12

The gift of an asset is not a disposal for capital gains tax purposes.

Q13

The gift of an asset is treated as if it had been sold for market value when computing any capital gain.

Q14

The transfer of a chargeable asset form one spouse to the other gives rise to a capital gain or loss.

Q15

A married couple are entitled to one annual exemption only.

Q16

A couple who cohabit are entitled to one annual exemption only.

Q17

The inter-spouse exemption applies only to a married couple who are living together.

Q18

The sale of a chargeable asset by a parent to his/her child is a disposal at arm's length.

Q19

The indexation allowance is calculated by applying an indexation factor to the allowable expenditure of a chargeable asset.

Q20

The indexation factor is normally restricted to three decimal places.

Q21

Maximum taper relief for a business asset is obtained after the asset has been held for two complete years.

Q22

The most tax efficient manner in which a capital loss may be used is to offset it first against those assets which are entitled to the least percentage of taper relief.

Q23

Any capital losses arising in the tax year of death can be carried back for offset against capital gains of the previous four tax years.

Q24

Capital losses can be carried forward indefinitely.

Q25

A child under aged sixteen at the start of the tax year is not entitled to the annual capital gains exemption.

Q26

In computing an individual's capital gains tax liability for a tax year the last deductible item is the annual exemption.

Q27

An individual's personal allowance for income tax purposes can be used to reduce an individual's capital gains tax liability.

Q28

The amount of any annual exemption which is unused in a tax year can be carried forward for future use.

Q29

Payments of account are required for any capital gains tax liability for a tax year.

Q30

Any capital gains tax liability for a tax year is payable on the 31st January after the end of the tax year.

Q31

On the sale of shares in any company by an individual the matching rules require that the shares be matched with purchases of shares in the company which are part of the Finance Act 1985 pool before matching with purchases of shares on or after 6th April 1998.

Q32

One of the conditions for the capital gain on the sale of a business asset by a sole trader to be rolled over against the purchase of a business asset by the sole trader is that the new business asset must be purchased within two years before and three years after the disposal of the first asset.

Q33

Movable plant and machinery qualify as business assets for rollover relief.

Q34

Goodwill qualifies as a business asset for rollover relief.

Q35

To obtain full rollover relief on the sale of a business asset it is only necessary to reinvest the amount of the capital gain on the sale of the old business asset.

Q36

Gift relief applies to the capital gain on the sale of any type of chargeable asset.

Q37

Gift relief will automatically cause taper relief to be lost on the capital gain which would, in the absence of gift relief, otherwise arise on the gift of the chargeable asset.

Q38

Gift relief can apply to a sale at an under-value.

Q39

For taper relief purposes in measuring the length of ownership of a rights issue of shares the date of acquisition is taken to be the date of the rights issue.

Q40

An issue of bonus shares is deemed to have occurred at the date of acquisition of the original shares in respect of which the bonus issue has occurred.

Q41

Taper relief is determined according to the length of ownership of the relevant asset.

Q42

The transfer of a sole trader's business to a limited company in exchange for an issue of shares enables the sole trader to rollover any capital gains arising on any chargeable assets transferred.

Q43

Capital losses of a tax year can be offset against a sole trader's trading profit for that tax year.

Q44

Capital gains of a tax year can be offset against a sole trader's trading loss for that tax year.

Q45

Capital gains of one spouse for a tax year can be offset against the capital losses of the other spouse for the same tax year.

Q46

Enhancement expenditure incurred prior to 6th April 1998 on a chargeable asset qualifies for indexation from the date it is incurred.

Q47

Quoted shares are valued at the higher of the average of the highest and lowest marked bargains and the value determined by the quarter up rule.

Q48

No chargeable gain arises on a "paper for paper" (i.e. where shares in one company are exchanged for shares in another company which is taking over the first company) takeover.

Q49

In calculating a capital gain on the sale of a chargeable asset any incidental costs of disposal may be deducted from the gross sale proceeds.

Q50

For taper relief purposes an asset which has been held for 11 months is treated as having been owned for 1 complete year.

QUESTIONS

Corporation Tax

Q1

Companies pay income tax on their taxable profits.

Q2

An accounting period of a company can be of any length for tax purposes.

Q3

Corporation tax is levied on a company's Profit for an accounting period.

Q4

Companies are liable to corporation tax on dividend income from other UK companies.

Q5

Net dividend income plus any attaching tax credit on dividend income form other UK companies is referred to as franked investment income.

Q6

The tax credit attaching to a net dividend is 10% of the net dividend.

Q7

All companies pay corporation tax at the rate of 30% on all their taxable profits.

Q8

In calculating a company's taxable rental income interest on borrowings used to buy and/or improve the property is a deductible expense.

Q9

Profits of a company for an accounting period equal profits chargeable to corporation tax plus franked investment income for that period.

Q10

The marginal rate of corporation tax on profits between £10,000 and £50,000 is 23.75%.

Q11

30% corporation tax applies to profits above £1.5 million.

Q12

Patent royalties are treated as a charge on income for corporation tax purposes.

Q13

Income tax is withheld at source at 22% on the making of patent royalty payments by a company.

Q14

Companies are liable to capital gains tax on any capital gains.

Q15

Companies are entitled to an annual exemption when computing the tax liability on any capital gains.

Q16

Trading losses of a company for an accounting period can be carried back to the 36 months prior to the accounting period of loss.

Q17

Trading losses of a company for an accounting period can be carried forward indefinitely and offset against future trading profits.

Q18

Trading losses of a company for an accounting period can be offset against profits chargeable to corporation tax of the same accounting period.

Q19

Writing down allowances for plant and machinery of a company for a 15 month period of account would be [25% x 15/12] x tax written down value at beginning of the period of account.

Q20

Long life assets qualify for a first year allowance of 40%.

Q21

The rate of corporation tax is fixed for a tax year of assessment.

Q22

Group relief refers to the offsetting by one company in a group of another group company's capital losses.

Q23

A group for chargeable gains purposes is the same definition as a group for group relief purposes.

Q24

If three companies are associated then they will automatically form a group for group relief purposes.

Q25

Non-UK resident companies are included when working out the number of associated companies for UK tax purposes.

Q26

The number of associated companies affects the rate of corporation tax which will apply to each company's profits chargeable to corporation tax.

Q27

Corporation tax for an accounting period is always payable nine months after the end of the accounting period.

Q28

Companies receive bank interest on deposits without suffering any deduction of income tax at source.

Q29

Companies are entitled to a personal allowance.

Q30

Bank interest forms part of a company's franked investment income.

Q31

Dividends from other group companies form part of a company's franked investment income.

Q32

When computing the corporation tax on a chargeable gain arising from a sale of shares the matching rules require that the shares sold be matched first to shares acquired on the same day; then shares acquired in the previous nine days; and then shares in the Finance Act 1985 pool.

Q33

Companies are entitled to taper relief when computing chargeable gains.

Q34

Indexation allowances are available to companies for periods beyond 5th April 1998.

Q35

Companies can claim gift relief.

Q36

The loan relationship rules apply to interest income and interest expenses.

Q37

Losses for an accounting period arising an excess of expenses over income arising under the loan relationship rules can be group relieved.

Q38

Where a chargeable gains group exists chargeable assets can be transferred between companies at no loss and no gain.

Q39

Dividends are treated as franked investment income for the accounting period in which they are received.

Q40

The financial year runs from 1st April to the following 30th March.

Q41

Companies can claim rollover relief on the sale of, and reinvestment in, qualifying business assets.

Q42

Rollover relief can apply where the company selling the qualifying asset and the company investing in the new qualifying asset are in the same chargeable gains group.

Q43

Trading losses of the last twelve months in which the company's trade ceases can be carried back and offset against the company's profits chargeable to corporation tax for the previous three years.

Q44

Dividends received from overseas companies are not subject to corporation tax.

Q45

Underlying tax refers to the foreign tax paid by a foreign company on its profits which is attributable to the dividends paid to the UK.

Q46

A company can only obtain double tax relief for underlying tax on dividends received in the UK if the company owns at least 10% of the voting power in the overseas company.

Q47

Capital allowances are computed for accounting periods.

Q48

Where a motor car is made available to an employee that is likely to be used for both business and private purposes, in computing the capital allowances available to the company an adjustment must be made to take into account the private use of the car by the employee.

Q49

The writing down allowance on a second hand industrial building is 4% per annum.

Q50

A first year allowance of 100% is available for low emission motor cars.

ANSWERS

Income Tax

A1

False

STI is total income of an individual *after* a deduction for charges on income

Taxable income is STI less personal allowances.

A2

False

Non-savings income is taxed at rates of 10%, 22% and 40% compared to 10%, 20% and 40% for savings income.

A3

False

Dividend income is taxed at 10% and 32.5%.

A4

False

All individuals of whatever age are entitled to the minimum personal allowance of £4,895.

A5

False

Students are no different from other taxpayers and are liable to income tax on their taxable income.

A6

False

The only charge on income which an individual pays under deduction of income tax is a patent royalty.

Interest on a qualifying loan also ranks as a charge on income but is paid gross i.e. without deduction of tax at source.

A7

True

Savings income can only be taxed at the rates of 10%, 20% and 40%.

A8

False

Effective 6th April 2005 Schedule A is abolished. Rental income is now taxed under the provisions of ITTOIA 2005.

A9

True

The taxable element of the premium is given by the formula:

[Premium – Premium x 2% x (n – 1)] where n is the duration of the lease in complete years.

A10
False

Schedule E was abolished from 6th April 2003. Earnings from employment are now taxed under ITEPA 2003.

A11
False

The tax credit attaching to a net dividend is 1/9th of the net dividend. 10% of the gross amount of the dividend will give the amount of the tax credit.

A12
True

The accruals and not the receipts basis applies to income taxed under Schedule A.

A13
False

Effective 6th April 2005 Schedule D (all Cases) is abolished. Trading profit of a sole trader is now taxed under the provisions of ITTOIA 2005.

A14
False

Under no circumstances is client entertaining ever deductible in computing a sole trader's trading profit.

A15
False

No capital allowances are available re residential accommodation; instead a wear and tear allowance is available for furnished but not unfurnished accommodation.

A16
False

Tax at the lower rate of 20% is applied by banks when deducting income tax at source on bank interest credited to an individual on a cash deposit.

A17
True

A18
False

Where an individual's income tax liability falls below the amount of tax deducted from the making of a charge on income payment then the excess deducted may be recovered from the taxpayer by the Inland Revenue.

A19

False

Any unused element of the personal allowance available for a tax year cannot be carried forward or back to future or previous tax years; it is simply lost.

A20

False

The tax year or income tax year or year of assessment is the period 6th April to the following 5th April.

A21

False

Payments on account of an income tax liability for a tax year are payable in equal instalments on 31st January within the tax year and on 31st July after the end of the tax year.

A22

True

Strictly speaking, the payments on account are based upon the prior tax year's relevant amount which is the prior tax year's income tax liability less any tax deducted at source.

A23

False

Property business losses may only be carried forward against future property business profits.

A24

False

A reverse premium received by a tenant from a landlord is taxable on the part of the tenant either as part of trading profits or part of property business income.

A25

False

The number of rooms let out is not the test for application of the rent a room scheme; the key element is that the gross rents from the relevant rooms in total do not exceed £4,250.

A26

False

Minimisation of an individual's income tax liability is achieved by offsetting personal allowances against non-savings, then savings then dividend income.

A27

False

Savings income is taxed at the rates of 10%, 20% and 40%.

A28

False

Dividend income is taxed at 10% or 32.5%; never 40%.

A29

True

Dividend income is taxed after non-savings and savings income have been taxed.

A30

False

Gross dividend income is included in ascertaining an individual's income tax liability.

A31

False

A non-taxpayer may still not reclaim any attaching tax credits.

A32

False

The gross amount of earned income from employment taxed under ITEPA 2004 is included when working out an individual's income tax liability; any PAYE reduces the final income tax liability in arriving at income tax payable.

A33

False

Business profits are taxed under ITTOIA 2005. ITEPA 2004 taxes earned income from employment and pensions.

A34

True

A35

True

Pensions, however, are taxed under ITEPA on an accruals basis.

A36

True

A37

True

Effective from 6ᵗʰ April 2005 relevant foreign income includes rental income from overseas based properties (see ITTOIA 2005).

A38

False

Rental ncome is treated as non-savings income and is thus taxed at rates of 10%, 22% and 40%.

A39

False

Only interest payable on a qualifying loan is a deductible expense in working out an individual's taxable income; such a loan would include for example interest payable on a loan to purchase shares in an employee controlled company or an interest in a partnership.

A40

False

No income tax at source is deducted when an individual pays interest to a bank on bank borrowing.

A41

True

A42

False

Income tax at the rate of 22% not 20% is deducted on making patent royalty payments.

A43

False

Very rarely will the accounts profit equal the taxable trading profits; this is because of the need invariably to add back non-tax deductible expenses etc.

A44

True

Overlap profit relief may be available on a change of accounting date; whether in fact this is so will depend upon whether the length of the time period from the "old" date to the "new" date exceeds 12 months.

A45

True

A46

False

On a sole trader's cessation the basis period for the final tax year of cessation is the period from the end of the basis period for the previous tax year to the date of cessation.

A47

True

A48

True

A49

True

On the making of a personal pension payment a sole trader deducts income tax at source of 22% and if he is a higher rate taxpayer (i.e. is liable to tax at 40%) then his basic rate band is extended and extra tax relief of 18% (making 22% + 18% in total) is obtainable.

A50

False

The age of the taxpayer which is relevant for a tax year is the age on the 6th April (ie the first day of the tax year).

ANSWERS

Capital Gains Tax

A1

True

Capital gains are taxed after (i.e. on top of) non-savings, savings and dividend income.

A2

True

Capital gains are taxed at savings income rates.

A3

False

Current year capital losses are deducted from current year capital gains before capital losses brought forward are deducted.

A4

False

Capital losses cannot generally be carried back; only in the case of capital losses arising in the tax year of death may such losses be carried back but then only to the three tax years prior to the tax year of death.

A5

False

Taper relief reduces a capital gain of an asset after not before indexation allowance.

A6

False

Indexation allowances for individuals cease on 5th April 1998.

A7

True

An indexation allowance can reduce a capital gain to nil but cannot turn the gain into a capital loss nor can it increase a capital loss.

A8

False

See A7 above.

A9

True

See A5 above.

A10

False

Capital losses whether current tax year or brought forward are utilised before taper relief is calculated.

A11

False

To be deductible enhancement expenditure on an asset must be reflected in the value of the asset at the date of sale.

A12

False

A disposal for capital gains tax purposes includes a gift or a sale at undervalue as well as a normal arm's length sale.

A13

True

As there are no actual sale disposal proceeds the assumption is that a gift has been sold for its then market value.

A14

False

Inter-spouse transfers are made at no gain/no loss.

A15

False

Each individual, whether husband and wife or not, are each entitled to an annual exemption.

A16

False

See A15 above.

A17

True

A married couple not living together are not entitled to the inter-spouse exemption.

A18

False

Transfers amongst family members (e.g. father to son; mother to son; brother to sister) are between connected persons and therefore by definition are not at arm's length; thus, market values are used not actual sale proceeds to calculate any capital gain.

A19

True

A20

True

A21

True

The maximum taper relief for a business asset is 75% and applies where an asset has been held for a minimum of 2 years.

A22

True

Capital losses should be first offset against gains on assets entitled to the smallest taper relief percentage, then against gains entitled to the next lowest percentage etc. etc.

A23

False

Capital losses arising in the tax year of death may be carried back but only to the previous three tax years not four. See A4 above.

A24

True

A25

False

Every individual is entitled to an annual exemption.

A26

True

Indexation allowances and taper relief are calculated before the deduction of the annual exemption which is always the last deduction to be made.

A27

False

The personal allowance is an allowance for income tax purposes not capital gains tax purposes and cannot therefore reduce an individual's capital gains tax liability.

A28

False

Any unused part of the annual exemption cannot be carried either forward or back and is simply lost.

A29

False

Payments on account only apply to income tax and Class 4 national insurance contributions. Any capital gains tax liability is payable in one lump sum on the 31st January following the tax year of the gains.

A30

True

A31

False

The matching of shares sold requires matching with purchases on or after 6th April 1998 before those purchases falling in the FA 1985 pool.

A32

False

The time limits for the purchase of the replacement asset are 1 year before (i.e. not 2) and 3 years after the date of sale of the "old" asset.

A33

False

The plant and machinery must be fixed to qualify not moveable.

A34

True

This is the case for an individual sole trader; however, effective 1st April 2003 goodwill is not a chargeable business asset for corporation tax roll over purposes.

A35

False

For rollover of the whole of the gain to apply the whole of the asset sale proceeds must be reinvested not just the gain amount itself.

A36

False

Gift relief only applies to gifts of business assets not any chargeable asset.

A37

True

Gift relief results in the vendor's gain not being taxed and the base cost of the asset for the recipient being reduced accordingly; the gain is after indexation but before taper relief; thus, taper relief is lost by the vendor.

A38

True

However, on a sale at undervalue rather than an outright gift although gift relief may apply some part of the gain on the gift will be immediately subject to capital gains tax.

A39

False

Shares acquired under a rights issue are for taper relief purposes assumed to have been acquired at the same time as the original shares in respect of which the rights apply not the date of the rights issue itself.

A40

True

A41

True

However, if the asset was purchased prior to 6th April 1998 only the ownership period from 6th April 1998 is used in determining the percentage taper relief (subject to any bonus year).

A42

True

Assuming the various conditions are satisfied a roll over of any gains arising on the chargeable assets transferred is available; if the consideration for the transfer is an issue of shares in the acquiring company 100% roll over applies; if any part of the consideration is cash, not just shares, then less than 100% roll over applies.

A43

False

Section 92 FA 1991 enables a trading loss of a tax year to be potentially off-settable against capital gains for the same tax year.

A44

True

See A43 above.

A45

False

The capital losses of one spouse belong to that spouse and cannot be used by the other spouse.

A46

True

Original cost of an asset and subsequent enhancement expenditure are each indexed separately from the date on which each was incurred.

A47

True

A48

True

A take-over simply results in the new shares replacing the original shares with no capital gains tax liability arising at the date of the swap.

A49

True

A50

False

For taper relief purposes the ownership period of an asset is rounded down not up; thus, an asset owned for 11 months is deemed to have been owned for 0 years; an asset owned for 1 year and 11 months is deemed to have been owned for 1 year.

ANSWERS

Corporation Tax

A1

False

Companies pay corporation tax on their profits.

A2

False

An accounting period for corporation tax purposes cannot be longer than 12 months; where a company prepares its accounts for, say, a 15 month period for tax purposes this must be split into two accounting periods of 12 and 3 months respectively.

A3

False

Corporation tax is levied on a company's PCTCT for an accounting period not its Profit (which in fact equals PCTCT plus FII).

A4

False

Dividends received from other UK resident companies are not subject to corporation tax but are used in determining the rate of corporation tax to apply to the company's PCTCT.

A5

True

A6

False

The tax credit equals 1/9th of the net dividend.

A7

False

Only companies with taxable Profit of £1.5 million or more are subject to a rate of 30%; companies with smaller Profit pay at rates below 30%.

A8

False

Whilst the statement in the question applies to individuals, for companies any interest payable concerning the purchase or improvement of property for letting is treated as a deduction in computing the company's net interest income (or loss) under the loan relationship rules.

A9

True

A10

True

A11

True

A12

False

Patent royalties are treated as a trading expense not as a charge on income.

A13

False

No tax at source is deducted from such payments when made by a company.

A14

False

Capital gains tax only applies to individuals; companies do, however, pay corporation tax on any chargeable gains.

A15

False

The annual exemption only applies to individuals.

A16

False

Trading losses of an accounting period may be carried back only 12 months; however, if a company ceases to trade then any trading loss of the last 12 months of trading (referred to as a terminal loss) may be carried back for offset in the 36 immediately preceding months.

A17

True

A18

False

Trading losses of an accounting period may be offset against profits of the same accounting period but before deducting any charges on income (PCTCT is after deducting charges on income).

A19

False

Where a company's period of account exceeds 12 months it must be split (see A2 above) into two separate accounting periods and capital allowances must be computed separately for each accounting period.

A20

False

Long life assets are not entitled to a FYA; the WDA is 6% per annum.

A21

False

Corporation tax rates are fixed for financial years (i.e. 1st April to following 31st March) not tax years or years of assessment.

A22

False

Group relief refers to the offsetting of one company's trading losses against the PCTCT of another group company.

A23

False

The definitions of a group for chargeable gains purposes is different from that for group relief purposes; thus, companies may for example form a group for chargeable gains purposes but not for group relief.

A24

False

For associated company status companies must only be under common control (i.e. broadly more than 50% ownership) whereas for group relief companies must fall to be treated as 75% subsidiaries.

A25

True

Only dormant companies are excluded in arriving at the number of associated companies.

A26

True

The number of associated companies causes the normal corporation tax profit limits to be divided by the number of associated companies which in turn will affect the rate of corporation tax applying.

A27

False

Corporation tax is payable nine months after the end of an accounting period unless the company is one which pays corporation tax at the 30% rate; in this case corporation tax is payable by instalments typically in months 7, 10, 13 and 16.

A28

True

Banks do not deduct tax at source when making interest payments to companies.

A29

False

Only individuals are entitled to a personal allowance.

A30

False

FII refers to gross dividend income not interest income.

A31

False

FII comprises only dividend income from other UK non-group companies.

A32

True

The matching rules for companies are not the same as those for individuals.

A33

False

Companies are only entitled to an indexation allowance although unlike individuals the indexation allowance extends beyond 5th April 1998.

A34

True

See A33 above.

A35

False

Gift relief only applies to individuals.

A36

True

Note, however, that loan relationships are actually divided into trade and non-trade relationships.

A37

True

Although group relief mainly applies to trading losses it also applies to deficits on non-trading loan relationships.

A38

True

A39

True

The receipts basis applies to dividend income.

A40

False

The financial year runs from 1st April to the following 31st March not the 30th March.

A41

True

Assuming the relevant conditions are satisfied rollover relief is available to companies on qualifying business asset replacement.

A42

True

A43

False

Whilst a trading loss of the final 12 months of trading may be carried back to the previous 36 months (see A16 above) it is then offset not against PCTCT but profits before charges on income.

A44

False

Dividend income from overseas companies is subject to corporation tax; such income is not FII.

A45

True

A46

True

If the ownership in the overseas company is less than 10% then double tax relief is only available for any dividend withholding tax but not for any underlying tax.

A47

True

A48

False

No adjustment for any private use is necessary in ascertaining the amount of capital allowances claimed by the company; this is because the director/employee will be taxed on the car as a benefit under ITEPA 2004; for sole traders, however, an adjustment to the capital allowances claim would have been necessary.

A49

False

The 4% WDA applies to industrial buildings which are not second hand i.e. are new; the purchase of a used second hand industrial building gives rise to a WDA which depends upon the capital allowance position of the vendor.

A50

True

For motor cars which are not low emission cars only a WDA of 25% per annum is available.

Index

UK TAXATION FOR STUDENTS: A SIMPLIFIED APPROACH

The UK Tax System: an introduction

Malcolm James (University of Wales Institute, Cardiff)

Publication date: October 2005   Price: £39.95   ISBN: 1 904905 22 6

The UK tax system has developed over hundreds of years, and continues to evolve daily. This book will provide a guide to the structure of the tax system and its application to various classes of taxpayer, as well as explaining the roles of the government departments who administer it and the full range of taxpayers' rights and obligations.

The contents are arranged under the following headings:
- The Legal Framework of Taxation
- Administration of Personal Tax
- Self-assessment
- Self-assessment Enquiries, Discovery Assessments and Investigations
- Tax Appeals
- Interest, Surcharges, Penalties and Criminal Offences
- Income Tax Computation
- Overseas Aspects of Taxation
- VAT Administration, Appeals, Interest, Penalties and Surcharges
- Notification of Tax Avoidance Schemes

The book is for anyone advising on UK tax, from the experienced practitioner to the newly-qualified professional coming to tax advice for the first time, as well as being an ideal starting point for any students of the UK tax system.

About the author

Malcolm James is a Senior Lecturer in Accounting and Taxation at the University of Wales Institute, Cardiff and has lectured widely on the subject of taxation on both professional and undergraduate courses. He has also lectured for the Chartered Institute of Taxation and written a number of articles for their journal *Tax Adviser*. He also contributes regularly to CCH and Lexis Nexis tax publications. Before becoming a lecturer he worked for several large firms of accountants and also in industry.

Orders:

Turpin Distribution Services, Pegasus Drive, Stratton Business Park, Biggleswade, Bedfordshire SG18 8TQ

Tel: 01767 604951   Fax 01767 601640

E-mail: books@turpin-distribution.com

UK TAXATION FOR STUDENTS: A SIMPLIFIED APPROACH